THE NORTHERN SECTION

Seattle to Eureka

Not to be used for navigation

For southern section see rear endpapers

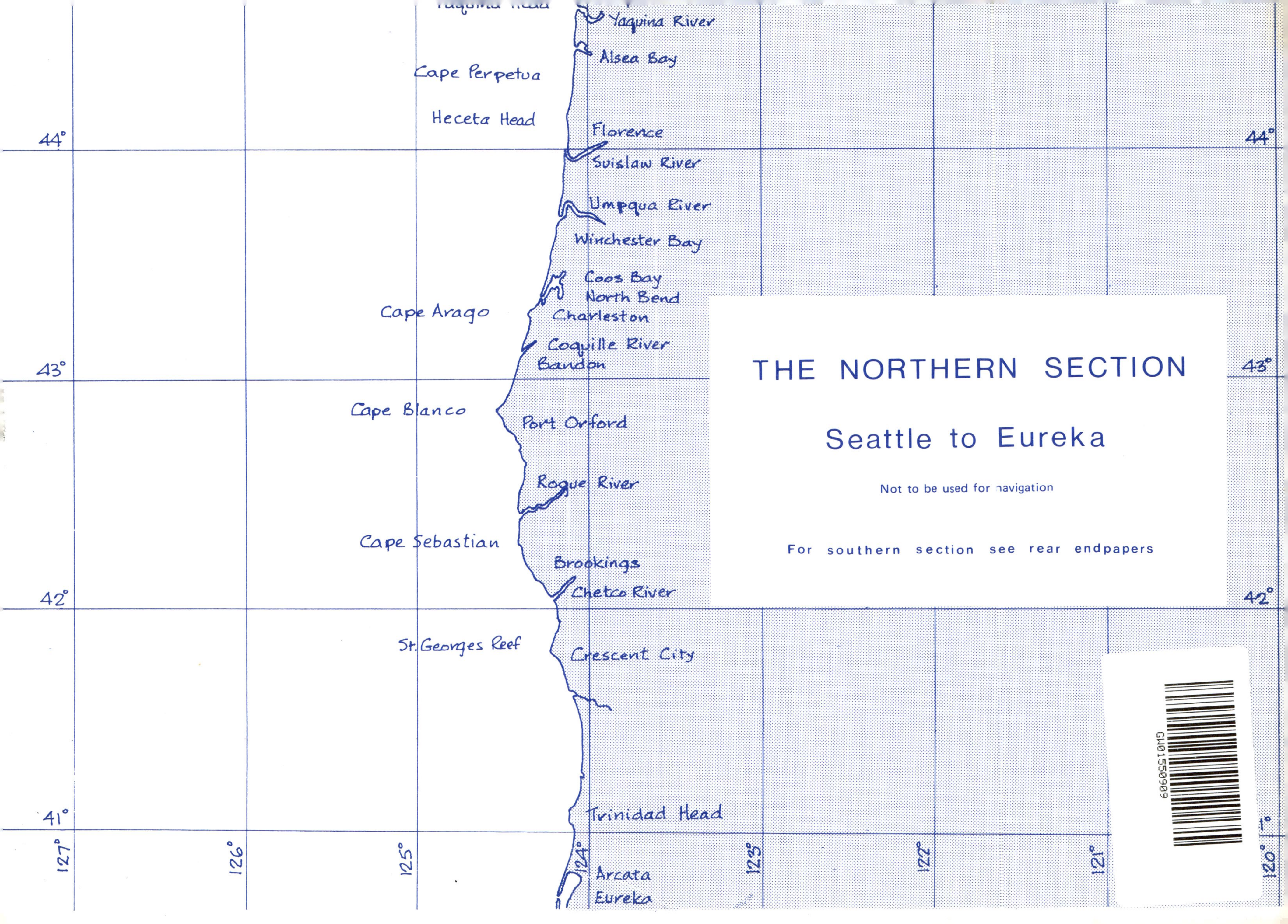

44° 43° 42° 41°

120° 121° 122° 123° 124° 125° 126° 127°

Yaquina River
Alsea Bay
Florence
Siuslaw River
Umpqua River
Winchester Bay
Coos Bay
North Bend
Charleston
Coquille River
Bandon
Port Orford
Rogue River
Brookings
Chetco River
Crescent City
Trinidad Head
Arcata
Eureka

Cape Perpetua
Heceta Head
Cape Arago
Cape Blanco
Cape Sebastian
St. Georges Reef

Other books by Charles E. Wood:

BUILDING YOUR DREAM BOAT, Published by Cornell Maritime Press
CHARLIE'S CHARTS of the Western Coast of Mexico (including Baja)
CHARLIE'S CHARTS of POLYNESIA
CHARLIE'S CHARTS NORTH TO ALASKA
CHARLIE'S CHARTS of the HAWAIIAN ISLANDS

SOUTHEAST FARALLON, FROM N., distant abt. 5 miles.

Canadian Cataloguing in Publication Data

Wood, Charles E. (Charles Edward), 1928-1987
  Charlie's charts of the Pacific Coast of
the United States : Seattle to San Diego

  Includes index.
  ISBN 0-9691412-5-4

  1. Nautical charts - Pacific Coast (U.S.).
2. Boats and boating - Pacific Coast (U.S.) -
Maps. 3. Pacific Coast (U.S.) - Description
and travel. I. Title.
G1461.P5W65 1988   623.89'22979   C87-091438-7

Published by: CHARLIE'S CHARTS, a division of POLYMATH ENERGY CONSULTANTS LTD.
               Box 1244, Station A
               Surrey, BC V3S 4Y5
               Canada

Printed by: D. W. FRIESEN & SONS LTD.
               5748 - 176 Street
               Surrey, BC V3S 4C8
               Canada

                    PRINTED IN CANADA

CHARLIE'S CHARTS

of the

U.S. PACIFIC COAST

(Seattle, WA to San Diego, CA)

By

Charles and Margo Wood

CHARLIE'S CHARTS

Box 1244 Station A

Surrey, BC, Canada

V3S 4Y5

ISBN 0-9691412-5-4

CHARLIE'S CHARTS of the U.S. PACIFIC COAST (Seattle, WA to San Diego, CA)
   First Printing, 1988

DEDICATION

   This book is dedicated to Charles E. Mason III, Executive Editor of
SAIL, who was the first person in the publishing business to encourage
my husband in the initial stages of his writing career. His early interest
and his continued support have been very much appreciated.

SAN FRANCISCO THROUGH THE GOLDEN GATE

Charts drawn by: Charles E. Wood   Sketches drawn by: Charles E. Wood
                   Richard Miller   Richard Miller
                   Robert L. Orcutt

Edited by Helen Scrivin   Photographs by the authors

ACKNOWLEDGEMENTS

In the midst of working on the fifth CHARLIE'S CHARTS cruising guide my captain and husband passed away. I was determined to complete the book he had started and there are many people whose help I relied on in order to finish his project. I would like to thank many people for their assistance and encouragement in particular,

Lieutenant M.A. Monteith, Commanding Officer, U.S. Coast Guard Station Cape Disappointment, for the ideas he shared related to crossing bars,

Jamie Kolbeck of Captain's Nautical in Seattle, Pete Peterson of Tradewind Instruments in Alameda, Janet Steele of Balboa Marine in Newport Beach, and Susanne and John Pew and Connie and Dave Wheeler of Seabreeze in San Diego whose commendation and encouragement came at a crucial time,

John Guzzwell, who read the text and made a few suggestions,

Fran Recht, through whose kind offices permission was obtained for reproducing material related to refuse disposal,

Helen Scrivin, whose counsel, careful editing, and meticulous proofreading have given polish where it was needed, and

Richard Miller, a talented young artist whose beautiful sketches have joined those of my husband, to enhance the pages of this book.

A special note of appreciation is due to Edith and Frank McCrady for the help and support they generously gave in many different ways.

DISCLAIMER

The word, "CHARTS," in the title of this publication is not intended to imply that these hand-drawn sketches are sufficiently accurate to be used for navigation. They and the accompanying text are meant to act solely as a handy cruising guide to local harbors and marina facilities. As a result of new marina developments and other changes in the areas covered by this book it is inevitable that some of the material is already out-of-date and inaccurate by the time it is used.

The use of National Ocean Survey (NOAA) Charts is mandatory for safe boating. DO NOT USE ANY OF THE DRAWINGS IN THIS BOOK FOR NAVIGATION. CHARLIE'S CHARTS and POLYMATH ENERGY CONSUL-TANTS LTD. are in no way responsible for loss or damages resulting from the use of this book.

ADDENDA

p. 22: **Deception Pass:** Para 3, Line 5 should read ...bridge with 144 ft. vertical clearance at the center; 104 ft. otherwise.

p. 35: **Neah Bay:** Chevron Dock on sketch no longer sells fuel. It is now available at the Big Salmon Dock.

p. 43: **Columbia River Entrance:** Sketch indicates that the Ilwaco detail is on the next page; it is actually on p. 45.

p. 58: **Coos Bay:** Para 7, Line 3 should read ...from Charleston opposite Dairy Queen; going ashore is easy any place on the beach.

p. 87: **San Francisco** - Marina Yacht Harbor: Sketch shows a fuel dock which has been reported as no longer in operation.

p. 96: **Monterey:** Para 4, Line 2 should read ...there is a flat rate of $15 per day.

p. 97: **Monterey:** H dock is no longer reserved for transients. Call the Harbormaster on Ch. 16 when within 10 miles for assignment of a slip.

p. 98: **San Simeon Bay:** Para 1, Line 3 should read ...23 miles northwest of Morro Bay. Para 2, Line 4 should read ...San Simeon Bay is about 27 miles northwest of Point Buchon.

p. 100: **Morro Bay:** Para 1, Line 1 should read ...Located 23 miles south of San Simeon Bay, and about 20 miles from Port San Luis .....

p. 103: **San Luis Obispo Bay:** The transient anchorage is now between the long pier with large mooring buoys and the pier marked "County Wharf." You will have to move if you anchor anywhere else in the harbor.

p. 106: **Santa Barbara:** Para 5, Line 5 should read ...but propane is about 12 blocks away at 7-Day Propane on Milpas Street.

CONTENTS

SYMBOLS

▬ ▬ ▬ ▬ Recommended approach

✦ Range, or Leading Direction

⚓ Anchorage

⚓ Reported anchorage

× Rock or reef underwater

⊗ Dangerous rock

Shoal area

Shoal, dries at low water

Steep rocky edges

Sand or pebbly beach

Land area

Underwater patches

❗❗, ☼ Navigation lights
(not necessarily lit)

▫▫ Buildings (indication only)

⌐10⌐ Depth contour in fathoms

s Sand bottom

6f Depth in fathoms

m Mud bottom

∿∿∿ Surf, where strong
Absence does not mean
lack of surf.

r Rock bottom

⟨ Kelp

⏚ Mooring buoy

NOTE: All depths are given in fathoms, except where specifically
mentioned in feet. For a conversion to metric,
approximately 1 fathom = 2 meters
exactly 1 fathom = 1.8 meters

Coming in with the day's catch at Crescent City, California

The vastness of the Pacific is interrupted by a vessel on the horizon.

INTRODUCTION

The Pacific coast of Washington, Oregon, and California is rugged, rock bound and generally mountainous. Between Cape Flattery in the north and San Francisco in the south there are few protected harbors, mostly located at various river entrances. At these river mouths shallow bars build, and even with modern improvements of breakwaters, protecting jetties, and other coastal works, the entrances continually suffer change. This can make entry hazardous under certain conditions of weather and tide.

Certainly the West Coast harbors have been much worse in the past, resulting in the popular appelation, "Graveyard of the Pacific," for the Columbia River entrance, for example. While this coast must be passed, no sailors can consider it a cruising area. However, the perception that only offshore passages should be considered needs to be modified.

Coastal passage from harbor to harbor is one good alternative to consider. Many improvements have been made and continue to be made at most harbors, and the U.S. Coast Guard offers advice and assistance. Together with a judicious selection of the time to travel using calm, settled weather, the coastal passage becomes a feasible alternative.

South of San Francisco there is an increased number of harbors suitable for small craft. But it is not till south of Point Conception, in the relatively benign conditions of Southern California, that the intensity of the yachting scene shows in the many well-appointed small craft harbors.

Travel south along the coast can be either by offshore passages taking advantage of the favorable wind and current, or a coastal passage using selected harbors in good weather, or a combination of the two. Usually such a combination utilizes a coastal passage along the Southern California coast. Any of these passages can be interesting and exciting, though all should be approached with care, preparation, and prudence. Both sail and power boats can make these passages.

Travel north offers fewer options. The coastal route becomes more favored because it offers occasional respite against the prevailing winds of summer. Offshore passages are possible, but they require a long offshore run to achieve the ability to make the needed northing. Sailing craft have either option, but powered craft usually stick to the coastal route when northward bound.

These options are examined in the following sections. The guide goes on to describe the harbors, anchorages, points of interest, and facilities useful to small craft along the coast. But the harbors are not all equally approachable and caution should be used in selecting and using those chosen for stop-overs.

Purpose and Limits of the Guide

This guide is intended to assist in selecting and identifying small boat harbors and anchorages between Seattle and San Diego for vessels transiting the coast. Descriptions of the harbors and facilities, local land form details, depth and land contour lines, lights and other navigational data are important to this use, but it is equally significant to remember that the sketch charts are hand drawn and are NOT meant to be accurate surveys. There are good nautical charts of the harbors, bays, and coast and these should be used for navigation. They are the basis for most sketches, augmented by such details or personal observations as may be of assistance to a small boat skipper. The chart sketches of this guide are intended to supplement proper harbor and coastal charts to provide information that may be useful to a skipper entering an unfamiliar harbor.

As in other guides published by CHARLIE'S CHARTS the sketches and drawings are based on personal visits. The information given is also from experience and has been chosen as that most useful to cruising sailors. Since we retain our pattern of having the text on a page dedicated to the sketched chart on the facing page, this sometimes means information has to be graded for importance and sometimes greatly edited to fit the space. This results in the omission of some general interest material. Similarly, the type of binding is chosen for its ability to remain open and lie flat on a chart table or seat. In these and other details our own cruising background has helped us choose data, style and presentation.

All suitable small craft harbors and anchorages along the coast are presented, except for a few rarely used ones. However, of those presented, some are not prudent selections for locally inexperienced visitors. This is particularly true of those harbors with bars subject to hazardous conditions at times of bad weather or an ebbing tide. Even those harbors deemed available as refuges for most conditions can become unapproachable if weather and sea conditions deteriorate. In such conditions we do not recommend any approach to the coast between Cape Flattery and San Francisco, for staying out at sea will be safer. Similar comments might be made for the few anchorages in this portion of the coast, where the problem is not that of a hazardous bar but rather of the anchorage being open to southerly winds.

Every effort has been made to provide correct and current information, but errors can easily occur, and things are always changing on such a popular and developing coast. Data, information, and lists such as those of the charts required, etc. can only be current as of the date of the publication of the guide. An indicative list of charts needed is given in Appendix 1. It will be most helpful if any errors or omissions, and constructive criticism, could be forwarded to the author at the address given for CHARLIE'S CHARTS. Later editions can be rectified and improved for future cruisers.

A good sailor is always prudent. It remains necessary for you to navigate and work your vessel safely from harbor to harbor. Naturally, this guide does not relieve a skipper of the responsibility of decision and of navigating his/her own vessel safely. Do not rely only on these charts or on any single aid to navigation. Check and verify all available data, and if variances occur use the greatest caution and make your own decisions in light of the conditions prevailing at the time.

Proceeding South

When leaving the Pacific Northwest, Puget Sound, and the Strait of Georgia to travel to southern U.S. ports the sailing instructions can very simply be given as, "Go to Neah Bay, pass Cape Flattery, then turn left....." But there is much more to consider than a straight offshore run.

The passage past Cape Flattery opening the Pacific Ocean is always exciting, no matter how often one has cruised offshore. It is even more thrilling if this is your first offshore cruise. But there are choices to make in the route south after clearing Cape Flattery.

Offshore Route

After standing well to the west of Cape Flattery the vessel turns to the south. The west coast of the United States tends to fall away to the east at a gradual rate till Cape Mendocino, then more rapidly thereafter. The vessel travelling south slowly leaves the coast further away to leeward as it carries the advantage of the California current and a favoring, prevailing northwest wind in summer months.

The California current has an average speed of 0.2 knots. It is stronger closer to the coast and its effect may be felt from about 10 miles off the coast to 300 miles offshore. It is a southerly proceeding stream of the main North Pacific current curving clockwise around the northern Pacific basin.

The prevailing northwesterly winds curve around the North Pacific High. The high is at its most northerly position during summer. However the pressure gradient between the offshore high and the continental low pressure system sometimes becomes very tight, and stronger winds and higher seas develop in offshore waters more than 60 miles from land. Conditions are generally a little less intense towards the coast. Gales and storms can still occur but are less violent and are of shorter duration during summer months.

The warmer winds passing over the cool water of the California current, together with coastal upwellings of colder water, are responsible for much of the reduced visibility and fog of summer and fall months. But since the coldest water is nearer the coast the densest and most frequent fog occurs closer to shore while the far offshore route is less subjected to fog. There are times when the fog banks can be extensive and occur for hundreds of miles.

As the coast recedes a vessel is further offshore with each mile travelled south. At Cape Mendocino it is common to be more than 60 miles offshore. Though this is beneficial in being sufficiently distant from this Cape with its fog banks and windy and disturbed conditions there is a drawback in that a vessel is in the higher wind (and resulting seas) caused by the pressure gradients. Once past Cape Mendocino courses are usually altered to begin to close the coast towards a destination such as San Francisco or San Diego.

Since north-south traffic lanes are usually densest towards the coast a skipper might assume that the vessel is clear of the shipping lanes, but as we have found, the north-south shipping lanes are not restricted to any narrow lane. Ships are widely dispersed and we have met vessels well beyond 60 miles off the coast. Therefore, a good watch is needed when travelling this route.

Briefly recapping -- a full offshore route appears more direct and less concerned with a lee shore, but strong winds and corresponding higher seas can be expected. Ships can still be met far offshore, though they are less prevalent than closer in. Advantages of this route lie in the clear sea room, less chance of fog, and in the possibility of a relatively fast passage when southbound.

Inshore Route

A route that stays between 15 to 30 miles off the coast offers several advantages, but has its own drawbacks. The effect of the California current is stronger, while the prevailing westerlies of summer are often steadier and less forceful here than further offshore. Thus the heavier seas of the offshore route can be avoided.

While a lee shore being closer at hand offers dangers, it is still sufficiently distant that any well handled vessel need not be disturbed and it is close enough to run to if an emergency situation arises.

The main drawback is a greatly increased seaborne traffic, for this is the area of the main coastal travelling zone. Vessels of all types, from the largest container ships and tankers to small fishing vessels, tugs, and other yachts can be met. Since this area is over the continental shelf, the trawler fishing fleets of several nations are also found here.

The other drawback is fog. The strength of the California current in this zone gives any south-going vessel a boost, but it also indicates the densest and coldest water. The cooled moist air of the westerlies over this cold stream produces dense fog and usually overcast conditions. This band of deep fog and weather can extend to 50 miles offshore, often moving seaward during the day and rolling back onshore at night. Though the areas of densest fog can vary along the coast, the entire zone from Cape Flattery to San Francisco and a little below can be considered as plagued with fog, often for as many as 8 to 10 days per month.

From Cape Flattery to the Columbia River entrance the westerly winds are steadier and skies are a little less overcast than south of the Columbia River. Fog, however, remains a problem and becomes more frequent after the middle of the summer. The entrance to the Strait of Juan de Fuca in particular, is made more difficult by the presence of fog at Cape Flattery.

Between the Columbia River entrance and San Francisco fog or haze can occur up to 25% of the time in summer, and overcast or obscured skies can be expected up to 40% of the time. Gales, though infrequent, can still occur, with strong winds occuring up to 10% of the time.

The quickest passages can be made along this inshore route, as the weather conditions and seas (but not the fog) are more benign. In addition, fishing for tuna and other fish can be most productive.

Recapping, the inshore route is usually the fastest when northbound, is less bothered by seas and high winds (except near Cape Mendocino), but heavier seaborne traffic will be met and fog is an annoying factor. A constant and careful look-out is essential.

Coastal, Harbor-Hopping Route

The bars that build up at the entrances to the harbors of the west coast, particularly those in Washington and Oregon make entry and exit rough and dangerous for all vessels under certain conditions. This has tended to give the coastal route a poor reputation. But provided the proper precautions are taken, the harbors are entered or left in favorable conditions and above all, that time is available to wait out bad weather, this route is quite practicable and offers several interesting aspects. It is probably the least exhausting route when a vessel is northbound.

The rocky islands that extend all along the coast make this a scenic delight for the shore-based photographer, but make it essential that most vessels travel well off the land. For most of the coast, a berth of 5 to 10 miles suffices, closing in to the offshore harbor buoy at the end of a particular run. Most offshore harbor buoys are laid one or two miles out from the breakwater jetties, and provide a point from which an entry line can be taken. It is always important to pick up the offshore buoy and not attempt to short-cut or otherwise avoid the proper approach.

San Francisco is a common destination point for a first step down the coast (even when coasting), then leaving for the passage past Point Conception to the warmer and less boisterous conditions of Southern California. Harbor-hopping is easier on this southern leg. Harbors are more numerous and access to them is generally less restricted by weather than those north of San Francisco.

The choice of route -- whether fully offshore, inshore, or harbor-hopping -- is usually determined by time and preference. The offshore routes, being direct, are shorter but are exposed to weather. The usual time from Cape Flattery to San Francisco varies from 6 to 10 days. The coastal route, on the other hand, is interesting but very much slower, as the harbor entrances north of San Francisco have bars which can be greatly affected by the state of the tide and weather. The harbor-hopping route could take as much as a month to complete.

While this guide describes and shows sketches for almost all useable harbors, strangers are not advised to use all of them because under certain combinations of sea and tides they become extremely dangerous. The Coast Guard has established a rough bar advisory sign which must be heeded. It is diamond shaped, painted white with an orange border, and with the words "Rough Bar" in black letters. The sign is equipped with two alternating quick flashing yellow lights which are activated when seas exceed 4 ft. in height and are considered hazardous for small boats. The Pilot cautions, however, that if the lights are not flashing, it is no guarantee that sea conditions are favorable. The Coast Guard may close an entrance when conditions become sufficiently hazardous.

RM

Dire whelk
(Searlesia dira)

Weather

The most important factor to consider when deciding the time of year to travel is the weather. The Pacific Ocean can be benign and seem to live up to its name, but it is a very large body of water that has significant inter-locking relationships with global weather.

The major meteorlogical feature that concerns travel along the Pacific Coast is the North Pacific High -- a high pressure area that is resident off the west coast of North America. At the perimeter of the high, and continuing radially beyond, the velocity of the winds increase as they are rotated in a giant clockwise direction resulting from the Coriolis forces of the Earth's spin. The North Pacific High does not remain stationary, nor is it the same size all the time. It moves as the overall planetary weather systems affect it, sometimes enlarging and building, moving, weakening and reducing, and rebuilding again. But statistically, the High shows a trend of annual migration from near 30°N, 130°W in January and February (winter) to more northwest, about 38°N, 150°W, in July and August (summer) before retracing southwesterly again. During any season the day-to-day position of the high can vary from these average positions, and its perimeters are reported in daily weather broadcasts.

The stable and normally larger highs of the summer period i.e. June to August, provide the best time for travel along the coast. Though bad weather can be encountered at any time of year, the generally good weather across the Pacific at this time also means that fewer gales are encountered near the coast. May and September are almost as good as the best summer period. As the advent of winter occurs the frequency of storms and the parade of lows with their bad weather increases, and voyages made during these times must expect to meet inclement conditions.

High pressure systems dominate the weather in California offshore waters, although an occasional storm disrupts the good weather, particularly in winter and early spring. In waters from San Francisco northward the pressure gradient between highs and lows is often very tight, creating strong northerly winds during spring.

The prevalence of fog from the Strait of Juan de Fuca to San Diego is another feature of the weather which is common throughout the summer months. The reduced visibility makes the entry of strange harbors not just difficult but often dangerous. Night entrances into strange harbors is never a good idea; but to do so during dense fog is foolhardy in the extreme. Remaining offshore until visibility improves and daylight arrives, or continuing along the coast is a much safer and wiser course of action to follow. One's navigation must be accurate, current NOAA charts must be used, and no short-cuts should be taken.

Santa Ana (Santana) Winds are local, violent winds that may occur from Santa Barbara to Newport. These hot, desert winds may increase from 0 to 40 - 50 knots in twenty minutes with little or no warning. Prior to their arrival there is often good visibility, the air seems noticeably dry, and a dark-brown dust cloud may appear. And then the wind.........

Currents

The massive ocean movement known as the California Current sweeps south along the Pacific Coast of the United States at about .2 knots. The direction of the surface winds can accelerate or retard its speed to a considerable extent. Extending offshore more than 300 miles, it gives a nice boost to southbound vessels while northbound boats must work harder for each mile gained along the route against the prevailing northwesterly winds.

A weak counter-current -- the Davidson Inshore Current -- flows in a northerly direction from San Diego to Point Conception from July to February and from Point Conception to Cape Flattery from November to February.

Tidal currents vary greatly depending on the inequality of the tidal differential (two high waters and two low waters) each day, the area of the waters being drained (or filled) by the tidal flow, and the size of the channel. Tidal Current Tables must be referred to before transiting a harbor entrance in order for passage to be made at the optimum time. Do not confuse high or low water with slack water for land-locked harbors, narrow channels, or tidal rivers as there are several factors which determine slack water. For the strength of the current and estimated time of slack water one must refer to Tidal Current Tables.

Dangers

Aside from the obvious and standard dangers of rocks, shoals, and heavy weather there are some additional dangers peculiar to these waters.

Sneaker Waves

Sometimes a very large breaking wave seems to suddenly appear out of nowhere. Offshore during heavy weather a particular pattern of waves will produce immense steep waves which are known as rogue or freak waves. These should not be confused with sneaker waves which sometimes form in shoaling waters along the coast. Such waves form as a result of a combination of factors: the speed of the ebb current, the size of the swell and the water depth.

Kelp

Kelp grows on rocky bottoms, and where it is seen in or on the water it should be taken as a sign of danger. Along this coast it is particularly heavy in parts of the Santa Barbara Channel and in the San Diego area. Living kelp usually indicates depths of less than 10 fathoms, and since it is attached to the bottom its tendrils stream out in a line with the surface currents. However, dead or detached kelp often seen floating freely on the surface obviously does not indicate the same thing, and should cause no alarm.

Deadheads and Log Debris

Logging is a major industry in coastal areas of Washington and Oregon. Much of this timber is transported by log booms, while spring freshets and heavy rains often add to the debris from logging operations. Thus it is no surprise to find logs, deadheads, and other detritus floating in coastal waters.

Dredges

The natural shoaling of many harbor entrances and channels makes regular dredging a necessity. But when a dredge is operating in what already seems like a narrow channel, the space available for passage seems small indeed. Judgement and skill are required when passing a dredge for its anchor lines must be given adequate clearance. Passage of an operating dredge in a channel must await safe conditions.

Some dredges have a barge nearby for collecting the dredged material, while others have a long system of large pipes for pumping the silt outside the channel area. Never pass between the dredge and the buoys or lights marking the pipeline.

Pipelaying Barges and Jetbarges

Clearance of a mile in all directions should be given to pipelaying barges and jetbarges as they have anchors which extend outwards 3,500 to 5,000 feet. Vessels associated with the pipelaying operation may be contacted on Ch. 16 if advice is needed for safe passage through the vicinity.

Fish Havens

Fish havens can be found anywhere along this coast but are more common in Californian waters. Usually marked by buoys, and relatively close inshore, they must be given adequate clearance.

Oil Wells

Many offshore operating oil wells and exploratory wells are to be found in Santa Barbara Channel and other coastal Californian waters. Though the main structure is normally well lit (resembling a huge meccano set creation strung with lights) any subsidiary structures within 100 yards of the main platform are marked only by reflective material. A vessel should give good clearance to such operations.

Congested Traffic

The thousands of pleasure craft in an around the large cities along this coast can be intimidating to vessels from smaller population centers. All one can do is to obey the rules of the road and be ready to take evasive action in the event that other boaters are not operating their boats safely. By moving with the flow of traffic and maintaining a safe distance from other vessels one can help to prevent collisions. In theory, this sounds reasonable but there is no doubt that freeway boat traffic adds a real element of stress by day's end.

Crossing Bars

As the ocean swells approach an area of shallowing water, the increased resistance of the ocean bottom causes the water to pile up forming increasingly steeper seas. When these seas become so steep that they become unstable and cannot support the water at the top of the swell, they collapse in the form of breaking seas. Thus, when crossing a bar a vessel may encounter anything from a gentle swell to towering, breaking seas only a few seconds apart.

The boathandling problems under these conditions are similar to those experienced in heavy following seas, the main difference being that they are steeper and much closer together. This results in the vessel slewing about and tending to broach. Of course this must be avoided, not only because of the potential damage, but also because of the possibility that the vessel may be carried out of the channel on to jetties or shoal areas. To control a vessel in such conditions demands seamanship at the helm and puts tremendous loads on the rudder and steering mechanism. Sailboats are easier to control than powerboats because of their straighter keels and greater weight below sea level. Also, their larger rudder area as compared with powerboats gives them an advantage.

The decision to enter any harbor which involves the crossing of a bar must not be taken lightly. Preparation of the vessel is necessary; careful planning by the skipper is essential. Most pleasure boaters are unprepared for the experience of crossing a bar under turbulent conditions no matter what is read prior to the passage. Let us examine a worst case scenario to visualize what can go wrong, so that preventive measures may be taken ahead of time.

The most common vessel failures are loss of steering from either shearing of the rudder stock or from steering gear failure. This leads to loss of control of the vessel's direction in heavy swells and/or breaking seas. Broaching of the vessel makes it vulnerable to the full force of the seas on the boatsides. The cabinsides may be stove in, ports and windows broken or the companionway damaged such that the vessel is flooded. With batteries in the bilge this usually means the loss of engine power and restart capability.

Another possibility is the reduction in available power if the engine becomes starved for fuel. The erratic motion while crossing the bar can cause the fine deposits in fuel tanks to plug strainers and screens thereby restricting the passage of fuel. Since most boats have only a single fuel filter this is a real possibility. In addition, modern light displacement sailboats with their fine rigging often suffer failure under heavy surf conditions and this can be another casualty.

Assuming that one has survived the worst of the bar there is still a possibility of engine failure occurring upstream from the bar. Fuel may run out because more has been used (or spilled through overflow piping) in making the passage. Many vessels are not equipped with sufficiently heavy ground tackle to set an anchor against strong tidal and river currents; as a result, they may be swept onto a shoal or breakwater by the current.

The skipper must plan his entrance such that it is only attempted during a flood tide -- the last of the flood being the best. Therefore it is critical that Tide and Current Tables be consulted to determine when the optimuim time has arrived for starting the entrance.

The Coast Guard have lookout towers and stations at all bar entrances. Contact them (Ch. 16) prior to committing the vessel when crossing a bar for the first time or if sea conditions are at all in doubt. Remember, when seen from seaward, the appearance of seas in the distance, especially when viewed from the backside, is greatly diminished and they appear to be more benign than the real thing. It is far better to get on-the-spot advice regarding the safety of attempting an entrance than to run into problems and then have to call for help. The Coast Guard will often escort a vessel into a harbor; they would rather aid a boat to make port than look for bodies following an unwise entry that results in tragedy.

Double-check that all deck gear is securely fastened prior to crossing a bumpy bar so that damage will not be done by gear stowed on deck that comes adrift, nor will it be lost overboard. The risk of sending someone forward to secure a loose object must be avoided. All crew on deck should wear safety harnesses and preferably, survival suits. No short-cuts should be taken where safety is involved as all resources may be taxed to the limit.

Hypothermia (Exposure)

The cold California Current sweeping the coast, and brisk, chilly winds are common phenomena for the entire Pacific Coast until south of Point Conception. Particularly in sailboats where crew are often exposed to the full effect of the wind, spray, and air temperature, the wind chill factor can render conditions equivalent to much colder temperatures.

Cool winds can cause a considerable chilling, while strong cold winds can lower body temperature by causing a loss greater than the replacement rate. As this condition is moderated by any barrier to the wind's effect, the value of a good dodger behind which to shelter and windproof clothing combined with several layers of underclothing is obvious. Except when the sun's rays beat directly down on calm days, it is worthwhile to wear one's foul weather suit as an outer windproof covering with several layers consisting of sweaters, flannel shirts, and longjohns underneath. Gloves are necessary at times -- wool being the best in cold, and rubber fisherman's working gloves best in wet conditions. Wool toques help to reduce a major heat loss from the head, while neck scarves and seaboots with woolen socks are also recommended.

Such cold weather clothing is needed even in summer because in addition to wind chill, one may be standing or sitting for long periods without sufficient activity to generate heat; and when travelling on cloudy or foggy days convective cooling can be another cause of body heat loss.

Every effort should be made to stay on board. Safety harness should be used whenever it is warranted. If a crew member does go into the water every minute counts in the recovery. It is especially important to realize that a person in cold water goes into shock quickly, and as hypothermia advances one may become disoriented and unable to assist oneself.

A periodic refueling of body heat for those on watch greatly helps to keep the energy level high and prevent chilling. By keeping one or two thermos bottles full of boiling water, hot drinks can be made by any of the crew without having to start the stove. But keep the Mexican coffee and hot toddies until one is off watch as alcohol gives an artificial feeling of warmth.

Provisions

The variety, quality, and price of food available in U. S. city super-markets ranks with the best in the world. However, many of the retail outlets within walking distance of marinas or anchorages are convenience stores having a limited selection, low turnover, and high prices. Thus, one is advised to stock the vessel in the home port with as many necessary provisions as can be stowed. Another factor which reinforces the foregoing is that when one is cruising a car is seldom at one's disposal and the carrying and ferrying of groceries to a vessel at anchor, or at the end of a slippery dock, can be tedious.

When, one arrives at a small community only a few perishable items or fresh baked goods need be purchased, and if one arrives at a moorage that is convenient to a supermarket having a good selection with competitive prices, one can have a major replenishment of provisions.

Reciprocal Mooring at Yacht Clubs

One of the advantages of membership in a yacht club is the possibility of reciprocal moorage at yacht club facilities when one arrives in a distant port. With a little bit of preparation one can help to make this a reality.

When planning your cruise, ask the secretary of the club to which you belong to correspond with the yacht clubs in cities that are along your route offering reciprocal docking privileges. Verify before leaving that your club is "on the list" so that you know which clubs to approach for moorage -- otherwise, you'll be out of luck. Because of the pressure of many boaters arriving in Californian ports on their way to warm cruising grounds the yacht clubs want to see proof of current club membership by the owner of the vessel so keep your membership card and ship's papers handy.

If it is known that a major regatta or race is being sponsored by a club to which you are going it would be advisable to arrange your cruising plans to arrive after the event in order to avoid a time when facilities will already be taxed to the limit by the special function.

Cruising Permits

All vessels of foreign registry must enter the United States and apply for a Cruising Permit at one of the specified Ports of Entry. These include Seattle, Anacortes, Bellingham, Everett, Port Townsend, Port Angeles in Washington; Astoria, Coos Bay and Newport in Oregon; Eureka, San Francisco-Oakland, Port San Luis, Los Angeles-Long Beach, and San Diego in California. Often Customs officers handle Immigration and Health requirements. Yachts from Canada, Australia, New Zealand, Argentina, the Bahamas, and West Germany will be given a cruising permit, valid for 6 months, which allows the yacht to travel in specified waters. The skipper is responsible for notifying Customs (by telephone) when arriving at Ports of Entry. Vessels from other countries have more complicated procedures to comply with as no reciprocal arrangements have been agreed to at present.

Disposal of Refuse

For centuries the oceans of the world have been considered as limitless, not only in size but also as a cheap and convenient pump-out station. Only recently has the ecological movement, sparked by the research of Jacques Cousteau and others, begun to publicize a need for concern. Cruising boaters now may go ashore on any beach in the world and find plastic debris. Since the advent of the plastic age in the 1950s the ocean's shores have been fouled and defaced by the indestructable evidence of the "disposable" attitude.

Newport, Oregon is a leader in the area of refuse collection and recycling. It is to be hoped that other cities in the United States and throughout the world will take similar action to prevent further pollution of our oceans.

Every boater has a duty not to discard non-organic garbage at sea. Since there was sufficient space on board to stow the containers at the beginning of the trip, there obviously is the same capacity available for returning them to shore-based recycling depots or garbage containers. It is hoped the photographs on the following page will encourage the reader to return bottles, cans, and plastic debris to shore so that recycling can be effected. The following poem, printed by courtesy of the author, says it clearly in a few words:

IN YOUR WAKE

What do you leave
in your wake?
The choice is many,
few stop to think.

A sparkling trail
on a shining sea,
gone in a trice
to eternity?

Or a beer can track
that staggers along
to mar and foul
a virgin beach?

Or do you leave
the plastic debris
of the packaged world
to smother a bird,
kill a fish,
foul a prop,
or litter a coast?

The wake you leave
tells it all.
What is the legacy
that you bequeath?

Carey Paige

Debris Harms Our Marine Life

Rex Herron

Brian Lawhead

Endangered species also suffer. Sea turtles mistake plastic bags for jellyfish.

Some 30,000 Northern Fur seals die yearly from entanglement in netting, a 50% population decline in 30 years has been noted.

Common items like six-pack rings, fishing line and strapping bands entangle and kill sea birds, fish and mammals. Plastics can last many hundreds of years, harming even large mammals like the gray whale.

Fishermen and boater safety is jeopardized when debris fouls propellers or causes engines to overheat. Heavy losses of time and money are reported from debris damage to vessels and equipment.

Pierce Harris

Jim Boeder

... AND THE ANIMALS ARE SUFFERING.

NASA

Plastics can last for hundreds of years in the ocean. A careless moment lasts generations.

Jim Boeder

Our Blue Ocean Is Becoming Pink, Yellow, White And Green . . .

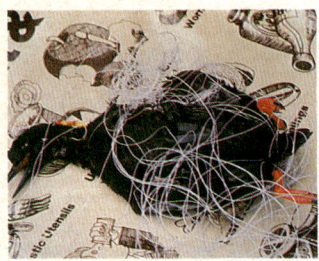

Dale Snow

Frans Lanting

Birds, fish and mammals mistake plastic for food. Some birds even feed it to their young!

With plastic filling stomachs, animals may die of starvation or poisoning.

You can help!

- Make it boat policy that no trash is discarded, washed or blown overboard.
- Minimize the amount of non-degradable products on board. Provision your vessel using bulk/refillable containers.
- Stow trash for disposal in port. Encourage your port to provide convenient refuse disposal facilities.
- Where possible retrieve trash encountered in the ocean.
- Share your concern with friends, fellow mariners and family.
- Participate in beach clean-ups, and leave the beach clean after visits.

DON'T TEACH YOUR TRASH TO SWIM!
WGM

The Port of Newport & Fishing Fleet Encourage All Boaters And Beach-Goers To Protect The Marine Environment.

This material has been reprinted (by permission) from a brochure published by the National Marine Fisheries Service, Marine Refuse Disposal Project, Newport, Oregon.

George Antonelis

Whale Watching

The grey whale migrates from the summer feeding grounds in Alaskan waters to the birthing and breeding havens in Mexican waters. The actual route is usually within 10 miles of the coast. The southbound trip is started by the pregnant females in the fall, followed by the rest of the herd making their passage as late as February. The northbound trip of the estimated herd of about 17,000 whales, begins in April with arrival in Arctic waters in June or July.

Those who travel along the coast in the areas covered by this guide will probably experience the joy and excitement of seeing whales from the deck of their own boat. Since there is a growing population of both whales and boaters, it is essential that some guidelines for viewing be understood.

Whales have never gone out of their way to follow, chase, or kill human beings, or to separate a mother from her child. Unfortunately, man does not have the same unblemished record. Man's actions have at times resulted in injured whales attacking boats, and frantic "mother whales" (cows) reacting in an erratic manner when separated from their calves. In the same way that we are startled by the sudden appearance of a hornet, a whale can be surprised by the quick arrival of a motor boat rushing into its immediate waters. Both humans and whales can react with alarm. Therefore, a few basic rules for viewing whales will make it a pleasurable, worry-free experience for both parties:

- stay at least 100 yards away from a whale

- approach the whale at engine-idle speed

- approach from the whale's side, never "head-on"

- travel parallel to and at the same speed as the whale

- avoid abrupt changes in direction or speed of the vessel

- do not cross the whale's path

- never get between two whales

- never "box in" a whale, i.e. have a boat on either side

- if a curious whale approaches your vessel, put the engine in neutral

Grey Whale

These stocky whales, which have no distinct dorsal fin, may reach 40 ft. and weigh up to 40 tons. Females are larger than males. They are a slate or mottled grey, with scattered whitish patches of barnacles or whale lice.

Surfacing & Blowing   Beginning a dive   Sounding

SEATTLE

The bustling city of Seattle is geographically located such that it enjoys protected boating on both salt and fresh water as well as skiing, hiking, and mountaineering on the nearby Cascade Range and Olympic Mountains. Surrounding Salmon Bay and Lake Union, it shares the shores of Lake Washington with the cities of Kirkland, Bellevue, and Renton. Seattle's western shoreline borders Elliott Bay and Shilshole Bay on Puget Sound. Since adjoining fresh water areas are above sea level it is necessary to transit the Hiram M. Chittenden Locks before proceeding via the 8-mile long Washington Ship Canal to Lake Washington. During this trip one is literally boating through the heart of the city, a feature which makes Seattle unique among west coast ports.

The city boasts of a wealth of facilities and services for the boating public. Two large moorage facilities operated by the Port of Seattle provide pleasure craft moorage for over 1,400 boats at Shilshole Marina on Shilshole Bay, and Fisherman's Terminal on Salmon Bay provides a large mooring basin for the huge fishing fleet which is based here. In addition, Seattle has 18 piers to service the deep-sea vessels which make this a busy commercial port. Private marinas, ship chandlers, repair and hauling facilities can be found lining the shores of Lake Washington. Many residences enjoy the luxury of a private dock built out from their waterfront property.

The Hiram M. Chittenden Locks consist of two locks for boat traffic -- a large one (825 ft. by 80 ft.) and a smaller one (150 ft. by 28 ft.). The lift varies from 6 to 26 ft. depending on the lake level and tidal fluctuations. On the south side of the small lock is a 21-weir fish ladder which allows migrating salmon and trout to swim upstream; an underwater viewing gallery is provided to watch the action. About 500,000 salmon and sea-run trout use the fish ladder while about 100,000 commercial and pleasure craft pass through the locks annually.

The only extra equipment needed for passing through the locks are at least two 50-ft. mooring lines having a 12-inch eye. The crew must be alert and attentive to taking in or paying out the line as the vessel is raised or lowered. A free booklet available at marine stores entitled, "Guidelines for Boaters," should be studied prior to locking through for the first time. It takes about 30 minutes for vessels locking through the large lock, about 10 minutes for those using the small lock.

Six bridges span the 8-mile long Washington Ship Canal; clearances range from 30 ft. to 57 ft. "Guidelines for Boaters" lists the horn signals required for the opening of the various bridges.

West Point Lighthouse

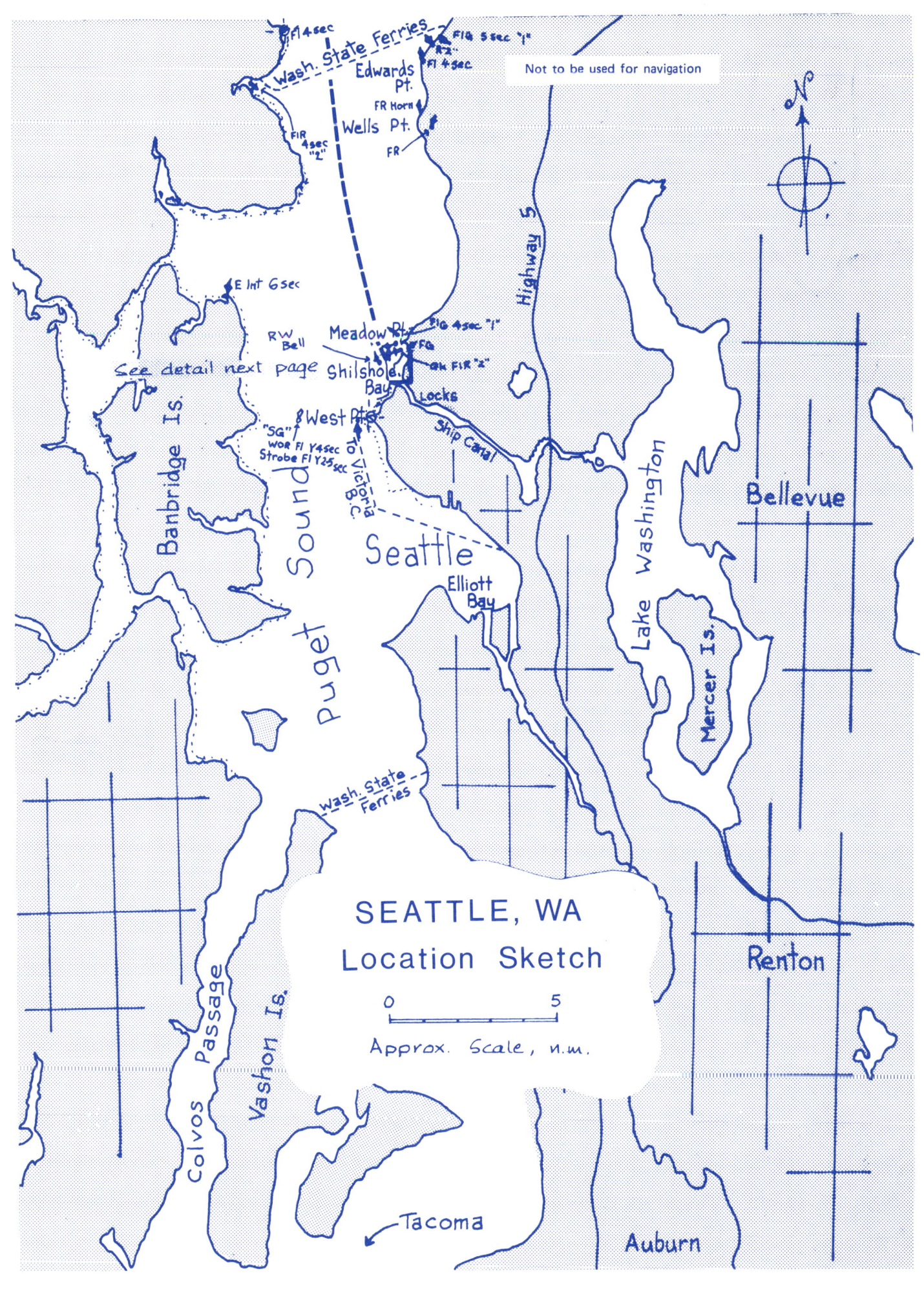

Fl 4sec

Wash. State Ferries

Fl G 5 sec "1"

Edwards
Pt.

"2"
Fl 4sec

Not to be used for navigation

FR Horn

Wells Pt.

F l R
4sec
"2"

FR

E Int 6sec

Highway 5

Fl G 4sec "1"

RW
Bell

Meadow Pt.

F G

Shilshole
Bay

Qk Fl R "2"

See detail next page

Locks

West Pt.

Ship Canal

"SG"
WOR Fl Y4sec
Strobe Fl Y25sec

To Victoria
B.C.

Puget Sound

Seattle

Banbridge Is.

Elliott
Bay

Lake Washington

Bellevue

Mercer Is.

Wash. State
Ferries

SEATTLE, WA

Location Sketch

Renton

0   5

Approx. Scale, n.m.

Colvos Passage

Vashon Is.

Tacoma

Auburn

The largest pleasure craft facility in Seattle is **Shilshole Bay Marina.**
Begun in 1960, the last addition was made in 1978. Not only can it be
reached easily when sailing down Puget Sound without having to pass through the
deep-sea port facilities (which are in Elliott Bay to the south), but the
vessels moored here do not have to line up to wait their turn to pass through
the locks as do boats moored on Lake Washington's shores. The marina has the
best of facilities including a tidal grid, while a boatyard at the southern end
can haul boats up to 42 ft. The Texaco fuel dock has limited picnic style
groceries; for major re-stocking one must take a bus or taxi to the nearest
supermarket. A bus stop is on the road next to the marina.

A vessel may enter at either end of the breakwater. As seen on the sketch
transient berths are on J dock, near the gas dock, and on the north and south
sides of the central pier. There are a number of registration stations
scattered around the marina where a form is to be completed and the correct
amount enclosed for moorage. Rates are 35 cents per foot per day. Several
restroom, laundry, and shower facilities are located throughout the marina.

Harbor Island Marina is a private marina located about 8 miles to the south.
To reach it one must proceed to the Duwamish River which empties into Elliott
Bay. The newest marina in Seattle, it is located under the West Seattle Bridge
(Cl. 41 ft.). Two spaces are available for transient vessels at 35 cents per
foot per day. A fuel station is located here but the nearest outlet for
propane is about 4 blocks distant.

When visiting this beautiful city it seems hard to believe that Seattle's
first settlers arrived as late as 1851 after rounding the Horn in the schooner,
"Exact." Named after Chief Seattle of the Duwamish Indian Tribe, Seattle has a
wealth of interesting attractions. Some of these are: the Museum of History
and Industry, Conservatory Volunteer Park (the Seattle Art Museum is located
here), Japanese Garden, Pacific Science Centre, Museum of Flight, Underground
Tour of Seattle, Space Needle (for spectacular views of the city), Pike Place
Market (an open-air market featuring produce, apparel, arts and crafts),
Seattle Aquarium and the Omnidrome (the last two being located on Pier 59).

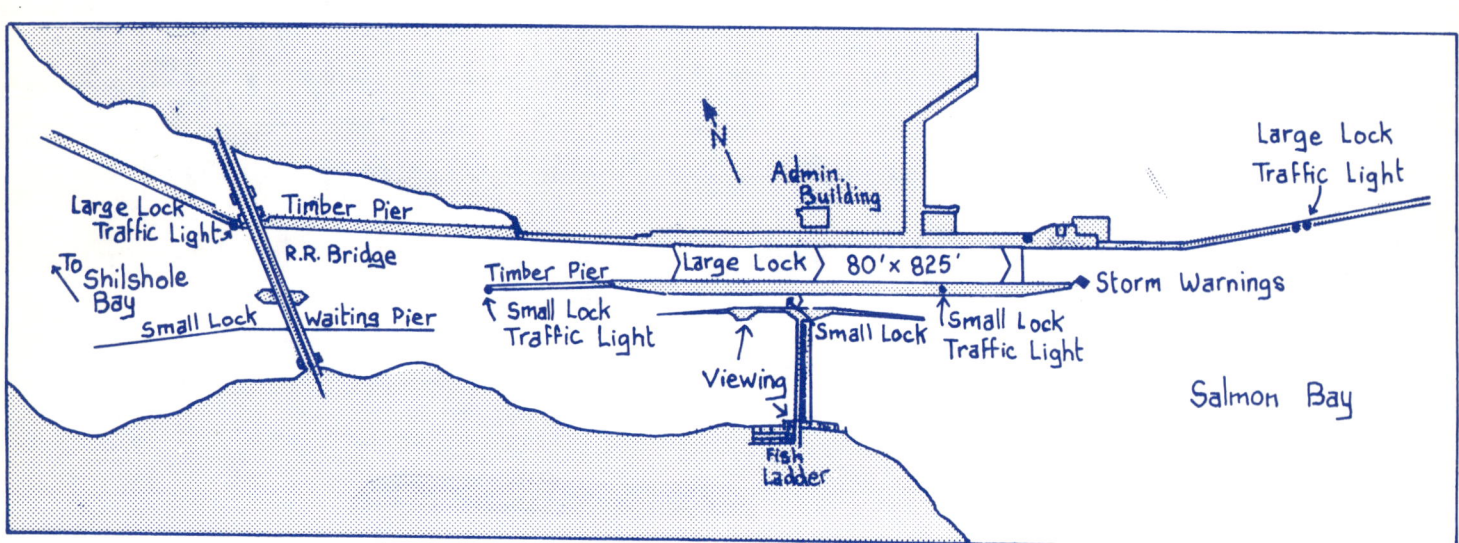

Hiram M. Chittenden Locks

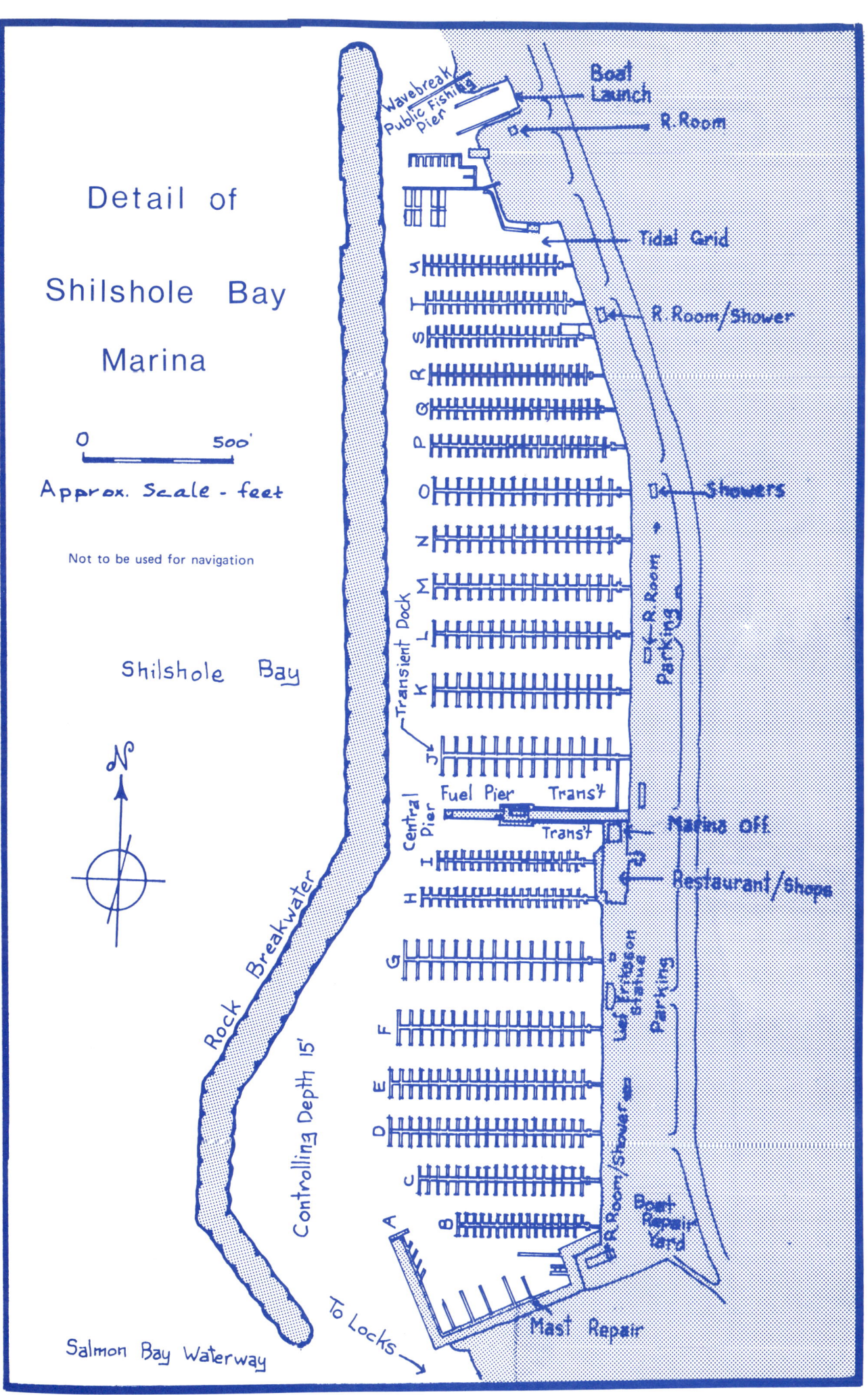

Detail of

Shilshole Bay

Marina

0   500'

Approx. Scale - feet

Not to be used for navigation

Shilshole   Bay

N

Rock Breakwater

Controlling Depth 15'

Salmon Bay Waterway

To Locks

Wavebreak
Public Fishing Pier

Boat Launch

R. Room

Tidal Grid

R. Room/Shower

Showers

R. Room → Parking

Transient Dock

Fuel Pier   Trans't

Trans't

Marina Off.

Restaurant/Shops

Central Pier

Fuel Friction Station

Parking

R. Room/Shower

Boat Repair Yard

Mast Repair

J S T S R Q P O N M L K J I H G F E D C A B

18

EVERETT

This city of 59,000 is strategically located on the doorstep of two cruising areas: Puget Sound and the San Juan Islands. The popularity of boating has made necessary the development of small craft facilities second only to the massive complex at Marina del Rey in southern California.

Everett is located about 25 miles north of Seattle on the edge of a fan-shaped shallow area in the eastern side of Possession Sound. The snow-capped mountains of the Olympic Peninsula make a stunning backdrop to the waters of Puget Sound while to the east are the tree-covered slopes of the Cascade range.

The shoal area near Everett extends south from Tulalip Bay to flashing buoy "1" and is marked further to the south by bell buoy "3". After rounding this buoy to port the vessel can proceed toward the entrance which is protected by two breakwaters. Lights are at the ends of each of the breakwaters which protect the dredged channel leading to the small craft harbor. The channel is marked by lights, buoys, and lighted and unlighted ranges.

The Snohomish River has a navigable channel which runs through the western side of the small boat harbor and continues for some distance to port facilities upriver. The huge smokestack of a pulpmill located upriver is prominent for miles. Though the river current becomes more evident during low tide, it is not normally a major problem when navigating in the small craft harbor area. Log booms are often moored to the eastern side of the long rock breakwater protecting the basin and channel from westerly winds. From fall to spring California sea lions congregate on this breakwater (Jetty Island) making their presence known with a continuous babble of barking.

The **Port of Everett Marina** has accommodation for over 1,500 boats, which includes some covered moorage. Numerous transient berths are available at 20 cents per foot per day. One may contact the Harbormaster on Ch. 16 for berth allocation or tie up to a vacant spot on the transient docks shown on the sketch. Stations where one may register and pay the moorage fee are along these docks. Repair facilities, hoists, ship chandleries, and yacht brokers are located on the north side of the docks, while on the south side is Everett Marina Village which is a collection of specialty shops and restaurants. As propane is no longer available at the fuel dock one must enquire about availability at an RV outlet in the city.

Of interest in the immediate area is Robert Louis Stevenson's ship, "Equator," which is on display while undergoing restoration. Further away on 13th Street is a Firefighter's Museum which offers through-the-window viewing while a self-guided walking tour of the Port Gardner district can be obtained from the Public Library. Transportation can be arranged to reach the Boeing 747/767 plant where 90-minute tours are held Monday through Friday. Here one can see the largest (by volume) building in the world which is 11 stories tall and covers 62 acres. For more information call 342 - 4801. Children under 12 are not allowed.

Looking to the future, completion of U.S. Naval Station Puget Sound is expected by the early 1990's when the aircraft carrier "Nimitz" will be based here along with numerous support ships and personnel.

EVERETT, WA

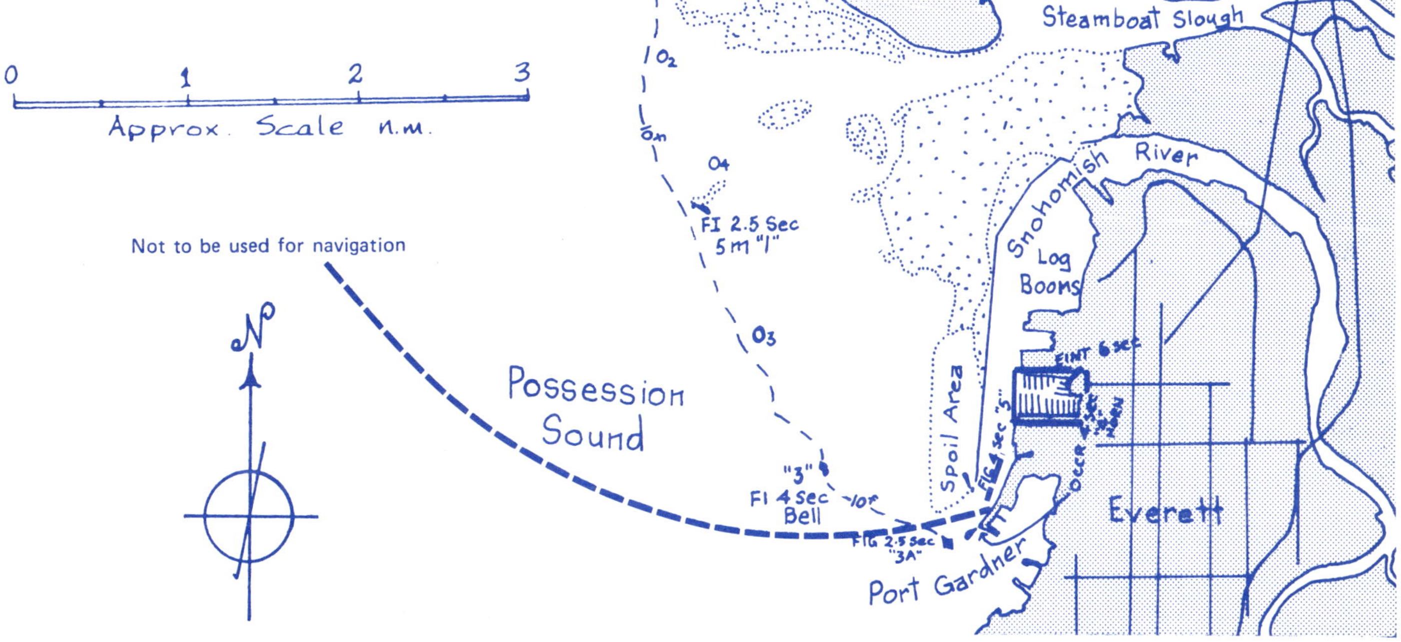

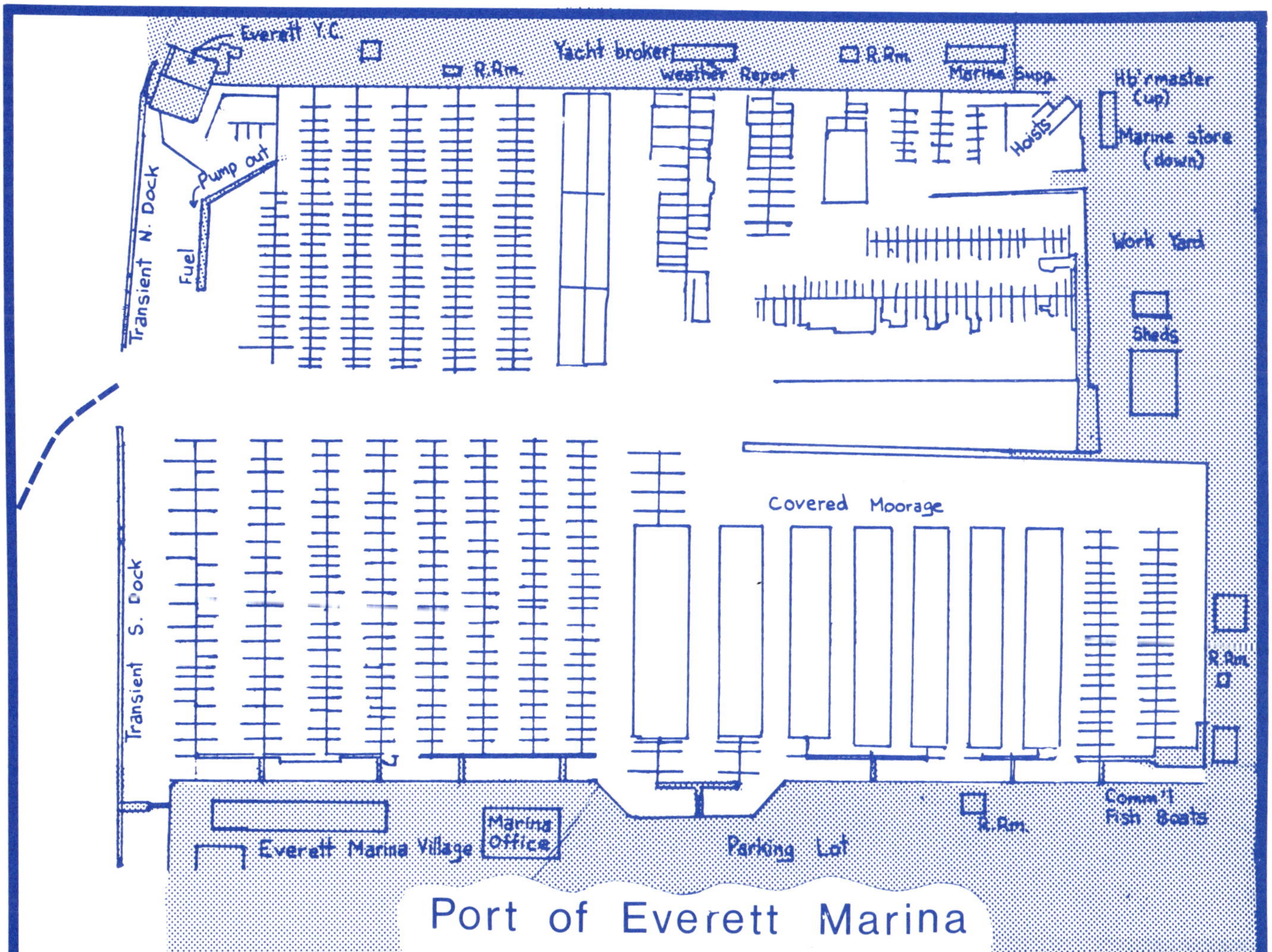

0 1 2 3
Approx. Scale n.m.

N

Hermosa Pt.

Tulalip Bay

Mission Beach

Steamboat Slough

Snohomish River

Log Booms

Fl 2.5 Sec 5m "1"

O2

Om

O4

O3

Possession Sound

Spoil Area

Fl Int 6 sec

Fl 4 sec "3"

"3" Fl 4 Sec Bell

Fl G 2.5 sec "3A"

Occr

Port Gardner

Everett

Everett Y.C.

R.Rm.

Yacht broker

Weather Report

R.Rm.

Marina Supp.

Hb'rmaster (up)

Marine store (down)

Hoists

Work Yard

Sheds

Pump out

Fuel

Transient N. Dock

Transient S. Dock

Covered Moorage

R.Rm.

R.Rm.

Comm'l Fish Boats

Everett Marina Village

Marina Office

Parking Lot

Port of Everett Marina

ANACORTES

Anacortes lies on the northern tip of Fidalgo Island and is connected to Rosario Strait via Guemes Channel. Rosario Strait in turn leads northward into the Strait of Georgia and thence to the extensive cruising areas of British Columbia, and also around the top of the main group of San Juan Islands to the Strait of Juan de Fuca. This strategic location attracted the ferry terminals that provide access to the San Juans as well as across to Vancouver Island.

The city used to be concentrated around its waterfront and the older part of Anacortes is characterised by brick and concrete buildings. Now it sprawls for some distance southward and westward along the highway, and the main activity seems to have shifted from the fishing town emphasis around its docks.

There are at least 3 marinas in and near Anacortes, the two largest being on the eastern shore of Fidalgo Bay. Across the bay the tanker docking facilities, refinery works, and massive storage tanks rise on March Point. The bay is shallow but dredged and marked channels lead to the two marinas. This is an excellent place to haul a boat as there is a large work area and equipment and supplies are readily available.

Anacortes Marina is less than one-half mile south of Cap Sante, and the marina is made obvious by the wooden piling breakwater that surrounds it. Enter at the south as shown on the sketch. Privately owned and operated, the marina has covered moorage areas, a fuel dock, facilities for haul-outs and maintenance, excellent security, and plenty of parking space. Transient vessels are welcome, though the available space fills rapidly on weekends.

Skyline Marina at Flounder Bay is part of a real estate development to the west of the main city center of Anacortes. Full services are provided here.

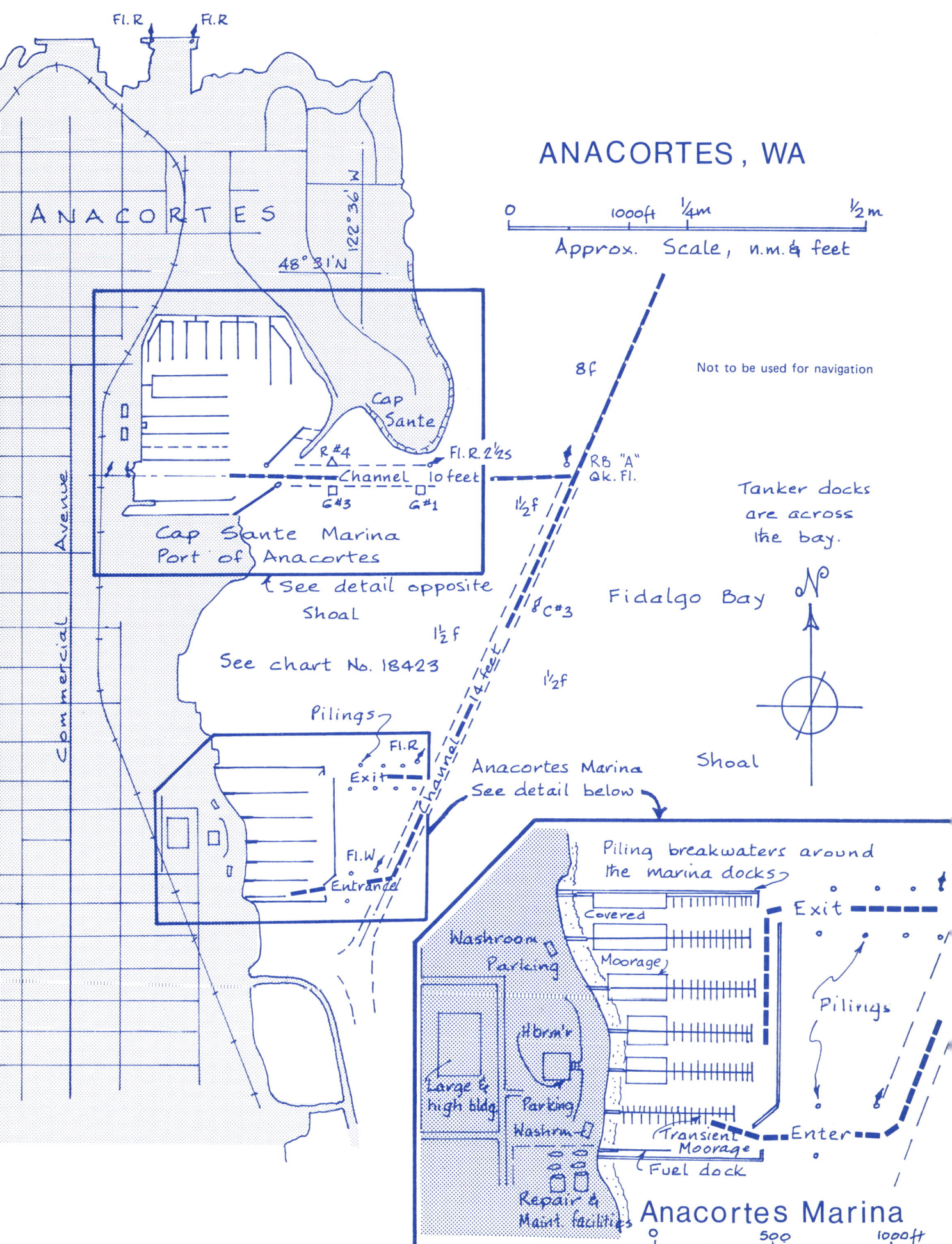

Guemes Channel

Fl. R   Fl. R

ANACORTES

122° 36' W

48° 31' N

ANACORTES, WA

0   1000ft   ¼m   ½m

Approx. Scale, n.m. & feet

8f

Not to be used for navigation

Cap
Sante

R #4   Fl. R. 2½S   RB "A"
Channel 10 feet   Qk. Fl.

□   □
G #3   G #1   1½f

Cap Sante Marina
Port of Anacortes

Tanker docks
are across
the bay.

See detail opposite
Shoal   8 C #3   Fidalgo Bay   N

1½f

See chart No. 18423   1½f

Channel 14 feet

Shoal

Pilings

Fl. R

Exit

Anacortes Marina
See detail below

Fl. W

Entrance

Piling breakwaters around
the marina docks

Covered   Exit

Washroom
Parking   Moorage   Pilings

H'brm'r

Large &
high bldg.   Parking

Washrm   Transient
Moorage   Enter

Fuel dock

Repair &
Maint. facilities   # Anacortes Marina

0   500   1000ft

Operated by the Port of Anacortes, **Cap Sante Marina (Boat Haven)** lies below the rocky bulk of Cap Sante which affords it excellent protection. Breakwaters protect the harbor entrance. This is a large and still developing marina, home to many of the fishing vessels that work the northern Pacific waters. Transient vessels should find a suitable spot to tie up on C Dock where signs indicate moorage. Register with the harbormaster whose office is just next to the C Dock shore walkway. Behind the marina road there is a marina hardware store, restaurant, and boat dry storage facilities.

ROUTES FROM SKAGIT BAY TO PADILLA BAY OR THE STRAIT OF JUAN DE FUCA

From Seattle or Everett two interesting routes are available which provide access to Padilla Bay or the Strait of Juan de Fuca: Deception Pass and Swinomish Channel. Each requires preparation and alertness, though only transit of Deception Pass is dependent on the tide.

Deception Pass is 5 miles south of Anacortes and separates Fidalgo Island on the north from Whidbey Island on the south. Two miles long, its narrowest section is 200 yards wide in the vicinity of Pass Island. Currents through the pass are very strong, reaching 8 knots, hence it is essential to travel at slack water. The pass is spectacularly narrow, steep-sided, and crossed by a bridge with 104 ft. vertical clearance.

Docks to await the tide can be found at the north end of Whidbey Island in Cornet Bay. A dredged channel marked by private daybeacons leads to the marina. Marine supplies, fuel, launching ramp, and a hoist are available. To the east of the marina is a state-run small craft facility where berthing and a launching ramp are available. Overhead power cables with clearances of 56 ft. cross the west end of the Bay.

Bowman (Reservation) Bay is a small bight between Reservation Head and Rosario Head on the Skagit Bay side of the Pass. When awaiting the tide here, anchorage may be taken in 2 1/4 fathoms, mud. Docks maintained by the Deception Pass State Park may be used on a temporary basis.

When westerly winds blow in from the Strait of Juan de Fuca, the ebb tide has heavy rips that can make the passage difficult for small boats. A further obstacle one may encounter is log booms transiting the pass at slack water, effectively narrowing the channel for other boats.

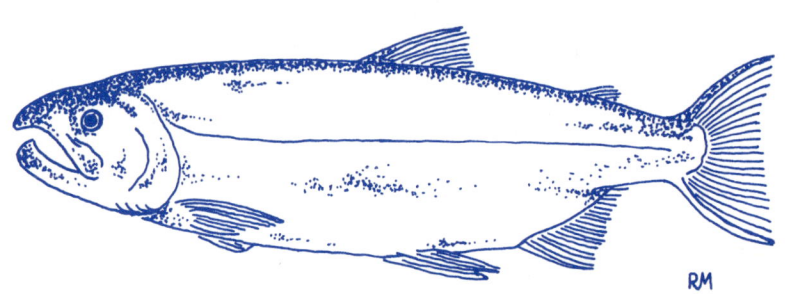

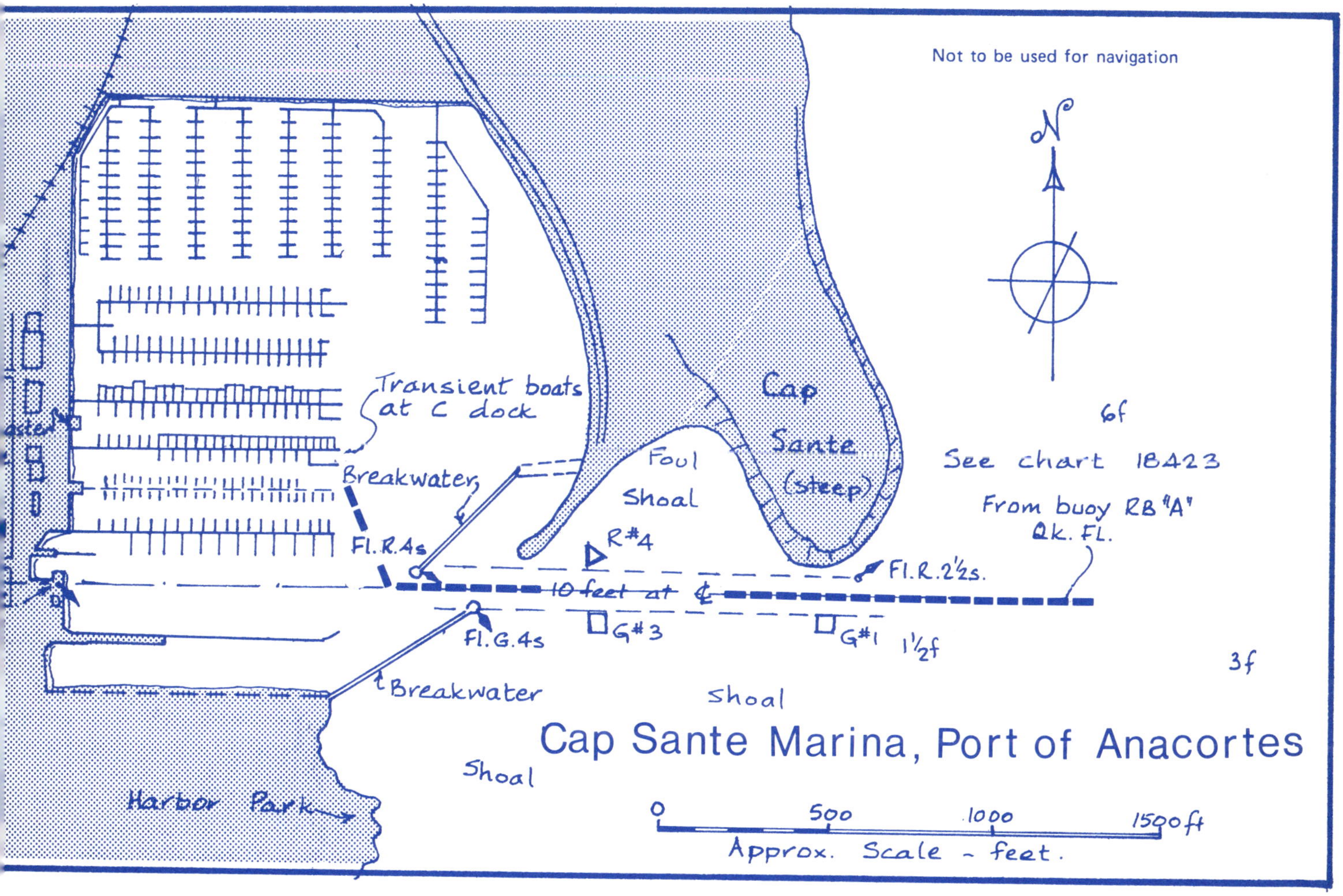

N

6f

See chart 18423

From buoy RB "A" Qk. Fl.

Cap Sante (steep)

Foul Shoal

Transient boats at C dock

Breakwater

Fl.R.4s

R#4

Fl.R.2½s

10 feet at ₵

G#3

G#1 1½f

3f

Fl.G.4s

Breakwater

Shoal

Shoal

Harbor Park

Cap Sante Marina, Port of Anacortes

0   500   1000   1500ft

Approx. Scale - feet.

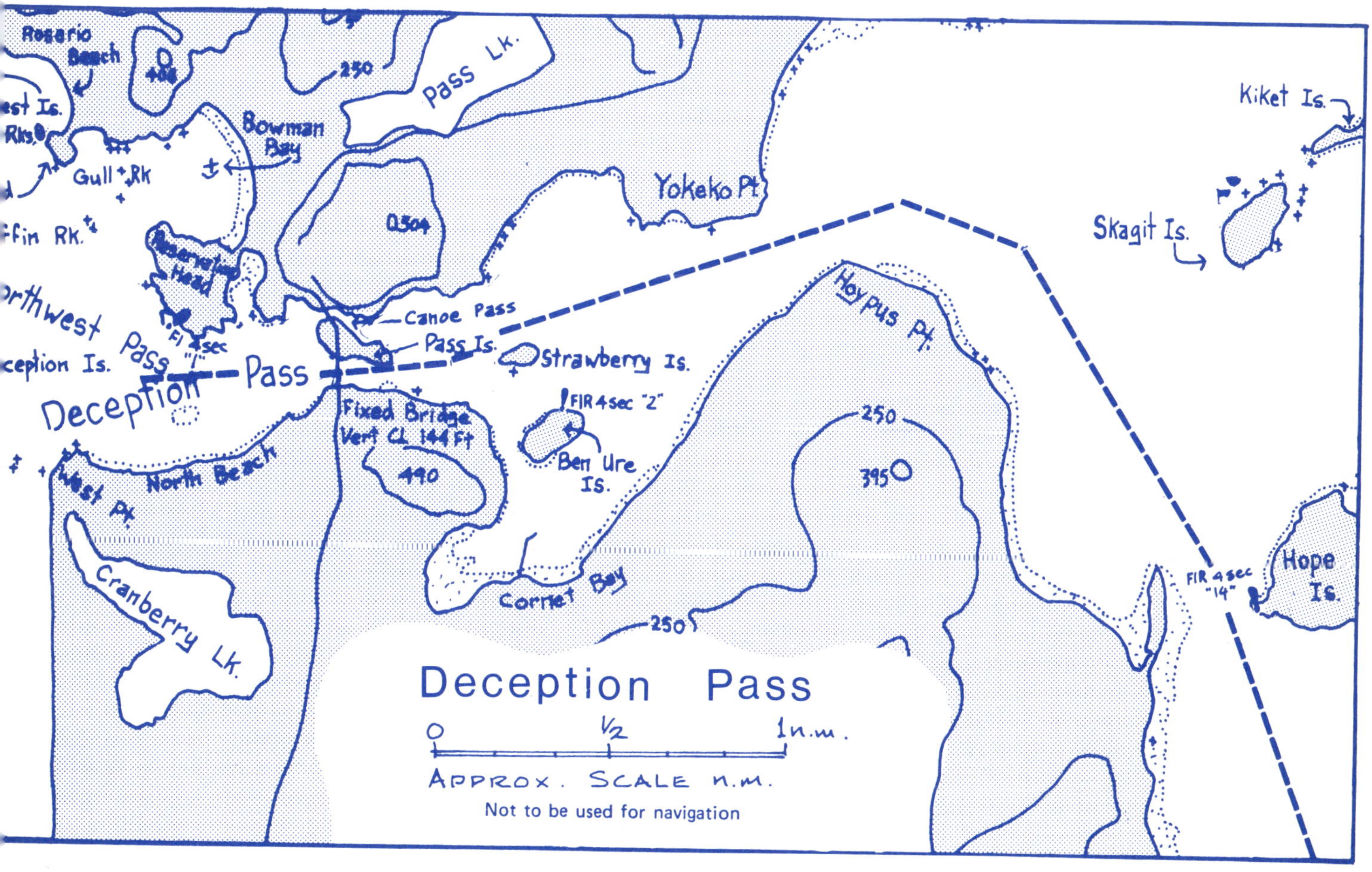

Rosario Beach

Pass Lk.

250

Kiket Is.

West Is.

Rks.

Bowman Bay

Gull Rk.

Yokeko Pt.

Skagit Is.

ffin Rk.

0.504

Canoe Pass

Pass Is.

Strawberry Is.

Hoypus Pt.

rthwest Pass

Fl sec "I"

250

eption Is.

Deception — Pass

Fixed Bridge Vert Cl. 144 Ft

Fl R 4 sec "2"

395

Fl R 4 sec "14"

Hope Is.

440

Ben Ure Is.

West Pt.

North Beach

250

Cornet Bay

Cranberry Lk.

250

Deception Pass

0   ½   1n.m.

Approx. Scale n.m.

Swinomish Channel is sometimes referred to as the "chicken route" between Seattle/Everett and Bellingham/Anacortes, since it provides a shorter, calmer run (unaffected by tidal conditions) than the more exciting and beautiful transit of Deception Pass.

Swinomish Channel connecting Skagit Bay to Padilla Bay is clearly marked and dredged. Entrance to the channel from Skagit Bay leads ENE between two jetties, then north of Goat Island. Caution: both jetties are submerged except for a short section, but they are well marked by daybeacons. A lighted range 072° – 252° marks the entrance from Skagit Bay. Take care to line up the range markers in Dugualla Bay before turning into the channel and keep to the north side of the red buoy marking the southern boundary. Keep to the channel, which has a controlling depth of only 8 ft., for it is very shallow on either side. Where the channel turns to the north at Hole In The Wall, a fork of the Skagit River is seen on the east side. One then passes an Indian settlement, Shelter Bay Development, and logging operations before entering the town of La Conner. The fixed highway bridge south of La Conner has a vertical clearance of 45 ft. (75 ft. for the center width of 310 ft.)

La Conner is an attractive tourist-oriented town which is also busy with logging, and smelt-fishing from October to March. Located in the midst of a rich agricultural area which is largely devoted to raising tulip bulbs, the country is a blaze of color during the spring. Transient moorage is available at the city-owned floats next to Pier 7 and the Lighthouse Inn. It is just a short walk to restaurants and stores.

Several power cables, and another highway bridge having clearances of 75 ft., cross the channel as one proceeds toward Padilla Bay. A railroad swing bridge at the Padilla entrance is left open unless a train is approaching. As long as a vessel stays in the well marked channel and keeps range markers lined up there are no problems in using this route.

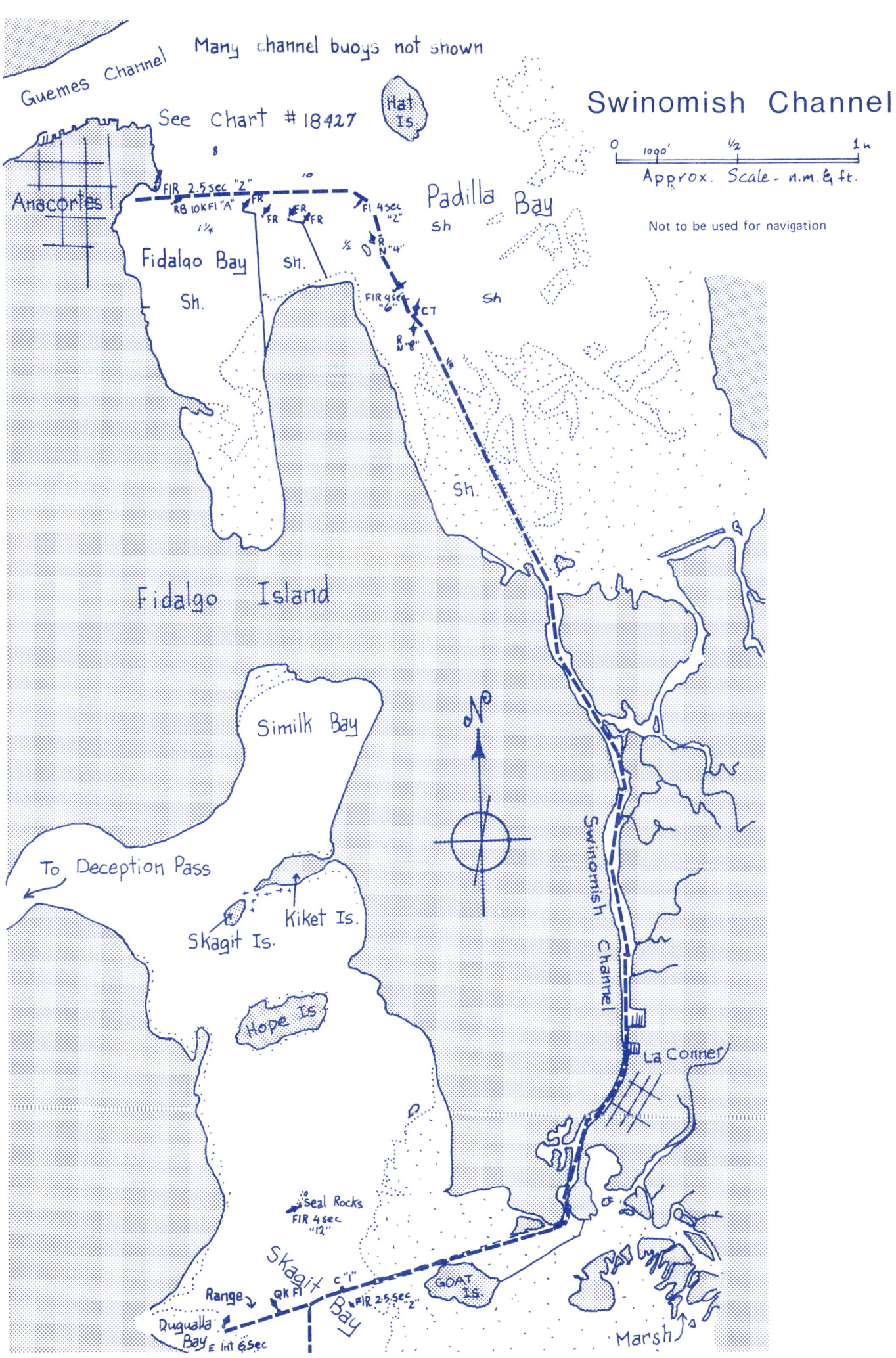

Guemes Channel   Many channel buoys not shown

Hat Is.

See Chart #18427

Swinomish Channel

Approx. Scale - n.m. & ft.

0   1000'   ½   1 n

Not to be used for navigation

Anacortes

Fl R 2.5 sec "2"
R B 10K Fl "A"
FR
FR   FR
FR

Fl 4 sec "2"   Padilla Bay
Sh

Fidalgo Bay
Sh.

Sh.

R N "4"

Fl R 4 sec "6"
C7
R N "8"

Sh

½

8

10

1¼

Sh.

Fidalgo   Island

Swinomish Channel

N

Similk Bay

To Deception Pass

Kiket Is.

Skagit Is.

Hope Is

La Conner

Seal Rocks
Fl R 4 sec "12"

Skagit Bay

GOAT Is.

Range   Qk Fl   C "1"

Duqualla Bay   Fl R 2.5 sec "2"
E Int 6 sec

Marsh

BELLINGHAM

From Anacortes it is only about 17 nautical miles to Bellingham, which is located on the northeastern curve of Bellingham Bay. This is a larger town than Anacortes, but its marina facilities have been a little slower in developing, mainly growing in 1985 - 86.

Squalicum Harbor is operated by the Port of Bellingham and now consists of two large basins. The outer and older basin has a breakwater with two entrances. Depths inside are 1 1/2 to 2 fathoms. The harbormaster's office is on the north side, near the main float walkway. The Bellingham and Squalicum Yacht Clubs also have quarters ashore nearby. The transient berths are just ahead of the seawall. A block behind these shore buildings is Harbor Mall, with several small marine specialty stores and a restaurant. Close by are large marine hardware chandleries such as LFS and Redden which cater to both pleasure and fishing craft.

The newer harbor basin is slightly to the east and behind the older basin. Enter from the southeast corner. Several large areas of floats are enclosed within. The transient berths lie off the Harbor Center on the northeast side. Nearby are boat launching ramps and a Coast Guard Station.

Roeder Avenue runs roughly east-west behind the harbor areas, as does the railroad. The downtown Bellingham area and shopping areas are to the east along this avenue, far enough away to require a taxi or bus ride. Bus service is hourly except Sundays and holidays.

Whatcom County Museum

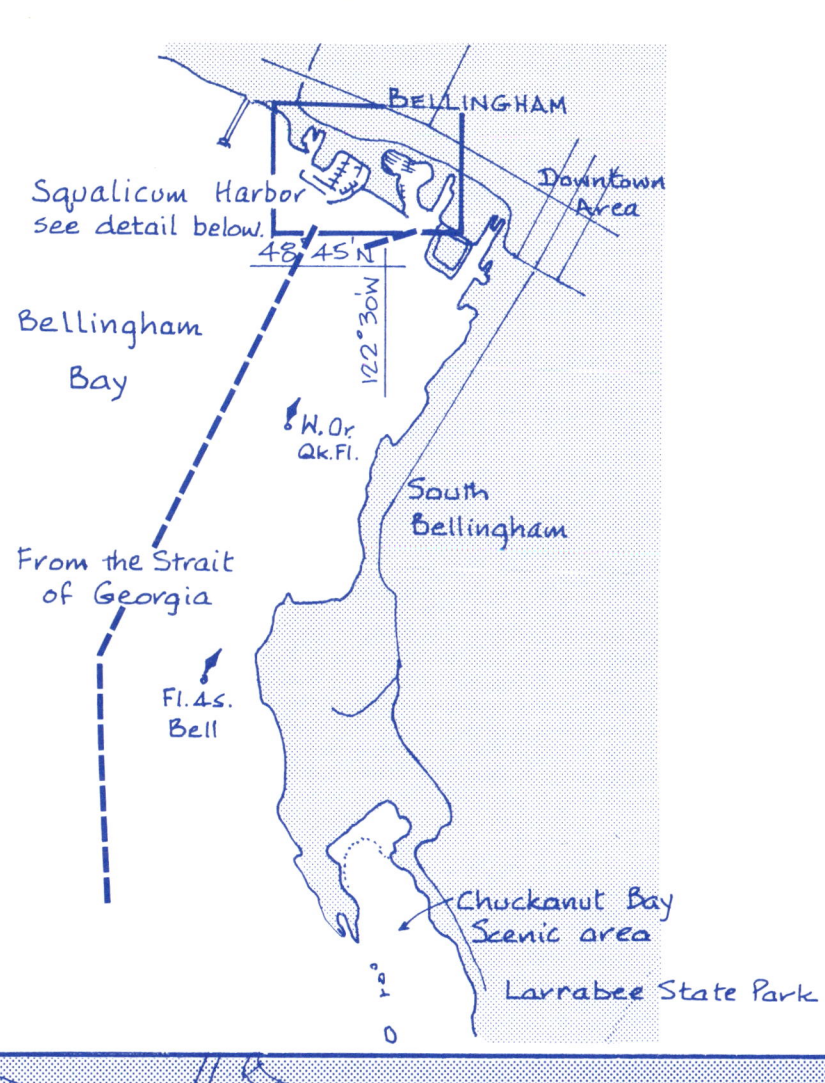

BELLINGHAM

Squalicum Harbor
see detail below.

Downtown
Area

48° 45' N

122° 30' W

Bellingham
Bay

W. Or.
Qk. Fl.

South
Bellingham

From the Strait
of Georgia

Fl. 4s.
Bell

Chuckanut Bay
Scenic area

Larrabee State Park

BELLINGHAM, WA

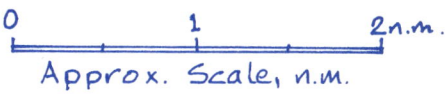

0   1   2 n.m.

Approx. Scale, n.m.

Not to be used for navigation

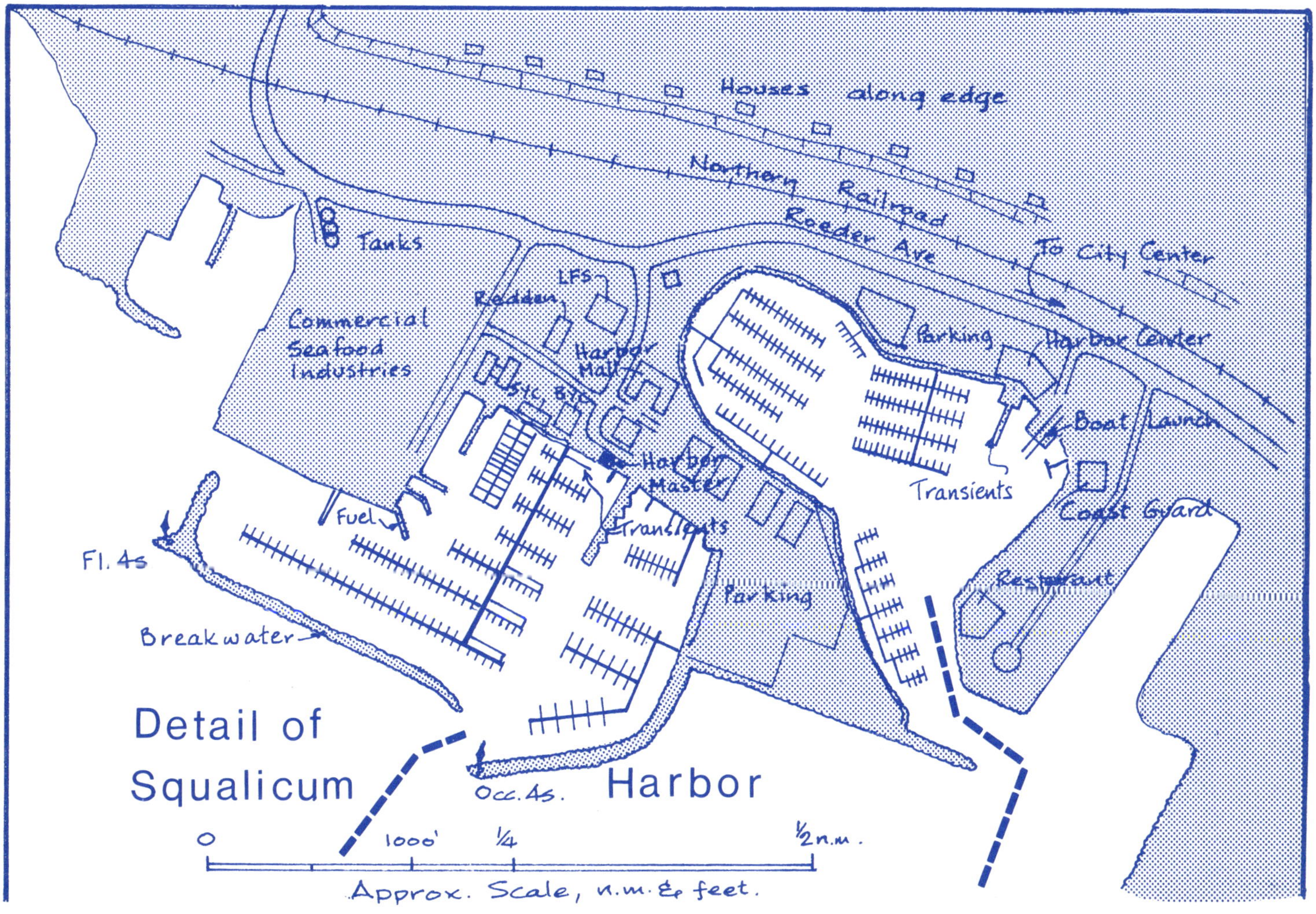

Houses along edge

Northern Railroad

Roeder Ave

To City Center

Tanks

LFs

Rodden

Parking

Harbor Center

Commercial
Seafood
Industries

Harbor
Mall

Sta. Bt.

Boat Launch

Harbor
Master

Transients

Coast Guard

Fuel

Transients

Fl. 4s

Parking

Restaurant

Breakwater

Detail of
Squalicum   Harbor

Occ. 4s.

0   1000'   ¼   ½ n.m.

Approx. Scale, n.m. & feet.

PORT TOWNSEND

The town of Port Townsend, a **Port of Entry,** lies at the mouth of an inlet having the same name. It lies at the threshold of the Strait of Juan de Fuca and can be recognized by the prominent light, foghorn, and radiobeacon at Point Wilson. A distinctive feature in the area is the long line of sand cliffs along Whidby Island just across Admiralty Inlet from the Port.

Port Townsend has many picturesque Victorian houses, and is now a National Historic Landmark City. The gray stone Customs/Post Office building, built in 1833, is prominent on the bluff above the sand cliffs behind the waterfront. The ferry terminal lies below, where one finds a ferry connecting Port Townsend to Keystone Harbor which is across the inlet on Whidbey Island. There are many restaurants, stores, and gift shops along the colorful waterfront.

Port Townsend Boat Haven lies a short distance southwest of the ferry terminal. A stone breakwater encloses the harbor, with the entrance on the northeast corner. Within the entrance a mole divides the harbor into a smaller and larger section. The harbormaster's office is on this mole, above a fuel float. Transient vessels can tie up here until assigned a berth. If the harbormaster is away a list of vacant berths is posted near the door, and vessels can fill out the forms supplied and take up one of these berths.

Point Hudson Harbor and Resort is a well protected indentation just southwest of Point Hudson. It is within easy walking distance of the main street of Port Townsend. A marine store is located at the west end of the harbor though the nearest fuel dock is at Boat Haven. The harbormaster's office is on the north side of the harbor. If one is staying at the Motel rates are a flat $5 per night; otherwise, rates vary depending on the size of the vessel, a 35 ft. boat costing $9. Showers and laundry facilities are available, and a restaurant is on the premises. If one is renting space at the motel, reservations may be made (385-2828 or toll free from Seattle call 622-5033) otherwise, moorage is first come, first serve.

Every year there are a series of popular events, including the Rhododendron Parade at the end of May, and the Wooden Boat Festival in early September.

Detail of

Point Hudson Harbor

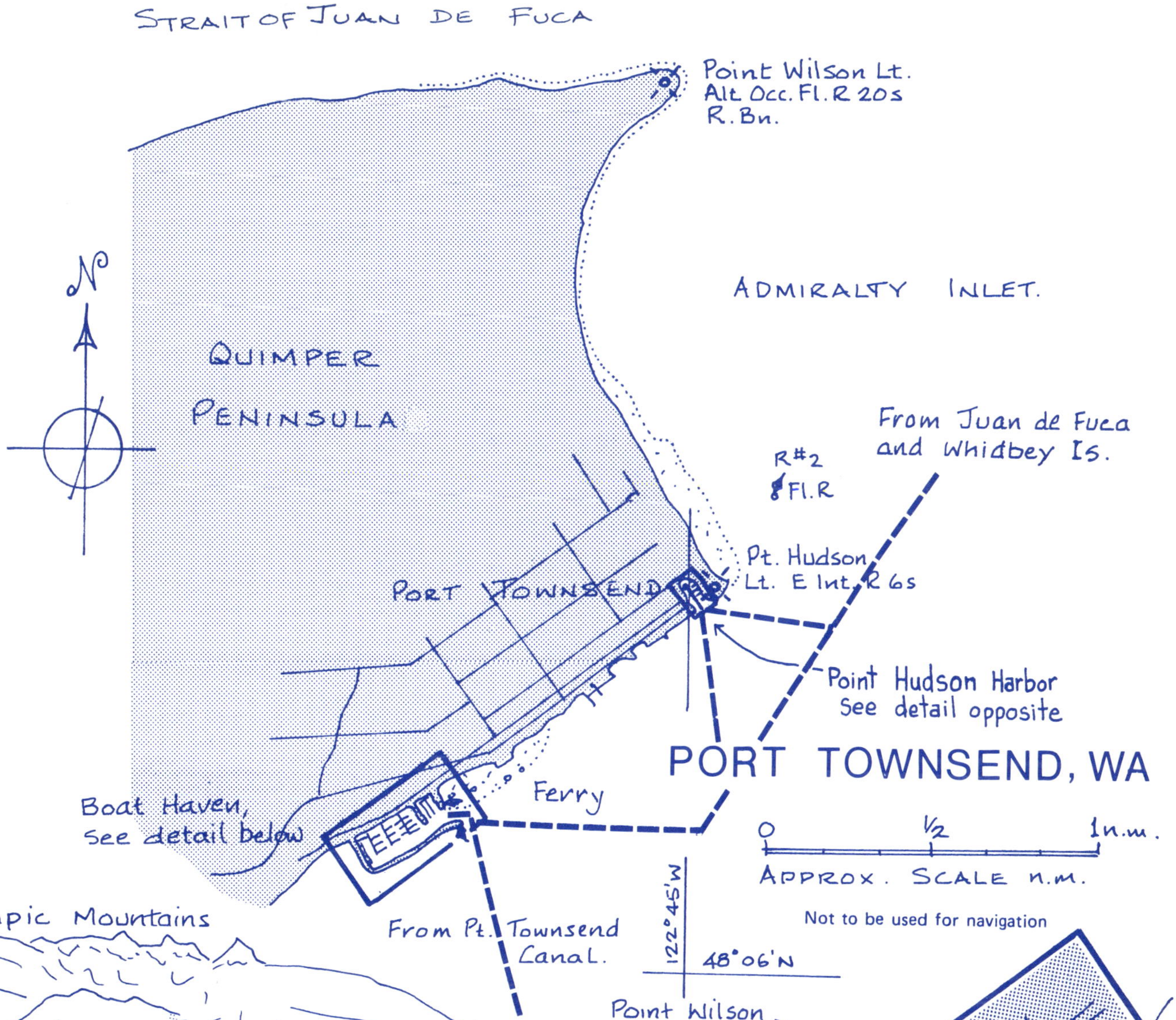

STRAIT OF JUAN DE FUCA

Point Wilson Lt.
Alt Occ. Fl. R 20s
R. Bn.

ADMIRALTY INLET.

QUIMPER PENINSULA

N

R #2
Fl. R

From Juan de Fuca
and Whidbey Is.

PORT TOWNSEND

Pt. Hudson
Lt. E Int. R 6s

Point Hudson Harbor
See detail opposite

PORT TOWNSEND, WA

Boat Haven,
See detail below

Ferry

From Pt. Townsend Canal.

122° 45' W

48° 06' N

Point Wilson

0   ½   1 n.m.

APPROX. SCALE n.m.

Not to be used for navigation

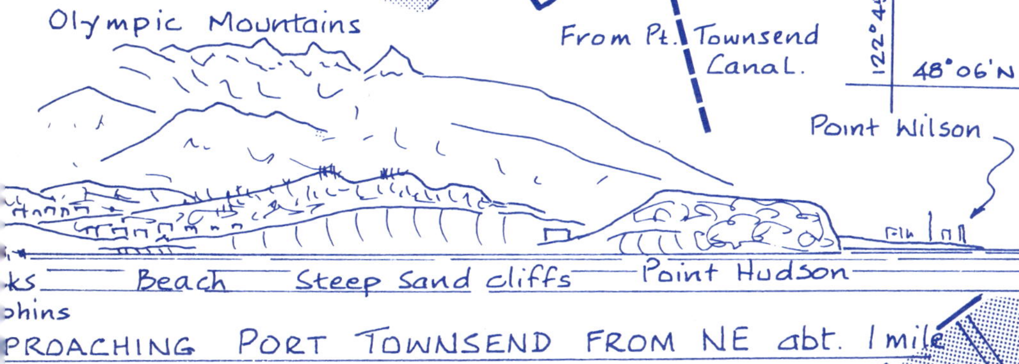

Olympic Mountains

ks   Beach   Steep sand cliffs   Point Hudson

ohins

PROACHING PORT TOWNSEND FROM NE abt. 1 mile

A very distinctive line of sand cliffs are seen
on Whidbey Is. across Admiralty Inlet.

Detail of Port Townsend

Boat Haven

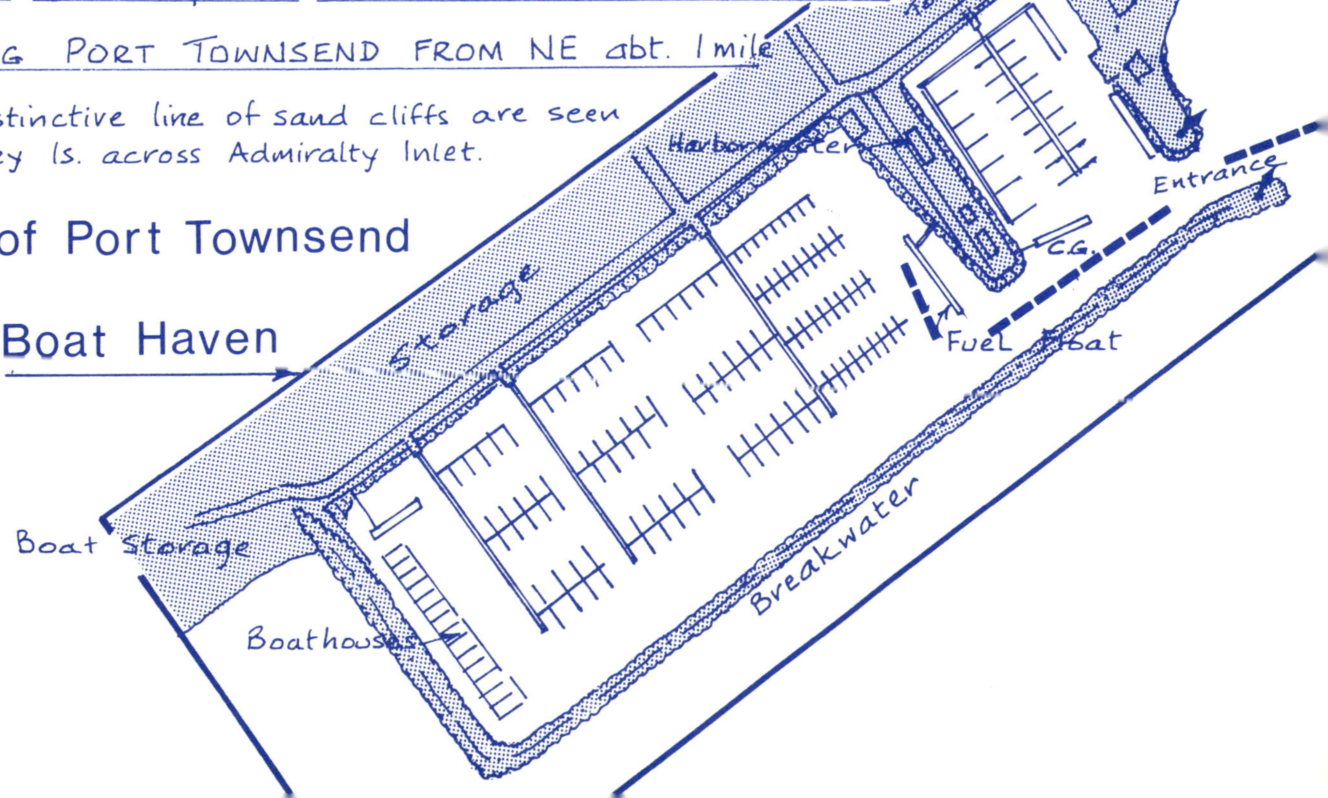

To Port Townsend

Harbormaster

Entrance

C.G.

Fuel Float

Storage

Boat Storage

Boathouses

Breakwater

SEQUIM BAY

The Olympic Peninsula forms the south side of the Strait of Juan de Fuca. Several deep bays and indentations are found along its shoreline including that of Port Townsend at its eastern end. To the west, Discovery Bay winds SSE'ly for about 8 miles. Protection Island lies off the entrance, and though there is a small harbor on the south shore of the island it has limited access. It is a haven protected for the birds. Captain Vancouver anchored "Discovery" and "Chatham" here in 1792 while refitting them to probe further northward. The bay is too deep for most small cruisers except towards its head.

Sequim Bay is next, about 6 miles to the west, and it penetrates the land for about 4 miles. At the entrance a long, low, sandspit extends westward from Kiapot Point to almost enclose the bay. Because of shoals extending almost half a mile from the western shore, vessels approaching the bay should aim towards Kiapot Point on the east side, then pick up the buoys marking the channel along the spit, turning it at the narrow passage on the west. Buoys mark the continuation of the channel to the west of Middle Ground Shoal. Once past the buoys the bay is open to anchorage in depths of 6 to 20 fathoms. Ebb currents can be strong, and use of Tide Tables is advised.

John Wayne Marina is about a mile into the bay on the west side, off Pitship Point. An oval rock breakwater encloses the floats. A fuel float and launching ramp lie just within the entrance. The modern marina being completed offers very clean and comfortable facilities. Transient floats are at the south end of the basin. The harbormaster's office is in the large marina building. Some marine and fishing hardware and limited groceries can be obtained in the store upstairs. More stores with a greater selection can be found in the small town of Sequim which is about a mile to the west.

Killer whale

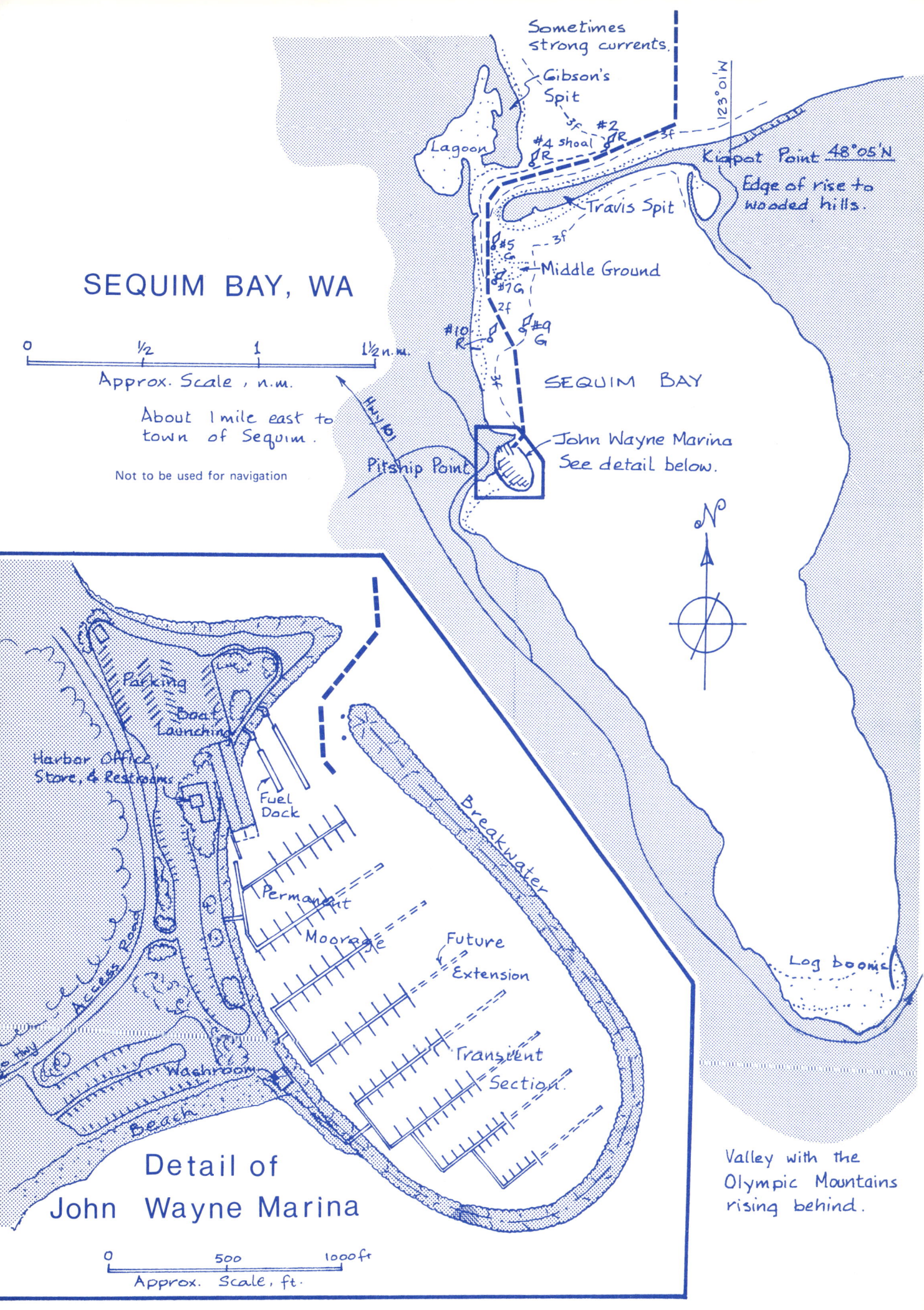

SEQUIM BAY, WA

Approx. Scale, n.m.

0   ½   1   1½ n.m.

About 1 mile east to town of Sequim.

Not to be used for navigation

Sometimes strong currents.

Gibson's Spit

3f   #2 R

#4 shoal   R   3f

Lagoon

123° 01'W

Kiapot Point 48°05'N

Edge of rise to wooded hills.

Travis Spit

3f

#5 G

Middle Ground

#7 G

2f

#10 R   #9 G

SEQUIM BAY

Hwy 101

Pitship Point

John Wayne Marina
See detail below.

N

Log booms

Valley with the Olympic Mountains rising behind.

Detail of John Wayne Marina

Parking

Boat Launching

Harbor Office, Store, & Restrooms

Fuel Dock

Access Road

Washrooms

Beach

Permanent Moorage

Breakwater

Future Extension

Transient Section

Approx. Scale, ft.

0   500   1000 ft.

PORT ANGELES

This important harbor lies along the Olympic coast of the Strait of Juan de Fuca, and is about 10 miles west of Sequim Bay. Ediz Hook is a long, narrow and curving sandspit almost 3 miles long that shelters the harbor of Port Angeles. Only easterly winds blow in, though strong winds from other directions can cause a sharp chop within the large expanse of the harbor. A further caution is called for due to the many logs adrift in this predominantly logging center. The U. S. Coast Guard maintains an air and helicopter station near the end of the spit.

This is the closest year-round **Port of Entry** to the entrance of the Strait of Juan de Fuca. Boats leaving Canadian waters must obtain a **U. S. Cruising Permit** when entering U. S. waters and travelling down the coast. It is far better to have the permit, so that if entry is made at any location which is not a Port of Entry one has already completed the necessary paper work and encounters no further problems related to entry regulations. Formerly, Neah Bay was often used as the Port of Entry for obtaining this Permit, but it no longer has a full-time Customs Officer, so one is strongly advised to obtain it at Port Angeles. Thereafter, foreign vessels must report by phone to the Customs Officer in each Port of Entry visited as long as the vessel is in U. S. waters; your Cruising Permit Number will be required, so have it handy. To call the Port Angeles Customs Officer the telephone number is (206) 457-4311.

Port Angeles Boat Haven is a large rectangular small boat harbor maintained by the Port. A breakwater protects the northwest section, a jetty covers the southeast section, and an angular breakwater protects the central entrance from some of the chop in the outer harbor. While there are floats and berths in both sections, the main transient area is on the central float of the southeast section. The harbormaster's office is in the building at the end of the east jetty, with a fuel and utility float directly beneath it in the harbor. A boat launching area, shipyard with marine ways, mobile hoist and some chandlers are located in the harbor area. As is common in most of these harbors there is a tidal grid.

The city center lies to the southeast of the basin and contains many stores with a wide variety of merchandise. The ferry terminal, for service connecting Port Angeles to Victoria, B.C. is towards the center of the town.

Edible mussel (Mytilus edulis)

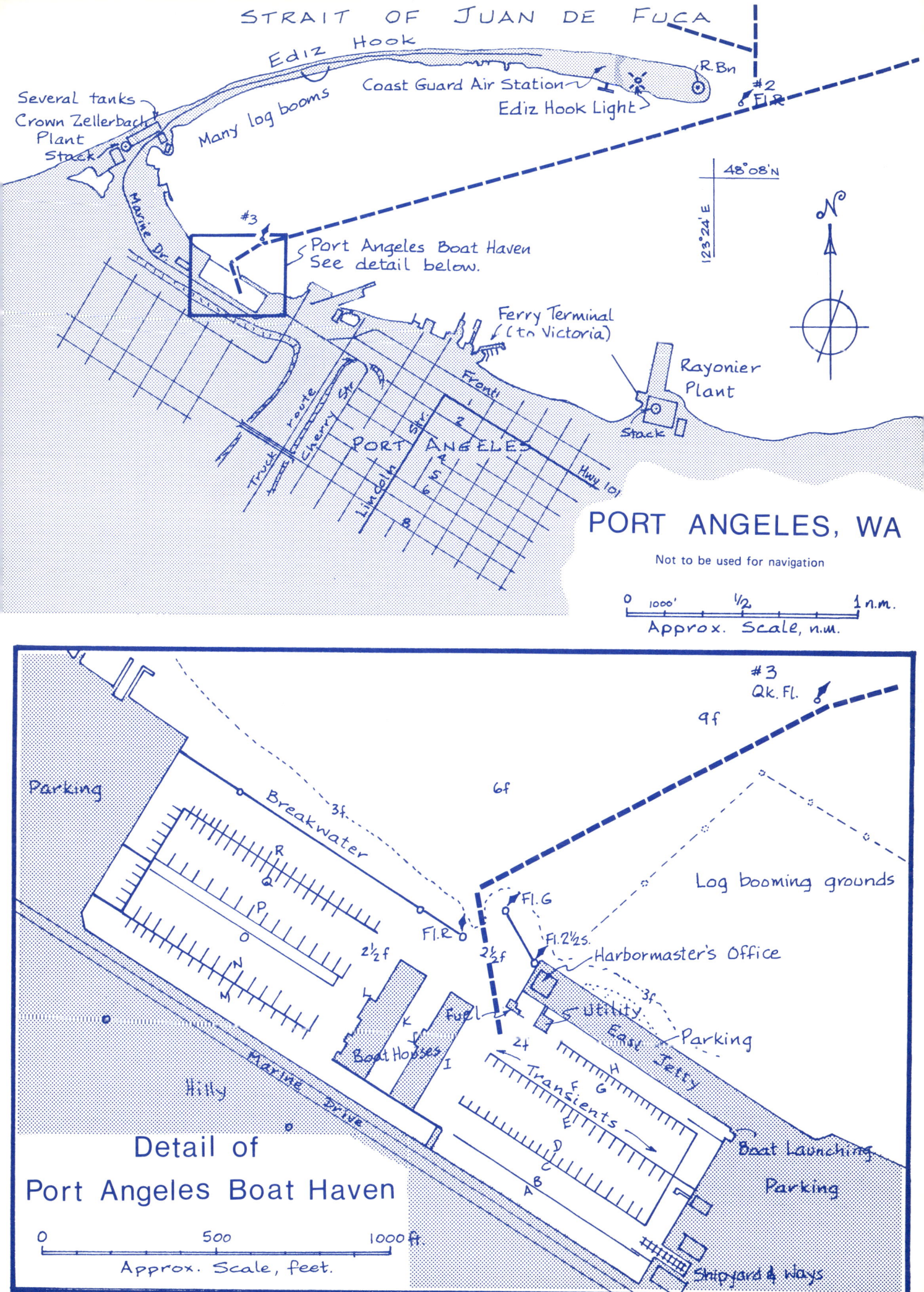

STRAIT OF JUAN DE FUCA

Ediz Hook

Several tanks
Crown Zellerbach
Plant
Stack

Many log booms

Coast Guard Air Station

Ediz Hook Light

R.Bn

#2
Fl.R

Marine Dr.

#3

Port Angeles Boat Haven
See detail below.

Ferry Terminal
(to Victoria)

Rayonier
Plant

Stack

48°08'N

123°24'E

N

Truck route

Cherry Str.

Lincoln

Front

PORT ANGELES

Hwy 101

1
2
3
4
5
6
8

PORT ANGELES, WA

Not to be used for navigation

0   1000'   ½   1 n.m.

Approx. Scale, n.m.

#3
Qk. Fl.

9f

Parking

Breakwater

3f

6f

R

Q

P

O

N

M

2½f

Log booming grounds

Fl. G

Fl.R

2½f

Fl. 2½s.

Harbormaster's Office

3f

Utility

Parking

Fuel

L

K

Boat Houses

I

J

2f

East Jetty

H

G

Transients

F
E

Hilly

Marine Drive

A

B

C

D

Boat Launching

Parking

Detail of
Port Angeles Boat Haven

Shipyard & Ways

0   500   1000 ft

Approx. Scale, feet.

NEAH BAY

This harbor is very handily located close to Cape Flattery, being about 6 miles east of the cape itself. It is a popular stop-over for cruising vessels entering or leaving the Strait of Juan de Fuca. Protection from the prevailing northwesterlies is given by a long, low, rocky breakwater connecting the west side of the bay to Waadah Island which lies just 1/3 mile off the east side of the bay. Waadah Island is 1/2 mile long, with extensive shoal areas around it and rocky ribs extending out northwesterly from the rocky island. Similar rock ribs run out from the mainland shore.

Entry into the bay is made via a buoyed channel between Waadah Island and Baadah Point. The least depth is about 15 feet through the channel. Just within the entrance a T-shaped pier lies off the Makah Tribal Office and Museum, with lights at each end. The remains of an old pier lie alongside, and further in the U.S. Coast Guard pier is located. In an emergency (if it is not occupied) the Coast Guard may allow one to moor to the pier temporarily for repairs.

Neah Bay is a U.S. Customs **Port of Entry** and foreign vessels are required to report to the Customs Officer. However, since this is not a full-time Customs Reporting Station, the officer is not always on duty. Try contacting him by phoning 645-2312. Otherwise, the skipper should call and report to the U.S. Coast Guard at 645-2236. If one is entering after regular hours (8 am - 5 pm) call the toll free number 1-800-562-5943 to report in. Overtime charges may be considerable if it is necessary for a Customs Officer to come to the vessel after hours. Paper work should be completed at Port Angeles where there is a full-time Customs Office.

Along the south shore of Neah Bay there are several small craft floats where transient moorage can be arranged. Anchorage is also possible in the bay in 4 to 6 fathoms, sand. Avoid the western and northern sides as well as the unmarked wreck near the middle of the bay. Two large piers belonging to co-operative fishing plants can supply fuel, water and ice.

When taking on water make sure that it is drinking water. On one occasion we were directed to a hose which turned out to be salt water for cleaning fish. As a result, one of our water tanks was spoiled and it necessitated our making an unscheduled entrance to another port to remedy the situation.

Neah Bay is within the Makah Indian Reservation and is the home port for many fishing vessels owned by the local inhabitants. Indian arts and crafts are available in one or two shops which are on the main street. This is not a major shopping center but basic food and supplies are available from the store on the main street behind the harbor.

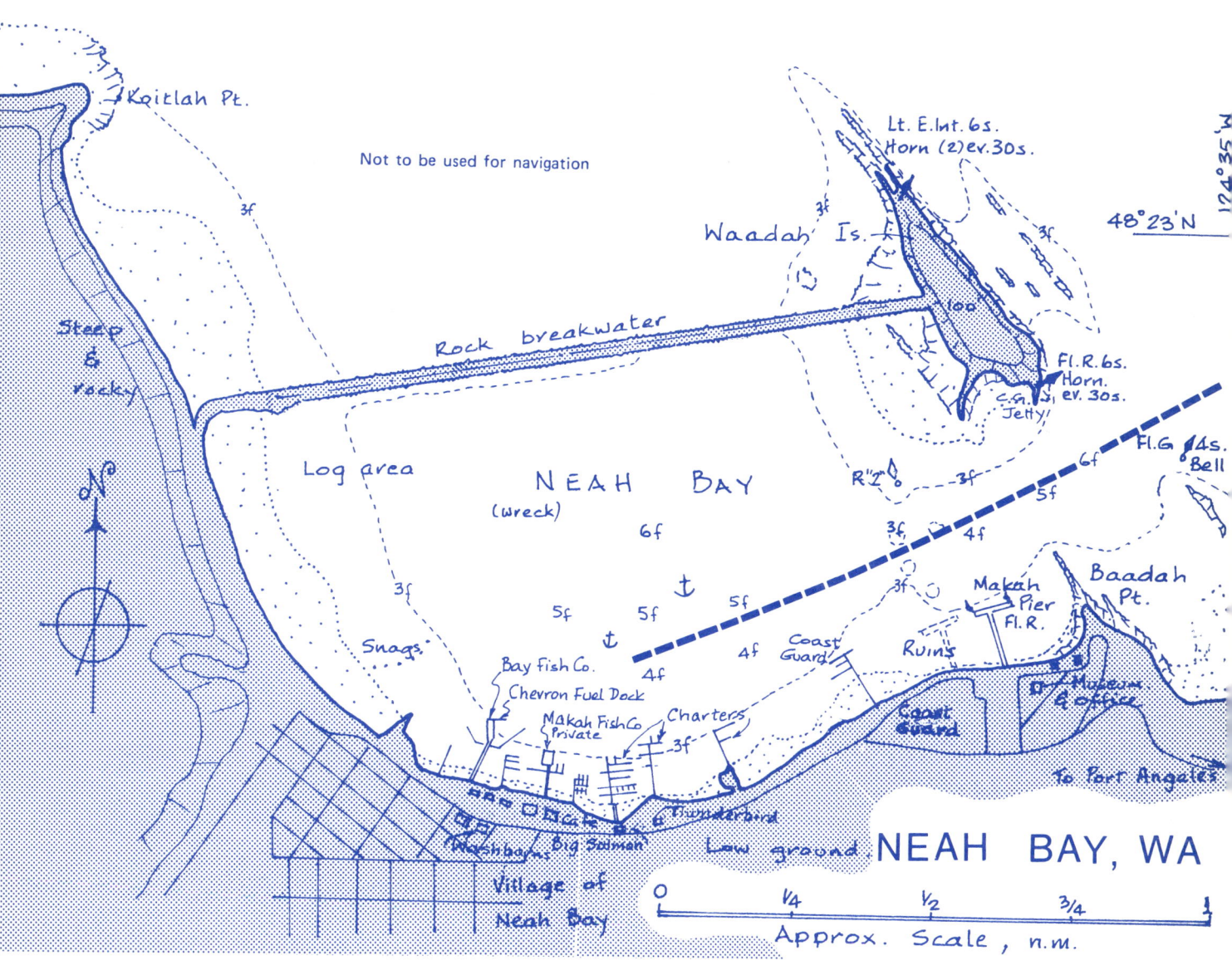

Koitlah Pt.

3f

Lt. E. Int. 6s.
Horn (2) ev. 30s.

Waadah Is.

3f

3f

48°23'N

124°35'W

Rock breakwater

100

Steep
&
rocky

Fl.R. 6s.
Horn.
ev. 30s.
C.G.
Jetty

Log area

NEAH   BAY

(wreck)

R"2"

3f

6f

Fl.G. 4s.
Bell

N

5f

6f

⚓

5f

5f

5f

3f

4f

3f

3f

4f

Makah
Pier
Fl.R.

Baadah
Pt.

Snags

⚓

Coast
Guard

Ruins

4f

Bay Fish Co.

Chevron Fuel Dock

Makah Fish Co
Private

Charters

3f

Coast
Guard

Museum
& office

Thunderbird

To Port Angeles

Washbarn

Big Salmon

Low ground

NEAH   BAY, WA

Village of
Neah Bay

0   ¼   ½   ¾   1

Approx. Scale, n.m.

CAPE FLATTERY - ENTRANCE TO THE STRAIT OF JUAN DE FUCA

Cape Flattery is a steep, 120 ft. cliff, rising behind to a rocky peak some 2 miles from the cape. Atop this peak a large radar dome is a prominent feature and a good landmark, even in fog when it tends to stick out above the lower clouds. Tatoosh Island is a flat-topped, steep-sided island about 1/3 mile northwest of the Cape. Two rocks awash lie in the center of this passage, often called Hole-in-the-Wall. Though a vessel can cross through this passage holding closer to the Tatoosh side, cross currents and the often treacherous fog can make this hazardous.

In travelling northward around Cape Flattery stand well out from the land (at least 3 miles) to clear the buoy beyond Duncan and Duntze Rocks, the two main dangers lying about 1 1/4 miles further NNW of Tatoosh Island. A combination of fog and strong currents requires this clearance. In good weather it is possible to sail close past Tatoosh Island. However, as we can report, when sailing steadily against a current in fog it is very difficult to determine when one is clear of the dangers here, and it would be wise to power well past this threshold to the open sea.

Looking northwest from Tatoosh Island

Right: The snow-capped Olympic
Mountains make a beautiful backdrop for Port Angeles.

Below: Fighting the tidal current
in Deception Pass can be exciting.

Pinnacle rocks south of Cape Flattery discourage close inspection.

Driftwood on the beach north of Grays Harbor entrance resembles a ghost from the past.

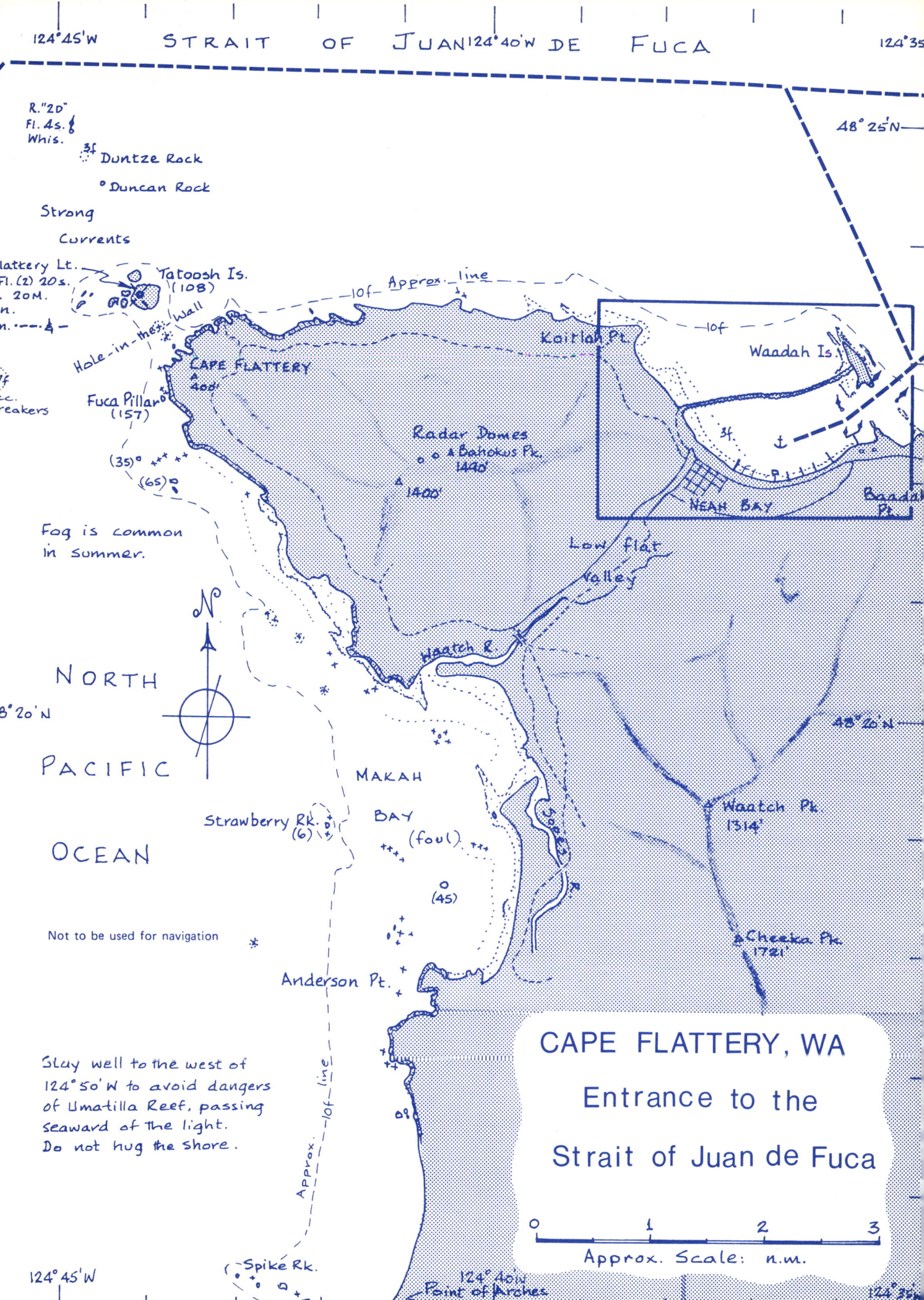

LA PUSH

This small Indian fishing village is about
35 miles south of Cape Flattery. During the
summer months there is increased activity in
the area as a result of the sports fishermen
who come to enjoy the simple pleasures of
unsophisticated life and good salmon fishing.

Entrance to the harbor is between James
Island on the west and a jetty extending south-
westward from the north end of a long curving
beach. Give good clearance to the outer end of
the jetty as about 25 feet is awash at high
water. An approaching vessel should pick up
the lighted whistle buoy which is almost 2 miles
southwest of the end of the jetty. A directional
light leads a vessel on the proper course until
one is past the end of the jetty, after which one
should favor the south side of the channel. A
light and seasonal buoys mark the channel which
is supposed to be 60 - 70 ft. wide but it seems
narrower. Keep a sharp eye for Indian fishing
nets after entering the river.

Do NOT attempt to enter at night even though seasonal floodlights illuminate the entrance channel between James Island and the jetty. An overhead cable
(clearance 100 ft.) crosses the entrance channel.

In heavy southerly weather the channel is dangerous. Fog often forms at
night and may be a problem until burning off around noon. A rough bar advisory
sign is maintained by the Coast Guard. If in doubt, ask the Coast Guard for a
report on current bar conditions. On request, they will guide a vessel into
the boat harbor if it is feasible. Re-read the section on crossing bars found
in the introduction (pp. 9 - 10).

The boat basin is seldom crowded. Pick a berth, then check in at the
harbormaster's office to ascertain that your location is satisfactory. He is
not always in the office so you may have to look for him or ask some of the
locals for his whereabouts. Fuel and limited marine supplies can be obtained.
A short walk takes one to the village of La Push where some groceries and a
good selection of fishing tackle are available at the general store. The U.S.
Post Office operates from a trailer near the store.

Destruction Island, which lies 15 miles SSE of La Push and 20 miles NNW of
Cape Elizabeth, is a flat-topped, brush-covered island having rocks and ledges
extending about 1 mile seaward from the cliffs on the north end. A light and
fog signal are on the island. Anchorage in 10 fathoms, sand may be taken off
the SE face of the island during settled northwesterly winds with the light
bearing 293° to 315°. This isn't a particularly good anchorage but it is the
only one available in the area. If the wind hauls W or S one must leave
immediately.

LA PUSH, WA

QUILLAYUTE RIVER

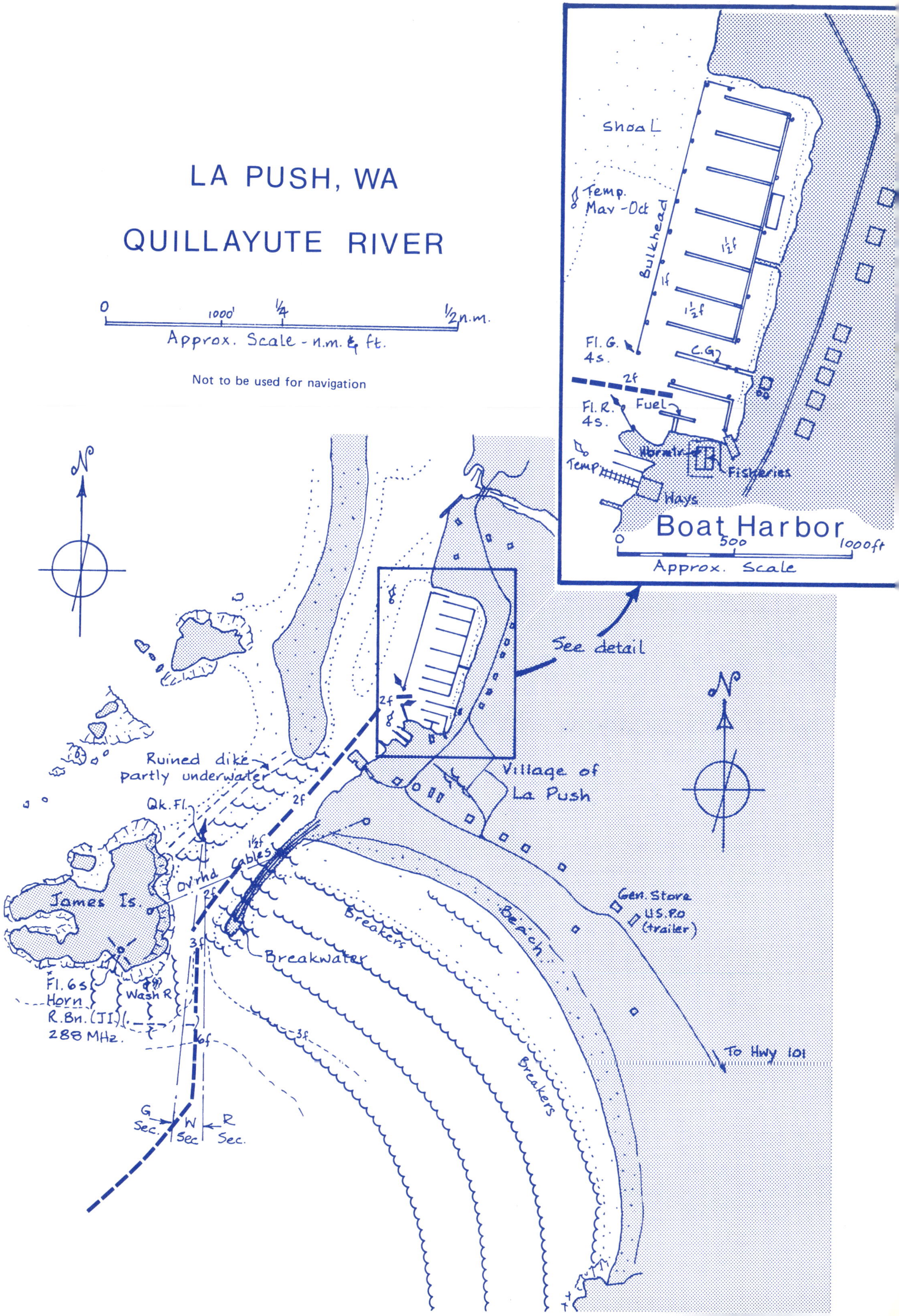

0 1000' ¼ ½ n.m.

Approx. Scale - n.m. & ft.

Not to be used for navigation

Boat Harbor

Shoal

Temp.
May - Oct

Bulkhead

1½f

1f

1½f

Fl. G.
4s

C.G.

2f

Fl. R.
4s   Fuel

Temp.   Unintr.

Hays   Fisheries

0 500 1000ft

Approx. Scale

N

See detail

2f

8

Village of
La Push

Ruined dike -
partly underwater

Qk. Fl.

2f

1½f

Ov'rhd Cables

2f

James Is.

3f

Breakers

Breakwater

Beach

Gen. Store
U.S. P.O.
(trailer)

Fl. 6s
Horn
R. Bn. (JI)
288 MHz.

Wash R

6f

3f

Breakers

To Hwy 101

G
Sec.

W
Sec.

R
Sec.

N

GRAYS HARBOR

The entrance to this large bay and harbor lies about 93 miles south of Cape Flattery and about 40 miles north of the Columbia River entrance. Though it is an important lumber port and deep sea charter fishing center, the approach, and entry into the harbor require a great deal of caution and deliberation. Please reread the section concerning crossing of bars in these Pacific ports on pages 9 - 10 of the introduction.

Two extensive rock breakwater jetties extend out from both entrance points. That of the South Jetty from Point Chehalis extends well out to sea, and is submerged at its end. The North Jetty, off Point Brown is shorter. Between these jetties the entrance is about 2 miles wide. A bar formed by shoals extending south and west from near Point Brown, together with the shoals off Point Chehalis causes rough water and breakers to occur, especially when the ebb meets the prevailing northwesterly winds.

The channel is subject to change, but a range is established leading in from the outer buoy. Though one should favor the south side of the entrance the prevailing northwesterlies put a vessel dangerously close to a lee shore -- great care is needed to stay out of trouble. A rough bar warning sign is shown on the north side of Westhaven Cove within the harbor.

Westhaven Cove is on the inner side of Point Chehalis, on the south side of Grays Harbor. Breakwaters, jetties, and reclaimed land areas form an extensive small boat basin, operated by the Port of Grays Harbor. There are a few transient berths. The harbormaster's office is on a side street (Lamb Street) as shown in the sketch.

There are many sportsfishing charter businesses along the main street, as well as restaurants, gift shops, and commercial shops. Grocery stores are a little further along, but still within walking distance. A visit to the museum in the old Coast Guard Station behind the waterfront is a must for all sailors.

A small craft basin also lies behind Point Brown and Ocean Shores on the north shore. It is accessible via a line of dolphins (some of which are lit), leading from the inner channels of Grays Harbor. Shoals all through this area do not recommend it to a stranger. A ferry service joins Ocean Shores and its seaside cabin areas to Westport.

The old Coast Guard Station

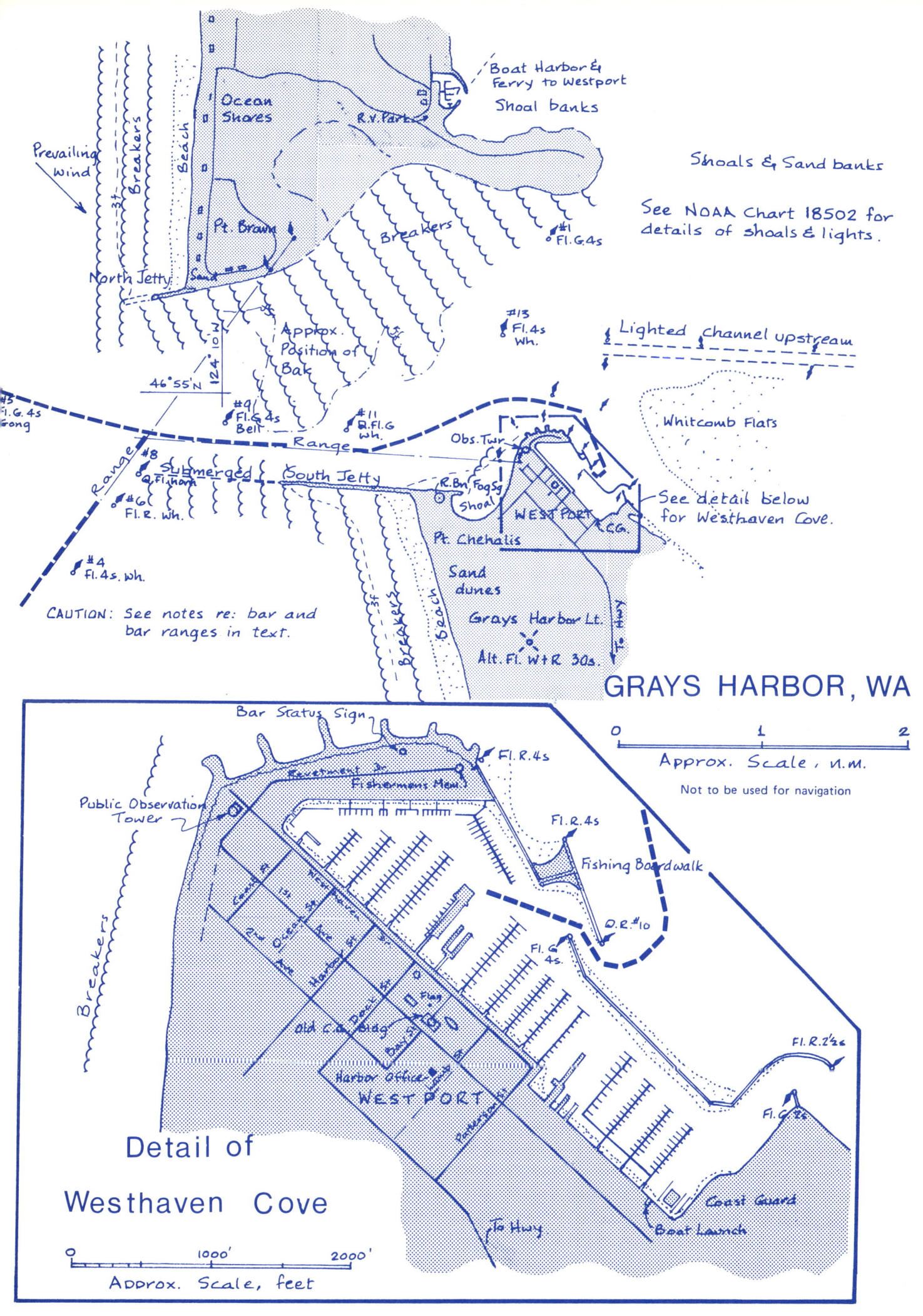

Prevailing Wind

Ocean Shores

R.V. Parks

Boat Harbor & Ferry to Westport
Shoal banks

Shoals & Sand banks

See NOAA Chart 18502 for details of shoals & lights.

Breakers

3'
Breakers
Beach

Pt. Brown

Sand

North Jetty

#1
○ Fl.G.4s

Approx. Position of Bar

124°10'W

46°55'N

#13
● Fl.4s Wh.

Lighted channel upstream

Whitcomb Flats

#3
1.G.4s
Gong

#9
○ Fl.G.4s Bell

Range

#11
● Q.Fl.G Wh.

Obs.Twr

See detail below for Westhaven Cove.

Range

#8
○ Q.Fl.hom

Submerged
South Jetty

#6
○ Fl.R. Wh.

R.Bn. FogSg
Shoal

WESTPORT

Pt. Chehalis

C.G.

#4
○ Fl.4s. Wh.

CAUTION: See notes re: bar and bar ranges in text.

Sand dunes

Grays Harbor Lt.
Alt. Fl. W+R 30s.

Breakers
3'
Beach

GRAYS HARBOR, WA

0   1   2
Approx. Scale, n.m.

Not to be used for navigation

Bar Status Sign

Revetment
3'
Fishermens Mem'l

Fl.R.4s

Public Observation Tower

Fl.R.4s

Fishing Boardwalk

Breakers

Q.R.#10

Old C.G. Bldg.

Fl.G 4s.

Fl.R.2'4s

Harbor Office

WESTPORT

Fl.G 2s

Detail of

Westhaven Cove

Coast Guard
Boat Launch

To Hwy

0   1000'   2000'
Approx. Scale, feet

COLUMBIA RIVER ENTRANCE

This is not a highly recommended stop-over. The entrance to the Columbia River is 145 miles south of Cape Flattery and 550 miles north of San Francisco. It is the most infamous of west coast bars because of the 250 vessels which have foundered while attempting to make or leave port. One must travel a long distance up a channel bordered by hazardous shoals in order to reach a moorage.

When the weather is relatively calm and settled -- just the time when one wants to make good mileage up or down the coast -- and it is a flood tide there are no major problems in transiting this wide and well-marked channel. The normal caution, to follow the navigation aids in their proper order and to maintain prudence and power, is sufficient.

When approaching the Columbia River a vessel should pick up the offshore navigational buoy "CR" which is about 5 1/2 miles southwest of the channel entrance. A fog signal, radio beacon, and radar transponder are at the 42-foot buoy. About 2 3/4 miles miles northeast of the Columbia River Approach Buoy is whistle buoy #2 which further identifies the beginning of the channel, while bell buoy #1 is about 2 miles west of the channel. On a clear day one can see Mount St. Helens (8,500 ft.) which is 75 miles to the east.

The Columbia River entrance lies between Clatsop Spit on the south and Cape Disappointment on the north. Clatsop Spit is a low sandy beach extending 2 1/2 miles northwest from Point Adams. The South Jetty extends almost 3 miles seaward from the end of Clatsop Spit. Take care not to confuse the low sand beach north of Cape Disappointment for the one south of Point Adams.

Cape Disappointment is a high, rocky headland having steep cliffs on the seaward side. Though the Cape Disappoirtment Light is 220 ft. above sea level, it is not always visible from the north. A radiobeacon is located at this light. The western point of Cape Disappointment is North Head, an unmistakable steep-sided cliff having a heavily wooded area behind. North Head Light is shown from a white conical tower almost 200 feet above the water.

The entrance to the Columbia River is between the South Jetty (extending westerly from Clatsop Spit) and the North Jetty which extends 800 yards in a southwesterly direction from the northern shore. The outermost mile of the South Jetty is submerged and the channel is clearly marked by buoys, lights, daybeacons, and lighted ranges. Great care must be exercised in identifying and following the various navigational aids in their proper order. Bar condition reports are broadcast 15 minutes before and after the hour on KVAS (1230 kHz) and KAST (1370 kHz) or one may call the Coast Guard for a report.

Peacock Spit is the area north and west of the North Jetty. This is the most dangerous area and has claimed the majority of the ships that have been lost while attempting the entrance. Breakers extending 4 miles to seaward are heavy in any type of current. Keep well offshore when approaching to avoid cutting across and into this shoal. Give the breakers more than 1/2 mile clearance even during calm, fair weather conditions. "Sneakers" are common up to 1/2 mile outside the usual breakers on the end of the North Jetty. Once in the channel, if power is lost one can be drawn onto Peacock Spit since the ebb tide runs across its tip.

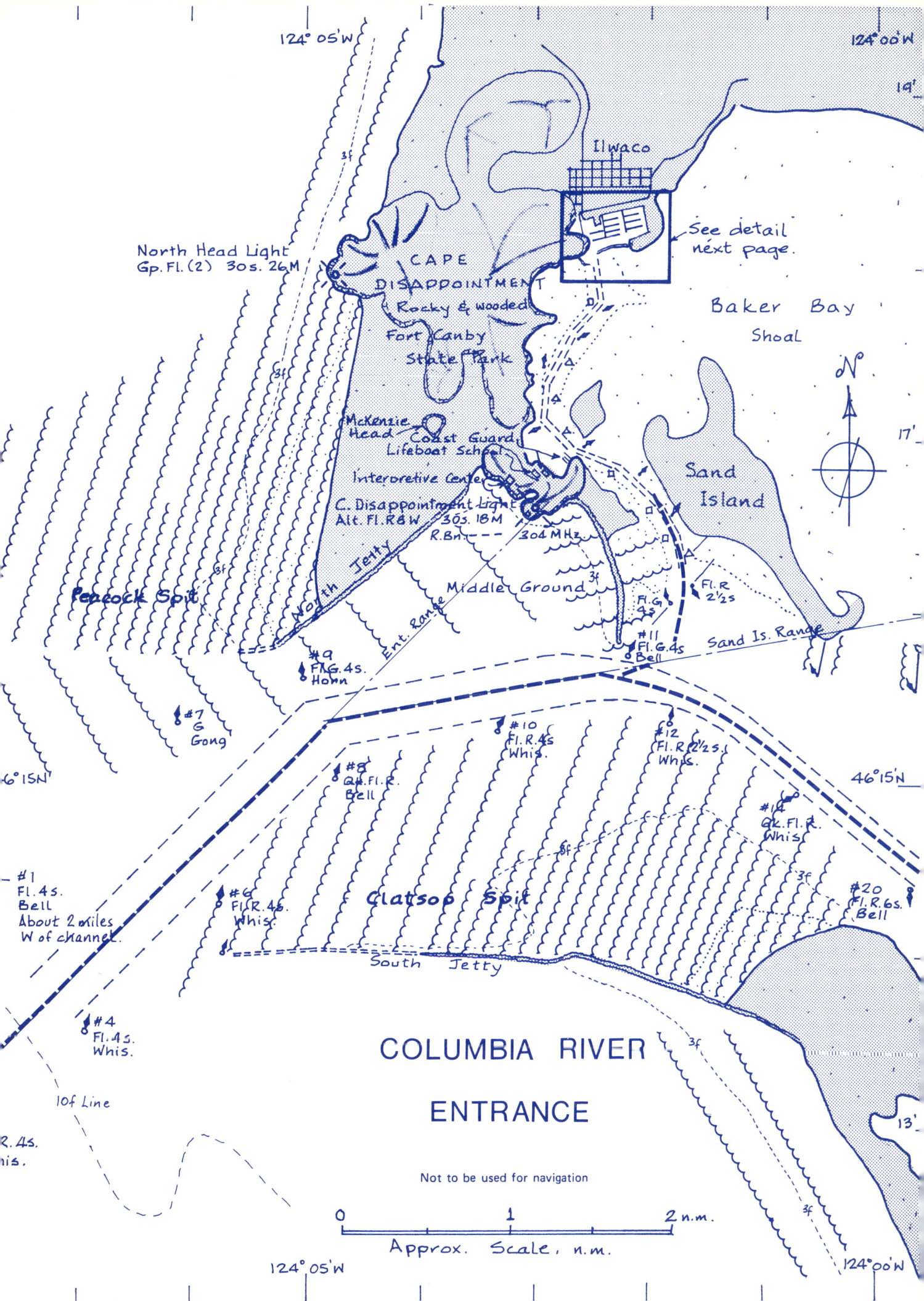

124° 05'W   124° 00'W

19'

Ilwaco

North Head Light
Gp. Fl. (2) 30s. 26M

CAPE
DISAPPOINTMENT
Rocky & wooded
Fort Canby
State Park

See detail
next page.

Baker Bay
Shoal

N

17'

McKenzie
Head   Coast Guard
Lifeboat School

Interpretive Center

C. Disappointment Light
Alt. Fl. R & W   30s. 18M
R. Bn. – – – 304 MHz.

Sand
Island

Peacock Spit

North Jetty

Middle Ground

Sand Is. Range

Fl. G.
4s

Fl. R
2½s

#11
Fl. G. 4s
Bell

Ent. Range

#9
Fl. G. 4s.
Horn

#7
G
Gong

#10
Fl. R. 4s.
Whis.

#12
Fl. R 2½2s.
Whis.

46° 15'N

6° 15'N

#8
Qk. Fl. R.
Bell

#14
Qk. Fl. R.
Whis.

3f

#1
Fl. 4s.
Bell
About 2 miles
W of channel.

#6
Fl. R. 4s.
Whis.

Clatsop Spit

3f

#20
Fl. R. 6s.
Bell

South Jetty

#4
Fl. 4s.
Whis.

10f Line

13'

R. 4s.
his.

COLUMBIA RIVER

ENTRANCE

Not to be used for navigation

0   1   2 n.m.

Approx. Scale, n.m.

124° 05'W   124° 00'W

To the south is Clatsop Spit which is also dangerous for a number of reasons. During flood or slack currents it may be comparatively calm but within a few minutes, when the current has started to ebb, it can suddenly have treacherous breakers extending far out towards the channel. Take care to maintain a course north of the red buoys. Another danger of this area is that if a vessel is set back while around the curve of the channel (resulting from engine failure, lack of fuel etc.) it is set onto the breakers of Clatsop Spit. During poor visibility take care not to cut across from buoy #6 to buoy #10 (thus missing #8).

Middle Ground is the area southwest of Cape Disappointment Light as well as the adjoining area south of Peacock Spit. This shallow area has breakers even when only a 4 ft. swell is running. Conditions can change drastically when the current changes to ebb.

Though the normal river current is 1 1/2 to 2 knots the velocity due to tidal outflow may reach as high as 9 knots. It is essential that the vessel is well founded and the crew is prudent in negotiating this long channel. Be sure to use the latest official NOS chart for navigating this entrance.

The first place where moorage can be obtained is at **Ilwaco**, a quiet town located northwest of Sand Island on the shore of Baker Bay. A dredged 3-mile channel marked by lights and daybeacons leads north from the Columbia River east of Buoy #11. The entrance to the harbor is between two jetties with lights at the ends. Depths in the mooring basin vary from 7 - 16 ft. in the western part to 1 - 4 ft. in the eastern part. The entrance is subject to constant change as a result of shoaling which fans out from the southern jetty. Be sure to stay in the channel as the water is <u>very</u> shallow alongside of it -- better still, pass through at high water.

Contact the harbormaster for assignment of docking space. Transients are usually assigned to Dock #1. Rates vary from $6 for boats up to 30 ft. to $15 for boats over 60 ft. Fuel is available at both a Union and an Exxon dock as shown on the sketch. The Port Docks can handle boats up to 100 ft. while marine supplies are available in the harbor area as indicated. This is an excellent place to haul a boat as rates are very reasonable. It is only a short walk to the town center where groceries and propane can be obtained.

It is well worth visiting local points of interest such as Cape Disappointment and North Head Lighthouses, and the Lewis and Clark Interpretive Center at Fort Canby. Views overlooking the Columbia River and bar can make one glad to be ashore when the tide is ebbing or strong winds cause breakers to form far into the distance.

Of particular interest to cruising sailors is the largest Coast Guard Station between Seattle and San Francisco which is based at Cape Disappointment. Also located here is the Coast Guard Lifeboat School where the training received is second to none. This location was deliberately chosen since very rough water for "practice" rescues is almost always available. Group Astoria is responsible for over 140 miles of coastline between Queets, Wash. and Cape Lookout, Ore. (about 90 miles to the south). The courageous men and women who are ready to assist mariners in distress do indeed deserve our admiration and appreciation for the work they do.

The Columbia River entrance from Cape Disappointment shows the extent of offshore breakers.

Seen from the West End Basin, the Astoria Bridge dominates the view.

Hopefully, this is the right wave to take for an entrance to Depoe Bay.

All essential shore necessities are conveniently located in one place at Depoe Bay.

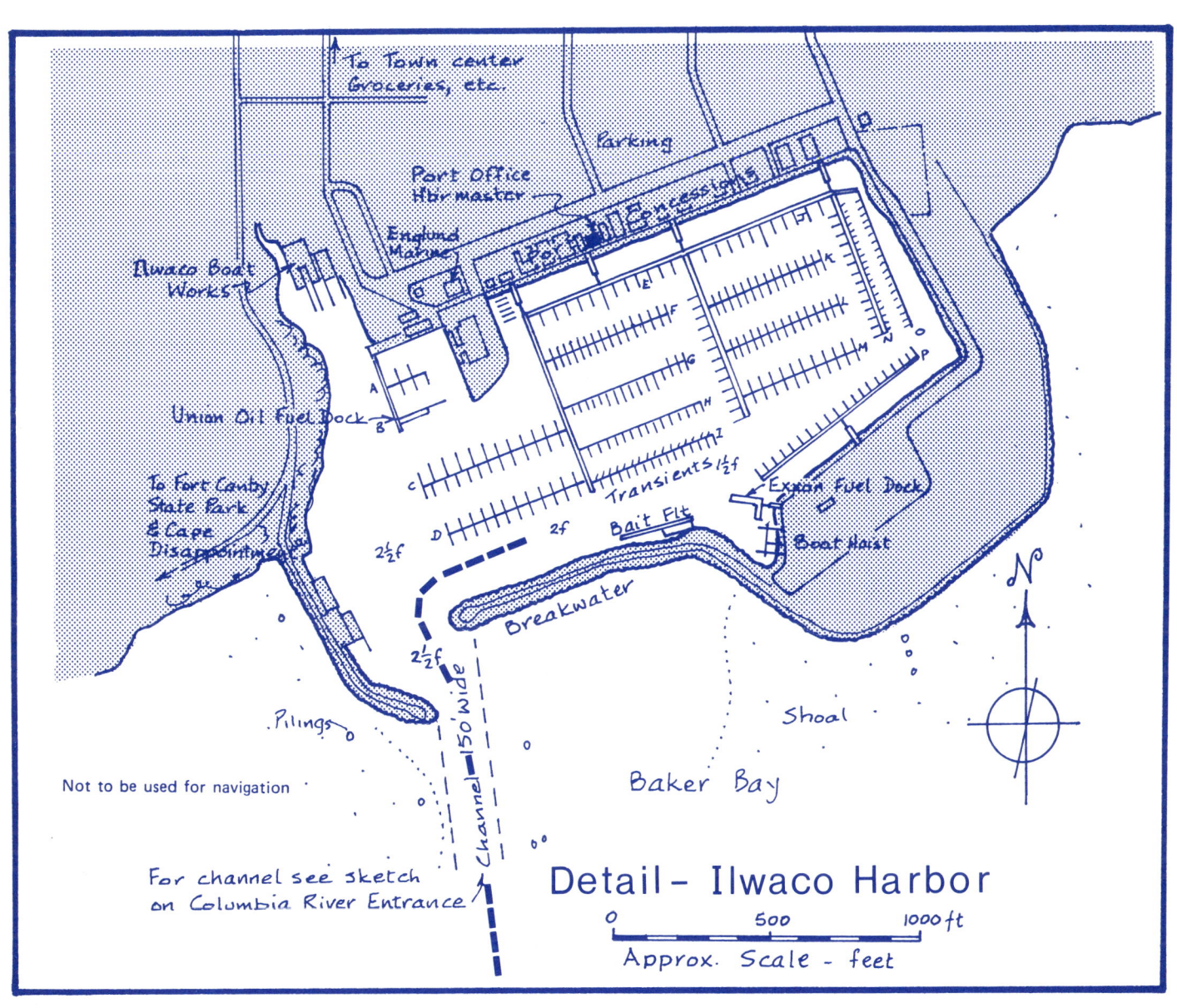

To Town center
Groceries, etc.

Parking

Port Office
Hbr master

Englund
Marine

Ilwaco Boat
Works?

Port Concessions

A
B
Union Oil Fuel Dock

To Fort Canby
State Park
& Cape
Disappointment

2½f
C
D   2f

E
F
G
H
I

K
L
M
N
O
P

Transients 1½f
Bait Flt
Exxon Fuel Dock
Boat Hoist

2½f
Breakwater

2½f

Pilings

Not to be used for navigation

Channel 150' wide

Shoal

Baker Bay

N

For channel see sketch
on Columbia River Entrance

Detail – Ilwaco Harbor

0   500   1000 ft

Approx. Scale - feet

ASTORIA

A **Port of Entry**, this historic city is located on the Oregon side of the Columbia River. As measured from Mile 0 (see detail drawing) it is at about mile 13. To reach it a vessel must follow the well marked channel passing through Lower and Upper Desdemona Shoal before following the Tansy Range. The impressive 4-mile long Astoria bridge which crosses the Columbia River and links Washington state to Astoria clearly pinpoints its location. Having a clearance of about 200 feet at the center, it was designed to withstand gusts of wind of 150 miles per hour and still have a safety factor. When it was completed in the 1960s, the era of ferry crossings came to an end.

Astoria had its beginnings shortly after the Lewis and Clark Expedition ended its trans-continental journey in Clatsop County in 1805. In 1811, when a group of fur traders landed and took up residence it became the first U.S. settlement west of the Rocky Mountains. The area is still settled mainly by people of Scandinavian heritage, who remember its past with restored Victorian homes and several museums.

The Port of Astoria is a major log shipping center, and increasing bulk cargo trade is adding to its activity. It continues to be a wood and seafood processing center as well as a transportation terminal having rail, highway, air traffic, and commercial deep-sea port activities. Maintained by the U.S. Army Corps of Engineers, the Columbia River Channel extends 100 miles upriver to Portland, Oregon.

There are two small craft moorages though only one, the **West End Mooring Basin,** is open to transient traffic. It is located 1/4 mile west of the Astoria Bridge. The entrance is between two sets of pilings and wooden bulkheads with a private light located at the end of each bulkhead to mark the entrance. Moorage can be arranged by reporting to the harbormaster whose office is located at the head of the main walkway. Rates are $3 for boats 19 ft. or smaller and increase $1 for every additional 10 ft. in length. Restroom and shower facilities are available nearby at the Red Lion Inn. A 10-ton hoist at a packing company west of the basin can handle small craft in emergencies. Groceries and marine supplies are available in the city center which is a mile or so to the east.

The **East End Mooring Basin**, 2 miles east of the Astoria Bridge, has a launching ramp, but no other services are available. An appreciation of the colorful past of this area can be had by visiting some of the local points of interest, including the Columbia River Maritime Museum, Flavel House Museum, Heritage Center, the Astoria Column, and Fort Clatsop National Memorial.

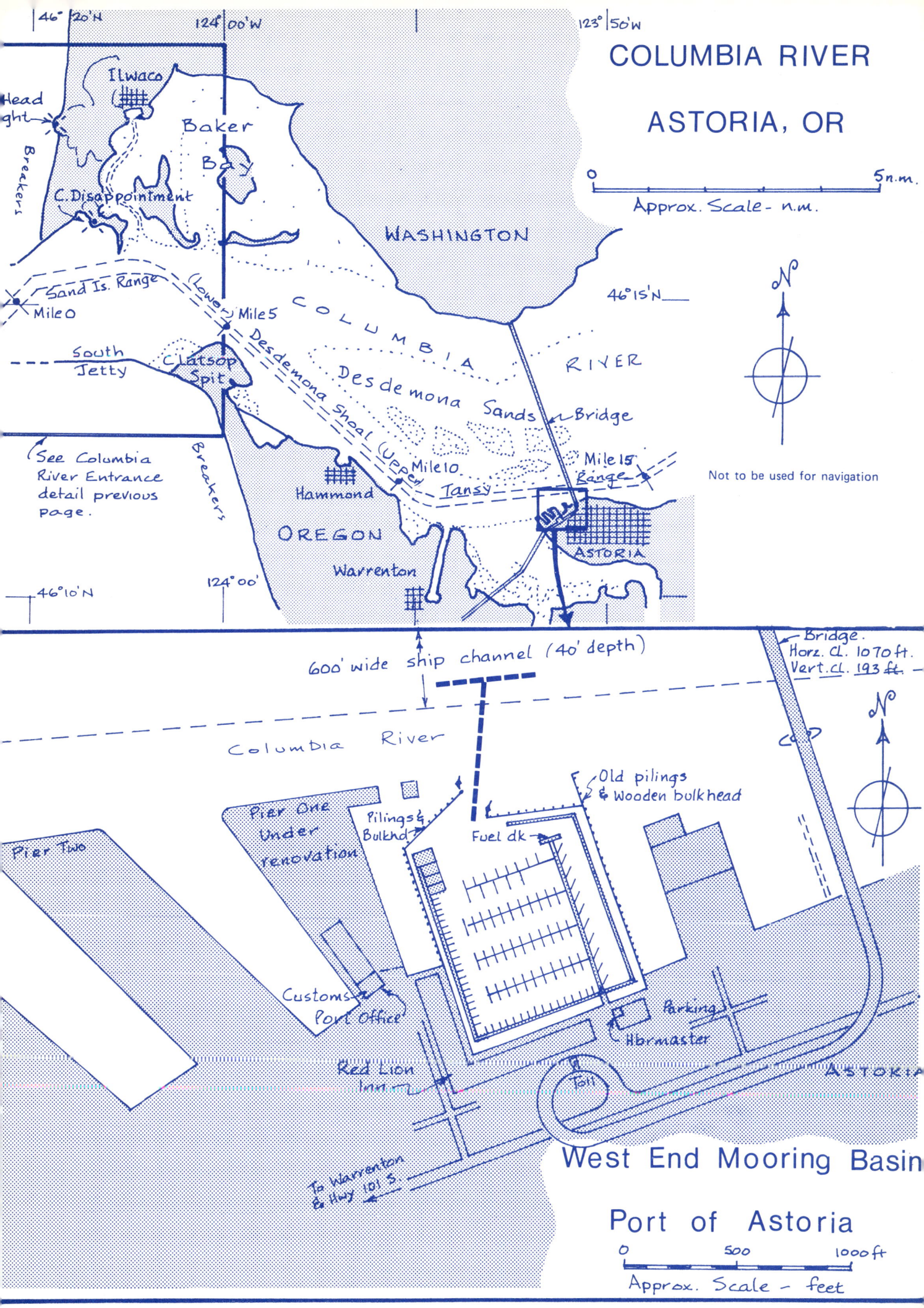

COLUMBIA RIVER

ASTORIA, OR

0 _____ 5 n.m.
Approx. Scale - n.m.

46°20'N   124°00'W   123°50'W

Head light

Breakers

Ilwaco

Baker Bay

C. Disappointment

WASHINGTON

46°15'N

N

Sand Is. Range
Mile 0

(Lower)   Mile 5

COLUMBIA

Desdemona Shoal (Upper)

Desdemona Sands

RIVER

Bridge

South Jetty

Clatsop Spit

Breakers

Mile 10

Mile 15 Range

Not to be used for navigation

See Columbia River Entrance detail previous page.

Hammond

Tansy

OREGON

ASTORIA

46°10'N   124°00'

Warrenton

600' wide ship channel (40' depth)

Bridge.
Horz. Cl. 1070 ft.
Vert. Cl. 193 ft.

N

Columbia River

Pier Two

Pier One Under renovation

Pilings & Bulkhd

Old pilings & Wooden bulkhead

Fuel dk.

Customs Port Office

Parking

Hbrmaster

Red Lion Inn

Toll

ASTORIA

To Warrenton & Hwy 101 S.

West End Mooring Basin

Port of Astoria

0 _____ 500 _____ 1000 ft.
Approx. Scale - feet

48

TILLAMOOK BAY (GARIBALDI)

Unless one has a very good reason for stopping here, this place should be
be avoided. At best, the entrance is not not easy; at other times, it is
impossible. Located 42 miles south of the Columbia River and 5 miles north of
Cape Meares, Tillamook Bay is adjacent to a rich agricultural area which is
famous for its cheese.

An offshore whistle buoy "T" is located about 2 1/4 miles from the west end
of the North Jetty while a flashing bell buoy #1 is a little over a mile closer
in. The entrance is protected by two jetties -- the North Jetty extending
about 1/2 mile westward from the shore while the South Jetty reaches out about
1 1/3 miles from the sand dunes of Kincheloe Point. Seasonal lights, a fog
signal, and horn are at the end of the North Jetty and a Coast Guard lookout
tower is adjacent to it. Note that Kincheloe Point appears to be a low island
when seen at some distance from the north. The channel is marked by a lighted
range, lights, buoys, and a daybeacon.

This is a very dangerous channel which must be navigated only with extreme
caution and local knowledge. This warning is given for two reasons: first,
the channel changes constantly because of natural silting and scouring; second,
one must not rely on the range markers without first checking with the Coast
Guard as to whether they mark the current location of the channel. A Rough Bar
Advisory sign is on the Coast Guard Station boathouse. Bar condition reports
are broadcast on KTIL (1590 kHz) twice daily and when conditions change. One
may call the Coast Guard for a report on the state of the bar.

Enter only on a rising tide, and once the vessel has started to cross do
not attempt to turn around if the bar is breaking. When the tide is ebbing the
current can run up to 6 knots, creating heavy breakers which extend over a mile
offshore. On the north side of the dredged channel there are a number of
visible and covered rocks. Note the location of Sow and Pigs ledge, which is
almost 500 yards off the north shore, in the vicinity of buoy #11. Caution:
on a flood tide the current sets towards this dangerous rocky ledge so a
helmsman must make the necessary adjustments to his course to avoid this
hazard.

Having passed this area of danger, the vessel may proceed to the boat harbor
as indicated on the sketch. Groceries, fuel, and some marine supplies can be
obtained in the town of Garibaldi which is a short walk away. A launching ramp
and dry dock are available. A spectacular 319 ft. waterfall -- Munson Falls --
is 1 mile to the east of the town. It is a treasure for photographers.

About 12 miles north of the entrance to Tillamook Bay is Cape Falcon. This
rocky cape jutting out about 2 miles from the general trend of the coast is
easily identified by the 200 ft. vertical cliffs on the southwestern tip. In
settled northwesterly weather anchorage may be taken in **Smuggler Cove** (a small
cove tucked in, just south of Cape Falcon). When approaching, avoid Falcon
Rock which is located about 3/4 mile west of the Cape. Anchorage should be
taken close to the northern shore of Smuggler Cove in 4 to 5 fathoms. Caution:
there are two isolated rocks about 150 yards from the north shore in otherwise
deep water, which are visible only at low low water.

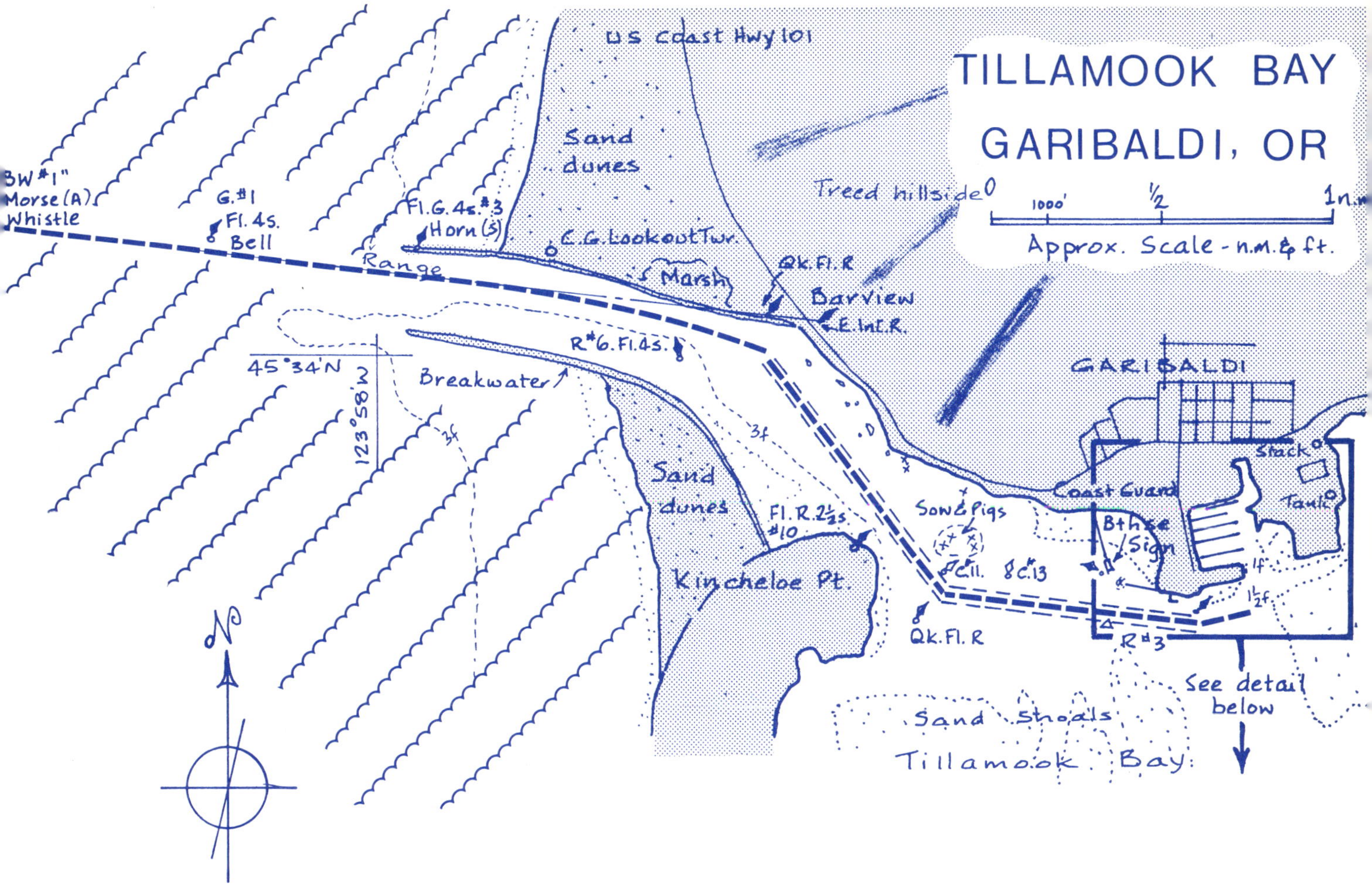

TILLAMOOK BAY
GARIBALDI, OR

US Coast Hwy 101

Sand dunes

Treed hillside

0   1000'   ½   1 n.m.

Approx. Scale - n.m. & ft.

BW #1"
Morse (A)
Whistle

G. #1
Fl. 4s.
Bell

Fl. G. 4s. #3
Horn (s)

C.G. Lookout Tur.

Marsh

Qk. Fl. R
Barview
←E. Int. R.

Range

GARIBALDI

45°34'N

Breakwater

R #6. Fl. 4s.

123°58'W

3f

Stack

Coast Guard

Tank

Sand dunes

Fl. R. 2½s.
#10

Sow & Pigs

Bthse
Sign

C. Ill. 8 C. 13

1f

Kincheloe Pt.

Qk. Fl. R

R #3

1½f

See detail below

N

Sand Shoals
Tillamook Bay

Not to be used for navigation

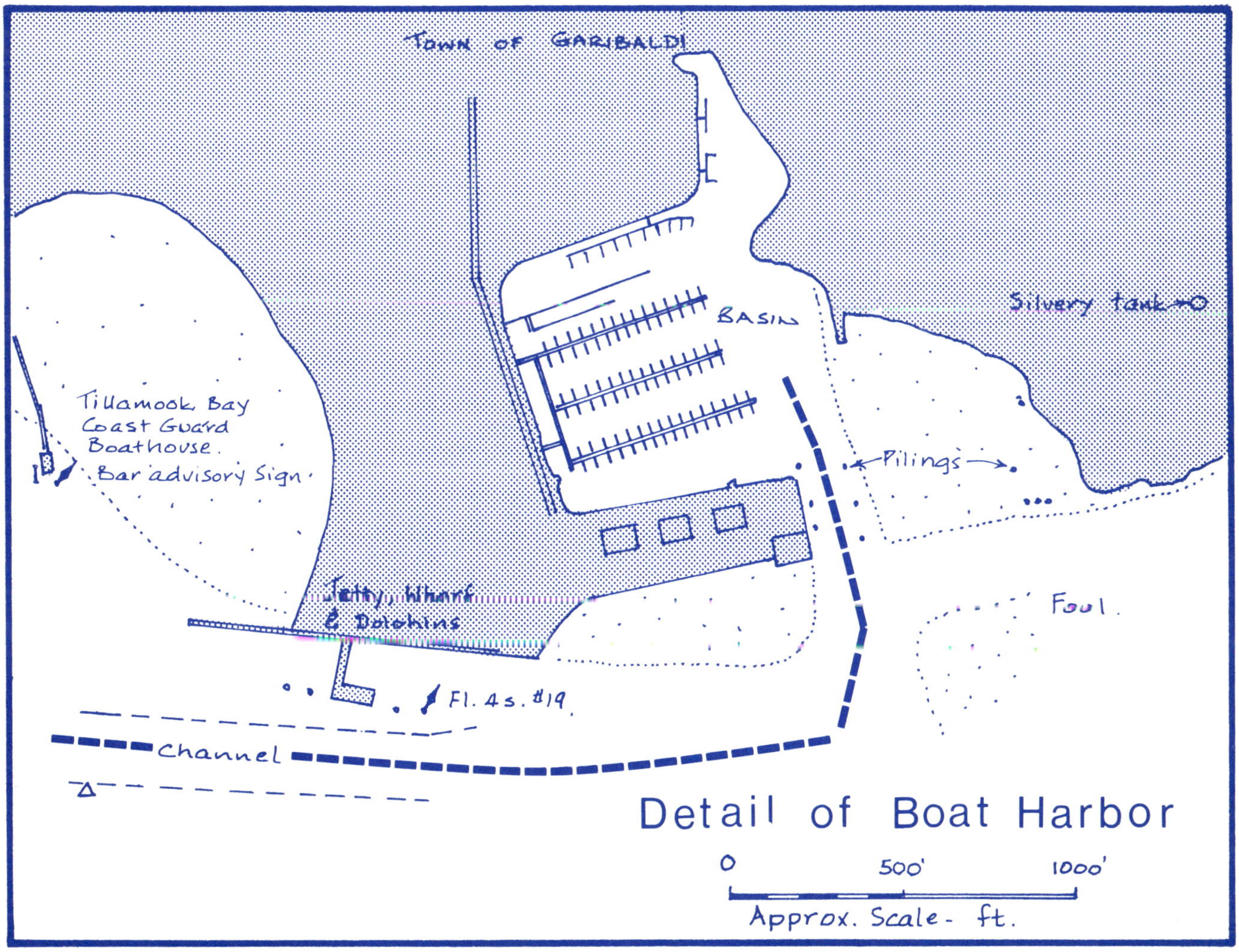

TOWN OF GARIBALDI

Silvery tank →O

BASIN

Tillamook Bay
Coast Guard
Boathouse.
Bar advisory Sign.

←Pilings→

Jetty, Wharf
& Dolphins

Fl. 4s. #19

Foul.

Channel

Detail of Boat Harbor

0   500'   1000'

Approx. Scale - ft.

DEPOE BAY

Having an area of only 6 acres, Depoe Bay has the distinction of being the world's smallest natural navigable harbor. Often referred to as "Hole-in-the-wall," it also has a well-deserved reputation for having one of the most intimidating entrances of any west coast harbor. It is about 100 miles south of Cape Disappointment and 12 miles north of Yaquina Bay and Newport. If one manages to negotiate its short but difficult entrance successfully, the vessel is treated to an excellent small boat haven.

The offshore lighted whistle buoy, "DB," is a little over a mile off the entrance to the bay, while bell buoy #2 is about 1/2 mile closer in. Since North Reef reaches out to within 100 yards of the bell buoy the approach must be made from the offshore buoy. The arched highway bridge over the entrance has a vertical clearance of 42 ft. which prohibits its use by many sailing vessels. The controlling depth of the channel is only 8 feet. Foul ground and breakers extend well offshore on each side of the entrance and at times breaking seas occur clear across it.

Unless you are <u>very</u> familiar with this entrance do not enter in rough weather or at night even though floodlights illuminate the passage to the inner basin. There is a dangerous surge in the narrow, curved 50 ft. wide entrance. The vessel must wait for a period of smoother waves when entering to avoid being pushed on to the rocks on the south side. Then in order to pass under the bridge into the harbor apply power to avoid the surge effects.

A rough bar advisory sign is located 25 ft. above the water on a building on the north side of the entrance channel. If in doubt, call the Coast Guard for an up-to-date report on bar conditions. Think carefully about what you are taking on before starting to enter, for once you have commenced this short entrance there is absolutely NO turning back.

If you are unable to contact the harbormaster prior to entering, tie up at the first dock. His office is a small building next to a garbage can and a johnny-on-the spot. If he isn't in the office or around the docks it is but a short walk up the hill to the north of the basin to his house. Marine supplies and a launching ramp are handy and a small shipyard is available for repairs. A grocery store and a laundromat are a short walk up the hill, in the town which borders the highway. Many fishing and whale-watching charter boats operate out of Depoe Bay.

On the north side of the entrance is a restaurant and observation platform from which one can watch the boats as they make their exciting transit of this unique entrance.

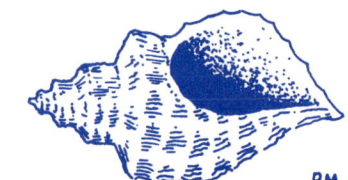

Sculptured rock whelk
(Ocenebra interfossa)

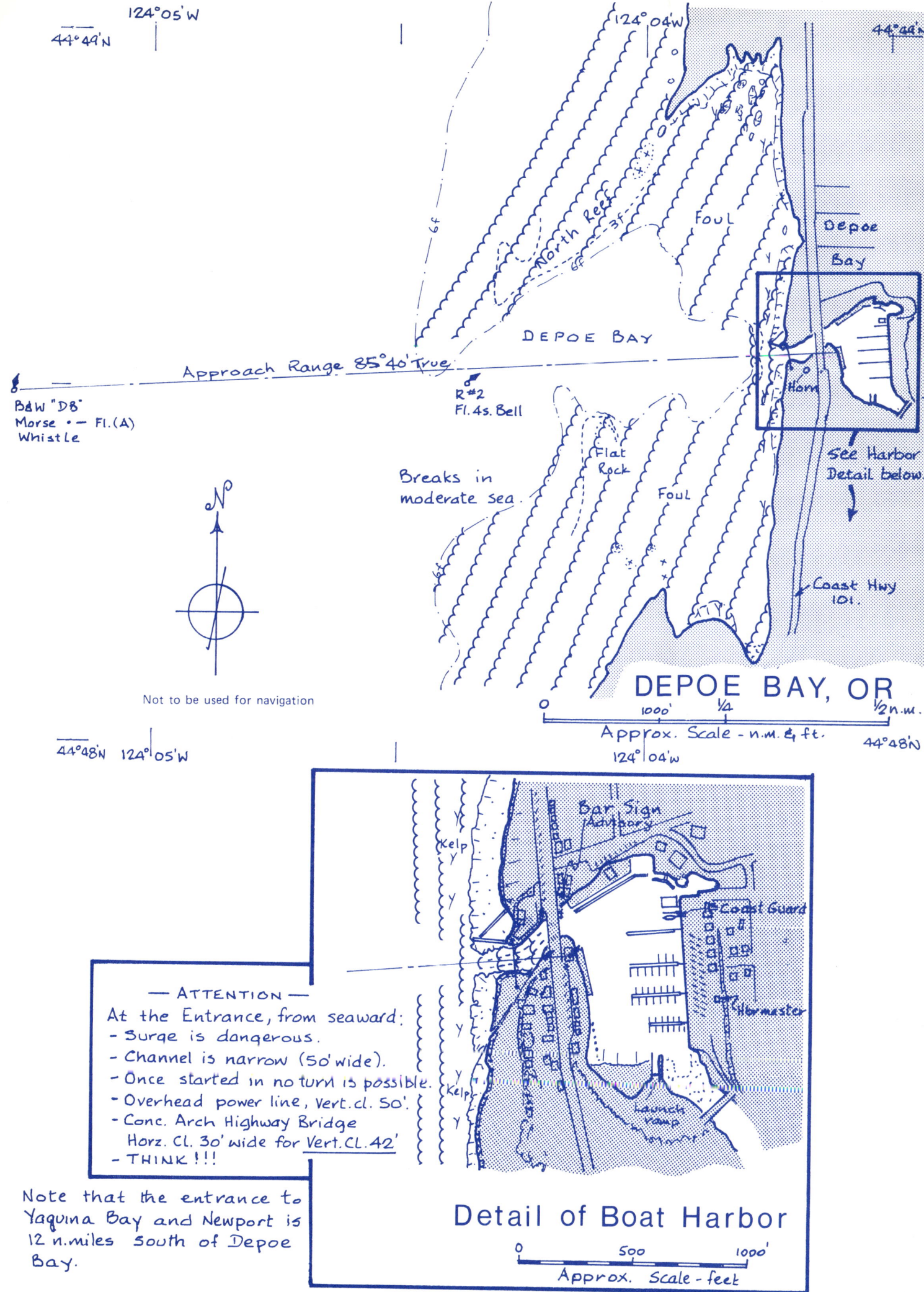

124°05'W
44°49'N

124°04'W
44°44'N

North Reef

6f
3f
6f

Foul

Depoe Bay

DEPOE BAY

Approach Range 85°40' True

B&W "DB"
Morse •— Fl.(A)
Whistle

R #2
Fl. 4s. Bell

Breaks in
moderate sea.

Flat
Rock

Foul

6f

Horn

See Harbor
Detail below.

Coast Hwy
101.

N

Not to be used for navigation

DEPOE BAY, OR

0   1000'   ¼   ½ n.m.

Approx. Scale - n.m. & ft.

44°48'N 124°05'W

124°04'w

44°48'N

Bar Sign
Anthony

Kelp
Y
Y
Y
Y

Coast Guard

Hbrmaster

— ATTENTION —
At the Entrance, from seaward:
- Surge is dangerous.
- Channel is narrow (50'wide).
- Once started in no turn is possible.
- Overhead power line, Vert.cl. 50'.
- Conc. Arch Highway Bridge
  Horz. Cl. 30' wide for Vert.Cl.42'
- THINK!!!

Y
Kelp
Y

Launch
ramp

Note that the entrance to
Yaquina Bay and Newport is
12 n.miles south of Depoe
Bay.

Detail of Boat Harbor

0   500   1000'

Approx. Scale - feet

YAQUINA BAY (NEWPORT)

This is the first place south of the Columbia River one can easily enter, provided of course that one enters on a flood tide. Yaquina Bay is 12 miles south of Depoe Bay and 45 miles north of Florence. Tucked inside the northern entrance point of Yaquina Bay, Newport is the largest city on the central Oregon coast and calls itself the "Dungeness Crab Capital of the World."

When approaching, pick up offshore lighted whistle buoy "Y" which is 1 1/2 miles southwest of the entrance. It is followed by 3 buoys leading to the entrance. An unmistakable landmark is the 129 ft. high Newport Bridge over the Yaquina River about 1 1/3 miles upstream. An abandoned lighthouse and Coast Guard tower are on the sandy bluff on the northern side of the entrance. The channel is protected by two jetties -- the 3/4-mile long North Jetty being the longer one. A seasonal light and fog signal are near the end of the South Jetty. The channel is well marked with lighted ranges, lights, and buoys. When leaving port, clear bell buoy #1 before turning north or south.

Two moorages are in this area: the Port of Newport Commercial Boat Moorage on the north shore is used by fish and charter boats, while the **Southbeach Marina** caters to pleasure craft. Easy entrance can be made from the main channel as shown on the sketch. In the commercial boat area fuel, ship chandleries, repairs, groceries and various supplies are readily available as are numerous restaurants, bars and souvenir shops. Anchorage may be taken up the river, but watch your depths. The dinghy may be tied at the City Dock.

Of interest to boaters from the Pacific Northwest is the former Swiftsure Lightship which can be found at Southbeach Marina now doing service as a restaurant. Interesting exhibits are in the Mark O. Hatfield Marine Science Center and the Lincoln County Historical Museum. Rock-hounding on the beaches north of Yaquina Bay normally rewards one with a pocket full of agates.

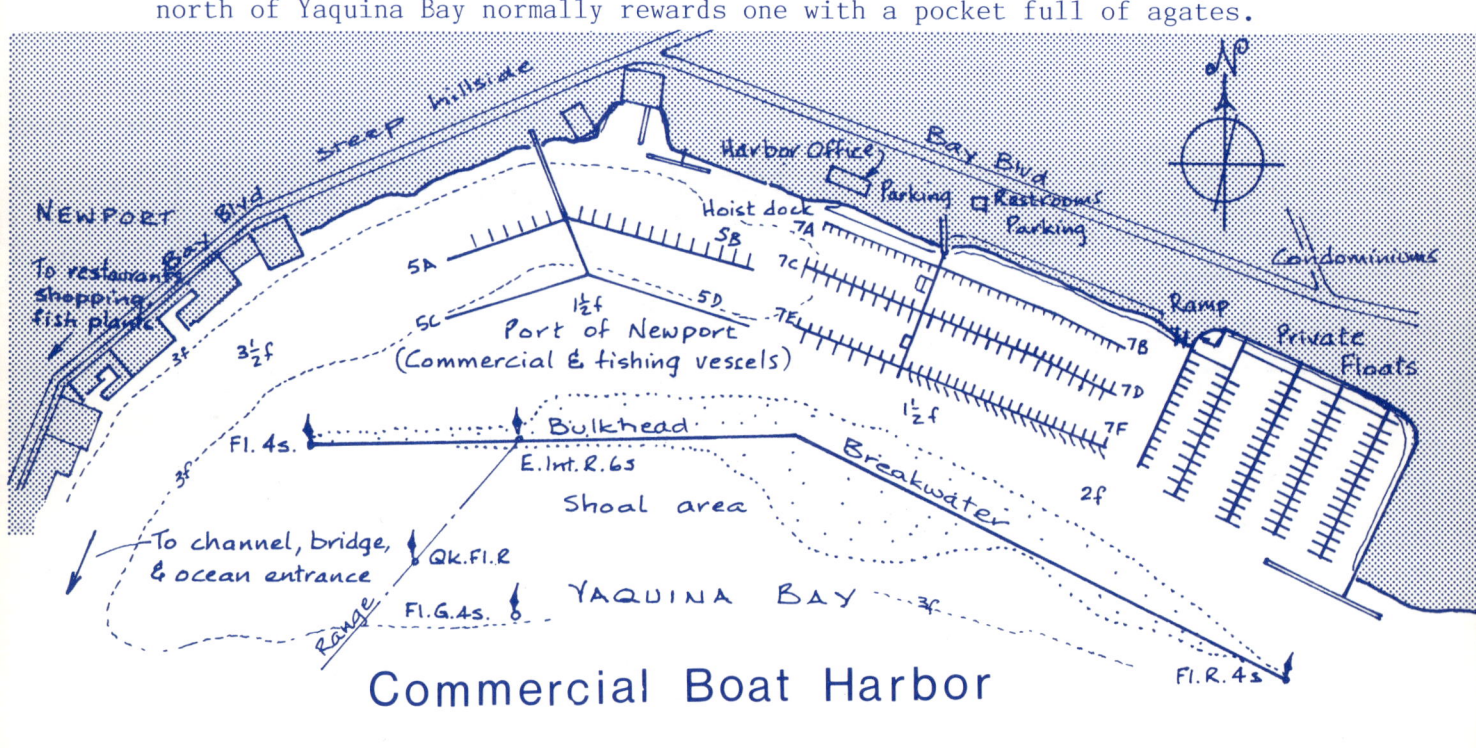

Commercial Boat Harbor

Port of Newport

Not to be used for navigation

0   500'   1000'

Approx. Scale - feet

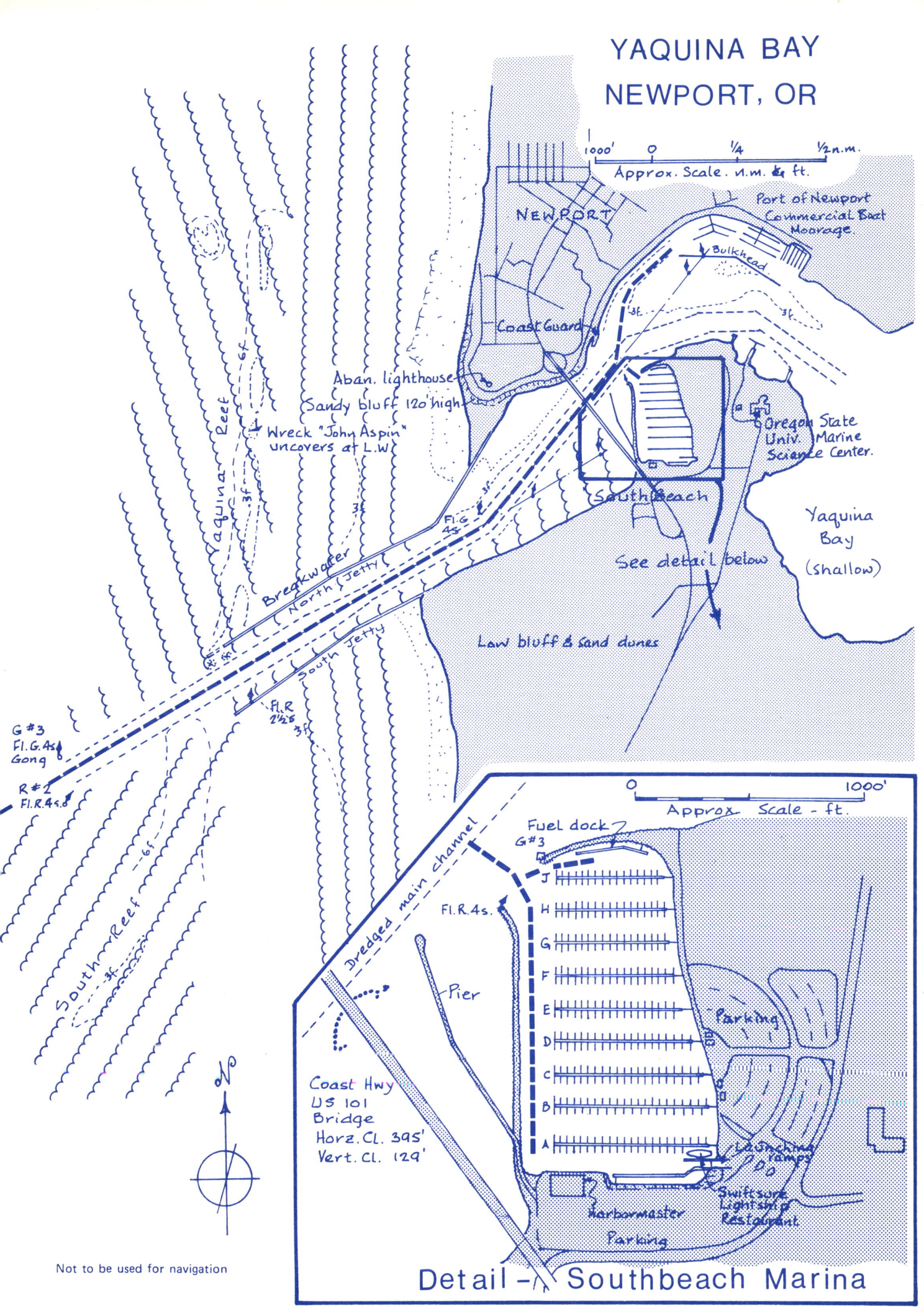

YAQUINA BAY
NEWPORT, OR

1000' 0 ¼ ½ n.m.
Approx. Scale . n.m. & ft.

NEWPORT

Port of Newport
Commercial Boat
Moorage.

Bulkhead

Coast Guard

3ft.   3ft.

Aban. lighthouse
Sandy bluff 120'high

Wreck "John Aspin"
uncovers at L.W.

Oregon State
Univ. Marine
Science Center.

Yaquina Reef

3ft.

3ft.

Fl.G
4s

Southbeach

Yaquina
Bay
(shallow)

See detail below

Breakwater
North Jetty

Low bluff & sand dunes

South Jetty

Fl.R
2½s   3ft

G #3
Fl.G.4s
Gong

R #2
Fl.R.4s.

South Reef

6f

3ft

N

Not to be used for navigation

Detail - Southbeach Marina

0   Approx. Scale - ft.   1000'

Fuel dock
G #3

Dredged main channel

J

Fl.R.4s.   H

G

Pier   F

E

D

C

B

A

Parking

Coast Hwy
US 101
Bridge
Horz.Cl. 395'
Vert.Cl. 129'

Launching
ramps

Swiftsure
Lightship
Restaurant

Harbormaster
Parking

SIUSLAW RIVER (FLORENCE)

Don't stop at this spot unless it is essential; if you must attempt to enter, do so with extreme caution. This is a very dangerous entrance not only because the depths over the narrow channel constantly change as a result of shoaling and freshets, but also because the bar becomes impassable even during a moderate swell.

This area is a transition point where coastal scenery abruptly changes from heavily vegetated mountains to a long chain of sandy beaches and dunes. The Siuslaw River entrance is about 40 miles south of Newport and 21 miles north of the mouth of the Umpqua River.

The offshore whistle buoy "S" is about 3/4 mile west of the end of the jetties protecting the entance. Closer in, but NOT in line with the entrance is gong buoy #5 which is generally in place from May 1 to October 15. The channel is between two Y-shaped jetties which extend westward from the river mouth. A Coast Guard tower is located on the North Jetty which is about 1/2 mile long and has a light and fog signal. The South Jetty is slightly longer though the seaward ends of both jetties are even. The only other feature is Cannery Hill (150 ft.) which is a wooded hill on the east side of the river almost 1 1/2 miles south of the entrance. The Coast Guard Station is located just to the south of this landmark.

Before entering the channel be aware of the hazards that will be faced. When seas are from the west or southwest, breakers extend off the ends of the jetties as far as the gong buoy. Breakers are usually experienced off the ends of both jetties, especially on an ebb tide or when seas are 3 ft. or more. There is a large area of shoal water on the south side of the channel well in from the bar. Breaking seas are common here, as shown on the sketch. Another area of shoal water is on the northeast side of the channel where depths are a little as 2 1/2 ft. at high tide. Because of the constantly changing channel, uncharted buoys are frequently shifted to mark the best water. The helmsman must take great care to stay in the middle of the channel as marked.

The Coast Guard operates a rough bar advisory sign on a 37 ft. tower situated on the North jetty. If in doubt, call them for a report on current bar conditions.

On the northern shore, the town of Florence is about 4 1/2 miles upriver from the entrance. A bascule bridge with clearance of 17 ft. connects Florence to a small settlement on the south shore. This bridge is unique because of its large Gothic columns and decorative concrete etchings on each arch.

There is a marina on each side of the bridge; the **Waterland Marina** on the west side, and the **Port of Suislaw Sport Marina** on the east. Both have fuel, water, marine supplies, and a launching ramp. It is only a short walk to the town for groceries, postal services, and restaurants.

It is worthwhile taking a walk through the carefully preserved Old Town just east of the bridge. North of Florence are the well known Sea Lion Caves which are a shelter for the Steller Sea Lion; picture-perfect Heceta Head Lighthouse lies just beyond. To the south of Florence, the Oregon Dunes National Recreation Area extends for 47 miles. Tribute must be paid to the foresight of those who have reserved this beautiful area for public use.

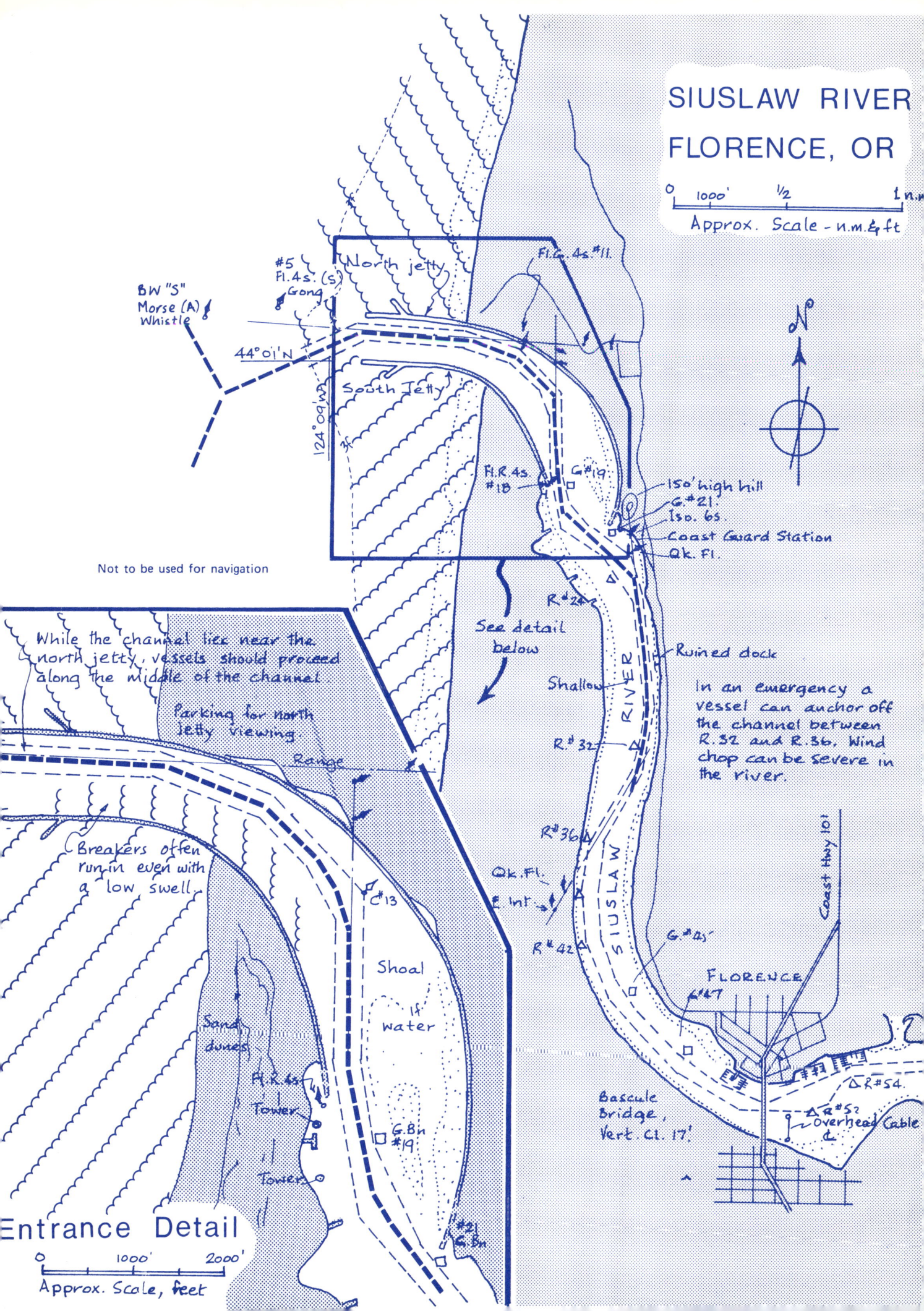

SIUSLAW RIVER
FLORENCE, OR

0   1000'   ½   1 n.m

Approx. Scale - n.m. & ft

BW "S"
Morse (A)
Whistle

#5
Fl.4s. (s)
Gong

North jetty

Fl.G.4s #11

44°01'N

124°09'W

South Jetty

N°

Fl.R.4s
#18

G#19

150' high hill
G#21
Iso. 6s
Coast Guard Station
Qk. Fl.

Not to be used for navigation

See detail
below

R#28

Ruined dock

While the channel lies near the
north jetty, vessels should proceed
along the middle of the channel

Shallow

In an emergency a
vessel can anchor off
the channel between
R.32 and R.36. Wind
chop can be severe in
the river.

Parking for north
jetty viewing

R#32

Range

R#36

Coast Hwy 101

Breakers often
run in even with
a low swell.

C#13

Qk.Fl.

E int.

R#42

G#45

Shoal
17'
water

SIUSLAW RIVER

FLORENCE

Sand
dunes

Fl.R.4s
Tower

G#47

R#54

G.Bn
#19

Bascule
Bridge,
Vert. Cl. 17'

R#52
Overhead Cable

Tower

#21
G.Bn

Entrance Detail

0   1000'   2000'

Approx. Scale, feet

UMPQUA RIVER (SALMON HARBOR)

This is not a highly recommended stopping point for cruising vessels because of its dangerous entrance. The mouth of the Umpqua River is 21 miles south of Siuslaw River and about 20 miles north of Coos Bay. The coast is a succession of sand dunes behind and on which the trees' dark foliage is seen.

When nearing the entrance a vessel must approach from the lighted offshore whistle buoy "U" which is almost a mile west of the South Jetty light. About 1/5 of a mile off the end of the jetty is gong buoy #2. The Umpqua River Light and a radiobeacon are south of the river's mouth in a treed area.

Two jetties form the entrance to the river: the 5/8 mile long North jetty extends seaward from sand dunes; the slightly longer South Jetty has a light and fog signal at its tip. About 160 yards of the outer end of the South Jetty is submerged. Connected to the seaward end of the South Jetty and bordering the channel some distance upriver is another breakwater sometimes referred to as Middle Jetty. The channel is marked by lights, daybeacons, and lighted ranges. A television monitor visible from the channel is on a pedestal next to the entrance front range light. When operating, it shows river traffic which may include barges hauling sand, fuel, or lumber. On Winchester Point is a Coast Guard rough bar advisory sign.

Caution is advised as there is considerable variation in the channel and basin depths, depending on how much time has elapsed since the last dredging took place. Dangerous breaking seas occur seaward of the North Jetty even when a low swell is running. These breakers may cover half of the distance between the jetties and often continue well around the curve of the North Jetty until past buoy "6A". Breakers may also be found between the entrances to Winchester Bay and Salmon Harbor. Before leaving the harbor some local boaters drive out to what is known as "Chicken Point," on the North Jetty, in order to check conditions before venturing out.

There are two moorages about 1 1/2 miles above the entrance, but only the second one should be entered by strangers, for it has a dredged channel. As shown on the sketch, **Winchester Bay** is the first one. It has varying depths of 8 ft. or less and the entrance is marked by a light and daybeacon. It is used by a few small power boats.

The second marina is in **Salmon Harbor.** A dredged channel leads in from the main river channel to a turning basin almost 1/2 mile from the harbor's entrance. Two lights mark the marina entrance -- the westernmost having a fog signal. There is usually space available on the long dock which is often called, "Sailboat Dock." Fuel, water, fishing and marine supplies are available as well as an 8-ton crane for hull and engine repairs. It is only a short walk to the village of Winchester Bay for some shopping.

The village of Winchester Bay is a resort known for its excellent steelhead fishing. The river is a busy one, with fuel oil barges serving the large paper and lumber mills upriver at Gardiner, and lumber barges working out of Reedsport, 10 miles from the entrance.

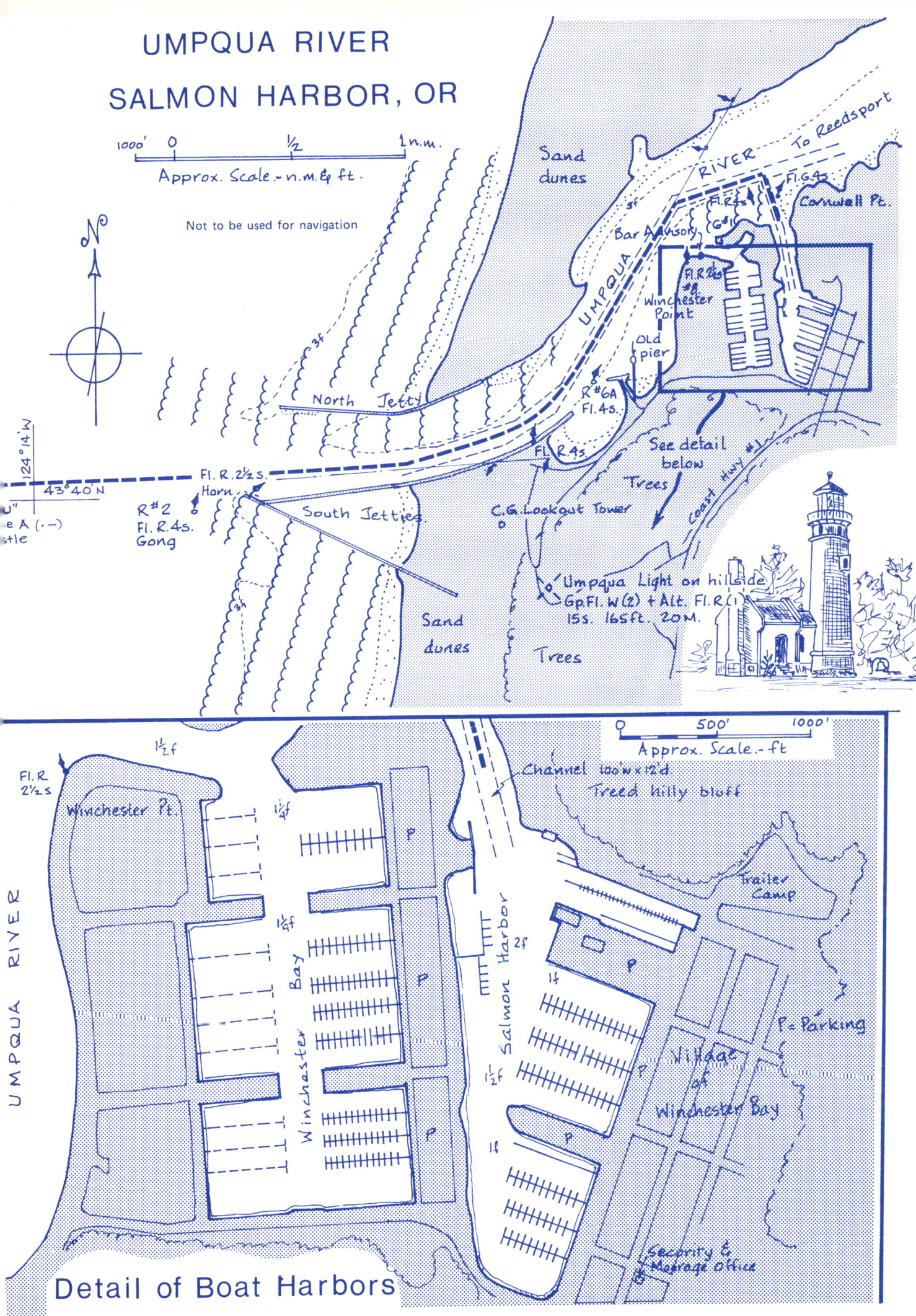

UMPQUA RIVER
SALMON HARBOR, OR

1000' 0   ½   1 n.m.

Approx. Scale - n.m. & ft.

Not to be used for navigation

N

Sand dunes

To Reedsport

UMPQUA RIVER

Fl. G. 4s

3f

Cornwall Pt.

Bar Advisory (G) Fl. R. 5s

G #1

Fl. R. 4s
#8

Winchester
Point

Old
pier

R #6A
Fl. 4s.

North Jetty

3f

See detail
below

Coast Hwy #101

Trees

124°14' W

43°40' N

Fl. R. 2½ s.
Horn

R #2
Fl. R. 4s.
Gong

South Jetties

C.G. Lookout Tower

e A (·−)
stle

Fl. R. 4s.

Sand dunes

Umpqua Light on hillside
Gp.Fl. W(2) + Alt. Fl. R(1)
15s. 165ft. 20M.

Trees

0   500'   1000'
Approx. Scale - ft.

Channel 100'w x 12'd.
Treed hilly bluff

Fl. R
2½ s

Winchester Pt.

1½ f

1¼ f

UMPQUA RIVER

Winchester Bay

1½ f

P

P

P

Salmon Harbor

2f

1f

1½ f

P

P

Trailer
Camp

P = Parking

Village
of
Winchester Bay

P

1f

P

Security &
Moorage Office

Detail of Boat Harbors

COOS BAY

Coos Bay is the most important harbor between San Francisco and the Columbia River, not only because it is a **harbor of refuge** but also because it is one of the largest wood products ports in the world. It is almost 20 miles south of Umpqua River and 33 miles north of Cape Blanco. It is easily identified by Cape Arago Light as well as Coos Head, a high, steep sided, rocky head on the south side of the entrance. The U.S. Naval buildings are conspicuous on the bluffs south of Coos Head.

The offshore lighted whistle buoy "K" is almost 2 miles WNW of the entrance. Bell buoy #1 is 1 mile closer in and then comes gong buoy #3 a short distance further. Bar reports are given each hour on KBBR (1340 kHz) or one may contact the Coast Guard (Ch. 12 or 16 or by telephoning 888 - 3102). The Coast Guard maintains a rough bar advisory sign on the east side of the breakwater near the fuel dock.

Two jetties form the entrance to the bay, the North Jetty having a light and fog signal at its seaward end. Both jetties are submerged at their tips -- the North Jetty for 300 yards, the South Jetty for 100 yards. Even moderate swells break heavily on the ends of the jetties -- those on the south side of the channel rolling in for a considerable distance along the edge of the jetty. Buoys, lighted ranges, lights and daybeacons mark the channels.

As usual, enter only on a flood tide, the best time being toward the end of the flood current. Caution: just off the ends of the jetties there is a current of variable strength sweeping either to the north or south, a southerly current being more common during summer months. The impressive size of the swells, coupled with breakers thundering on the two jetties, can make this an awesome entrance even during favorable conditions.

Heavy breakers occur in a wide arc off North Spit in the vicinity of bell buoy #5, and rogue waves are common in this area. Guano Rock (uncovered at low water) is on the south side of the channel about 280 yards northwest of Coos Head. Another danger is a submerged jetty which reaches out 1/3 mile off the east shore of Coos Bay. The sharp curve in the channel must be negotiated carefully in this area. Stay southwest of lighted buoy "1" when approaching or leaving the Charleston Boat Harbor.

The **Charleston Boat Harbor** is easily entered and the people are friendly. Call the harbormaster for assignment to one of the two transient docks. Moorage costs about $6 per night; showers are 25 cents. Fuel, propane (10% valve only), marine supplies, fishing tackle, laundry and washroom facilities are handy and groceries may be obtained from a store near the cafe. As this is the sportsfishing headquarters for the Bay area many charter and fishing boats are in evidence. It's worth obtaining a licence to enjoy the excellent crabbing.

Anchorage in Coos Bay can be taken outside of the dredged channels but it is a long trip by dinghy to pick up supplies. Alternatively, an anchorage is reported upriver from Charleston opposite MacDonalds; going ashore is easy any place on the beach.

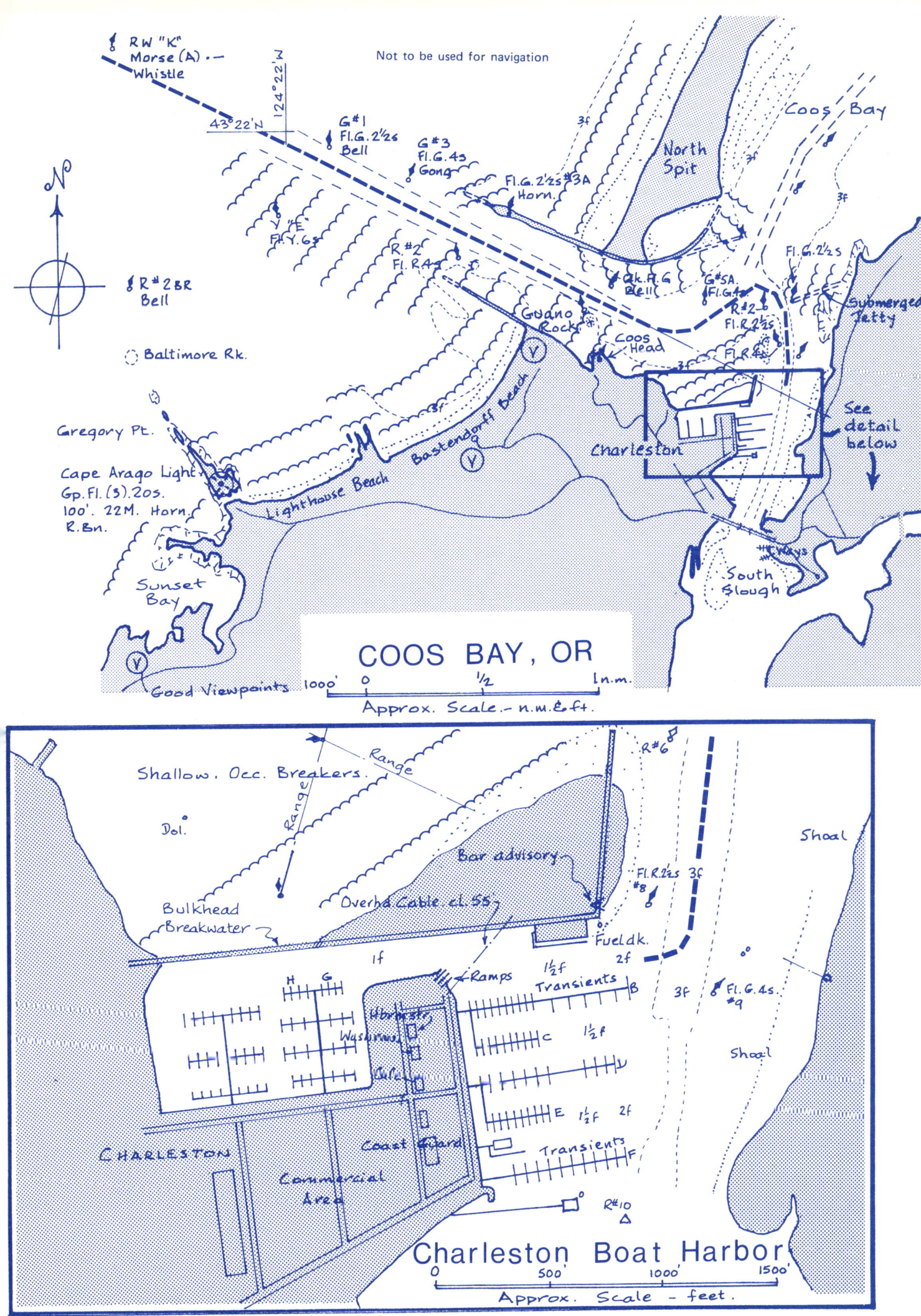

RW "K"
Morse (A) ·—
Whistle

Not to be used for navigation

124°22'W

43°22'N

Coos Bay

3f

3f

North Spit

G #1
Fl.G. 2½s
Bell

G #3
Fl.G. 4s
Gong

Fl.G. 2½s #3A
Horn

"E"
Fl.Y. 6s

R #2
Fl. R 4s

Ok.R.G
Bell

G #5A
Fl.G.4

Fl.G. 2½s

R #2-B
Fl.R.2½s

Submerged Jetty

R #2BR
Bell

Guano Rock

Coos Head

Fl.R.4s

3f

Baltimore Rk.

Charleston

See detail below

N

Gregory Pt.

Bastendorff Beach

Cape Arago Light
Gp.Fl. (3).20s.
100'. 22M. Horn.
R.Bn.

Lighthouse Beach

Sunset Bay

South Slough

Wkys

COOS BAY, OR

Good Viewpoints   1000'   0   ½   1 n.m.

Approx. Scale.— n.m. & ft.

Shallow. Occ. Breakers.

Range

Range

R #6

Range

Dol.

Shoal

Bar advisory

Fl.R.2½s 3f
#8

Bulkhead Breakwater

Overh'd Cable cl. 55'

Fuel dk.

2f

1f

Ramps

1½f

Transients

B

3f

Fl.G.4s
#9

H   G

Washrms

C   1½f

Shoal

Hbr.mstr.

E   1½f   2f

Office

CHARLESTON

Coast Guard

Commercial Area

Transients   F

R #10

Charleston Boat Harbor

0   500'   1000'   1500'

Approx. Scale - feet.

COQUILLE RIVER (BANDON)

Bandon calls itself the "Storm Watching Capital of the World." That should tell you something!

The Coquille River entrance is about 15 miles south of Coos Bay and 30 miles north of Port Orford. The area's economy relies mainly on the lumber-mills in addition to fishing, cheese and cranberry industries.

The offshore lighted whistle buoy "2" is about 2 miles northwest of the entrance to the river. About 1/4 mile SSE of this buoy is Coquille Rock where breakers occur in heavy weather. Approximately 5/8 mile closer to the entrance is bell buoy "4" followed in another 5/8 mile by whistle buoy "6", which is in turn about 5/8 mile from the ends of the jetties. The entrance is about 5/8 mile northeast of Coquille Point. The countless upstanding rocks, ledges, and reefs which form a huge fan-shaped area of spume and breakers off Coquille Point are a great encouragement to stay on course and not to take short-cuts. Breakers over a mile offshore are seen in this area.

The entrance is protected by two jetties on which the sea breaks heavily. A horn (operating June 1 - September 15) and light are on the South Jetty. Breakers roll up the southern shore of the channel where submerged rocks are evident. Caution: a current in the channel sets a vessel towards the south. On the North Jetty, just inland from the shore, is an abandoned lighthouse; partially submerged rocks extend from it to the end of the jetty. The channel is marked by a lighted range, lights, and buoys. Local knowledge is advised since the channel changes frequently, and so the range does not always indicate the deepest water.

From May 15 to October 15 the Coast Guard operates a Boat Patrol. If in doubt, give them a call for up-to-date advice on the channel; out of season, call the Coos Bay Coast Guard. A rough bar advisory sign is located as shown on the sketch.

The well protected small craft basin is tucked behind a high breakwater with a boardwalk on top. The harbormaster's office is a short distance away. Fuel, marine supplies, fishing tackle, and a launching ramp are available.

A walk through restored Old Town Bandon (near the waterfront) is a pleasant way to work off one's sea legs, or one may prefer a hike along the beach to better enjoy the safe side of the spectacular offshore rocks. Unique to Bandon is a metaphysical exhibit known as the Continuum Center. The Coquille River Museum is located in an historic Coast Guard building across the river at Bullards Beach State Park.

LOOKING E INTO THE COQUILLE RIVER FROM THE ENTRANCE.

The rocks south of the Coquille River entrance make a spectacular display even on a calm day.

The beautiful coast south of Port Orford beckons.

The morning mist soon disappears from Charleston Boat Basin in Coos Bay.

Oregon coastal rocks are a treat for land-based photographers.

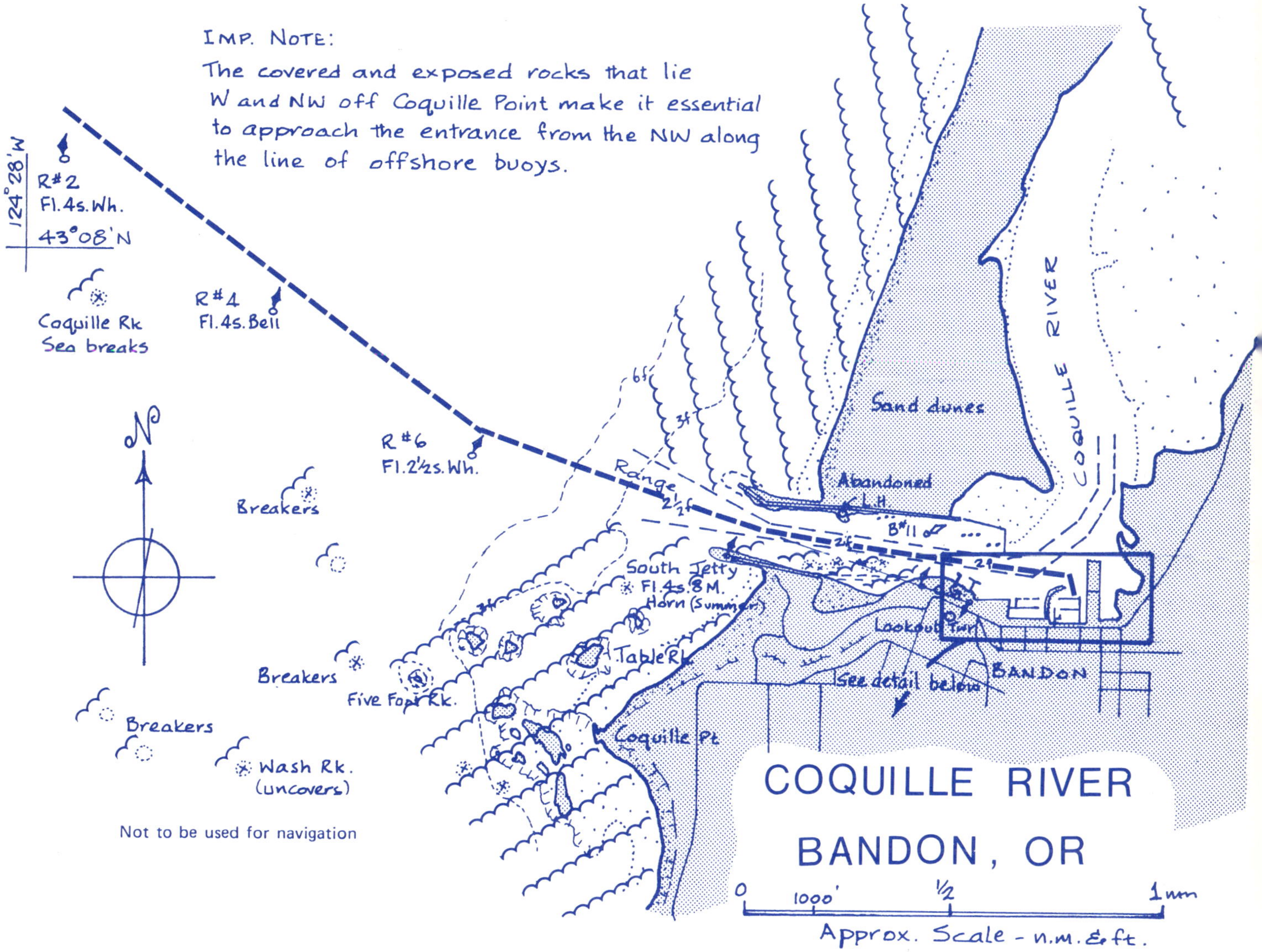

IMP. NOTE:
The covered and exposed rocks that lie
W and NW off Coquille Point make it essential
to approach the entrance from the NW along
the line of offshore buoys.

124°28'W

R#2
Fl.4s.Wh.

43°08'N

Coquille Rk
Sea breaks

R#4
Fl.4s.Bell

N

R#6
Fl.2½s.Wh.

Breakers

Range
2½f

6f

3f

Sand dunes

Abandoned
L.H.

B#11

2f

COQUILLE RIVER

South Jetty
Fl.4s.8M.
Horn (Summer)

Breakers

2f

Five Foot Rk.

Table Rk.

Lookout Tree

BANDON

Breakers

See detail below

Coquille Pt.

Wash Rk.
(uncovers)

Not to be used for navigation

COQUILLE RIVER

BANDON, OR

0   1000'   ½   1 nm

Approx. Scale - n.m. & ft.

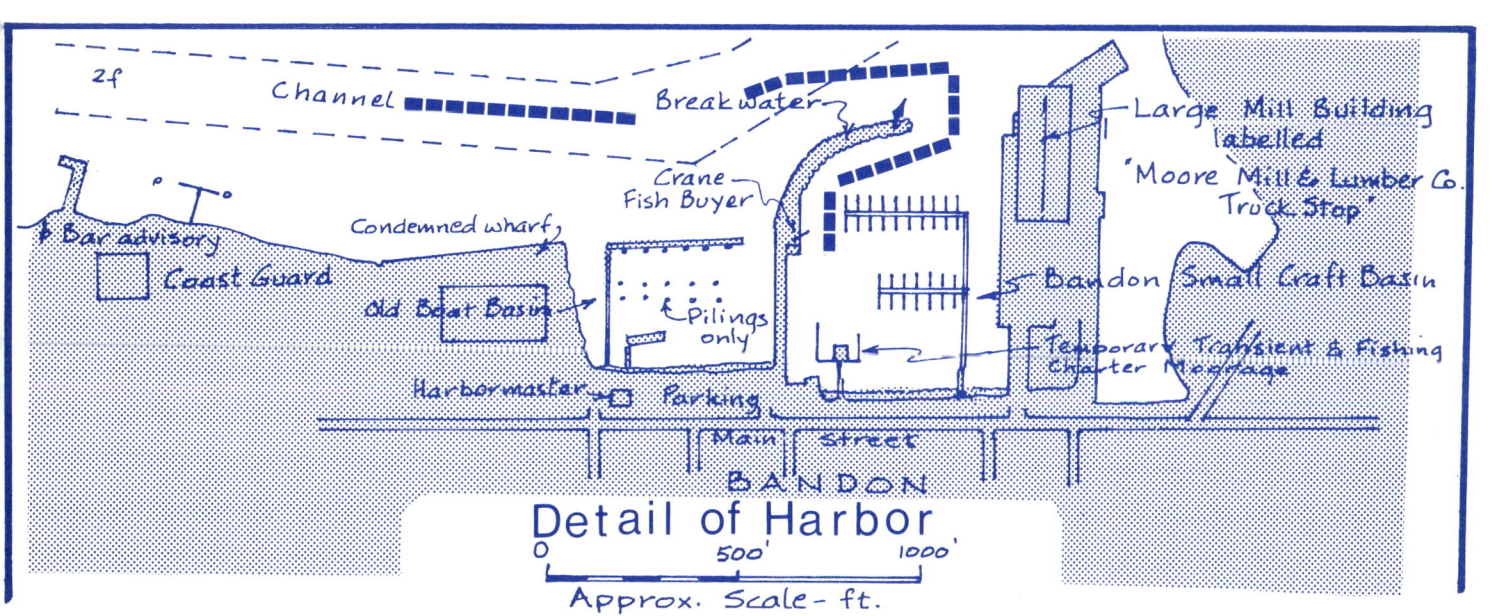

2f

Channel ▬▬▬▬▬   Breakwater

Large Mill Building
labelled
'Moore Mill & Lumber Co.
Truck Stop'

Crane
Fish Buyer

Bar advisory

Coast Guard

Condemned wharf

Old Boat Basin

Pilings
only

Bandon Small Craft Basin

Temporary Transient & Fishing
Charter Moorage

Harbormaster   Parking

Main   Street

BANDON

Detail of Harbor

0   500'   1000'

Approx. Scale - ft.

PORT ORFORD

A very good anchorage in northwesterly weather, Port Orford is 30 miles south of Coquille River and 19 miles north of Rogue River. Except in southerly weather it is the best anchorage north of Point Reyes. There is no bar to cross, no narrow channel between jetties through which one must thread one's way, and the coastal area is beautiful.

Identification of Port Orford when one is approaching from the north is best achieved by pinpointing Cape Blanco (Oregon's westernmost headland); from the south, Humbug Mountain is a reliable landmark. The anchorage is 6 1/2 miles south of the former and about 4 miles north of the latter. Offshore whistle buoy "2OR" is about 7 miles northwest of bell buoy "1" which is a mile from the anchorage.

When coming from the north, maintain a course well clear of the extensive areas of danger west and southwest of Cape Blanco. Blanco Reef and various other rocks are scattered in a large area west and southwest of the Cape. This hazard is followed by Orford Reef which covers an area 2 to 5 miles offshore between the Heads and Cape Blanco. Do not pass between these reefs or take a route between Orford Reef and the coast unless you have local knowledge.

When approaching from the south one should also maintain an offshore course to be well clear of Island Rock (a little over a mile southwest of Humbug Mountain) and Redfish Rocks (2 miles north of Island Rock and 1 mile offshore).

The cove is tucked behind The Heads which resemble a triple-lobed ridge from the south. Don't mistake the white tank on the top of The Heads with Cape Blanco lighthouse. Anchorage may be taken in 6 - 10 fathoms, sand. The preferred area is outside the breakwater in the lee of The Heads since the prevailing winds funnel across the draw and sweep the inner area. A dinghy landing is at the dock. Rocks border the cove up to 1/2 mile offshore, while a 550 ft. breakwater extends southeasterly from Graveyard Point.

Fuel and water are available at the wharf and there is a hoist capable of lifting boats up to 42 ft. A pleasant hike takes one to the community of Port Orford for groceries and other supplies.

Featured in local shops is a wide variety of goods made from beautifully patterned myrtlewood. This wood is also known by the following names: California laurel, California sassafras, California olive, myrtle, spice tree, pepperwood, bay, bay laurel, and yellow, black, or white myrtle. Port Orford yellow cedar is unique to this area and is also highly valued.

An interesting historical fact is that Battle Rock (almost attached to the shore south of the town) is the site of the first settlement in this area in 1851. Two attacks by local Indians were repelled before the settlers' enthusiasm and ammunition ran low and they escaped to a settlement on the Umpqua River. A larger, better equipped group returned the same year to establish permanent habitation.

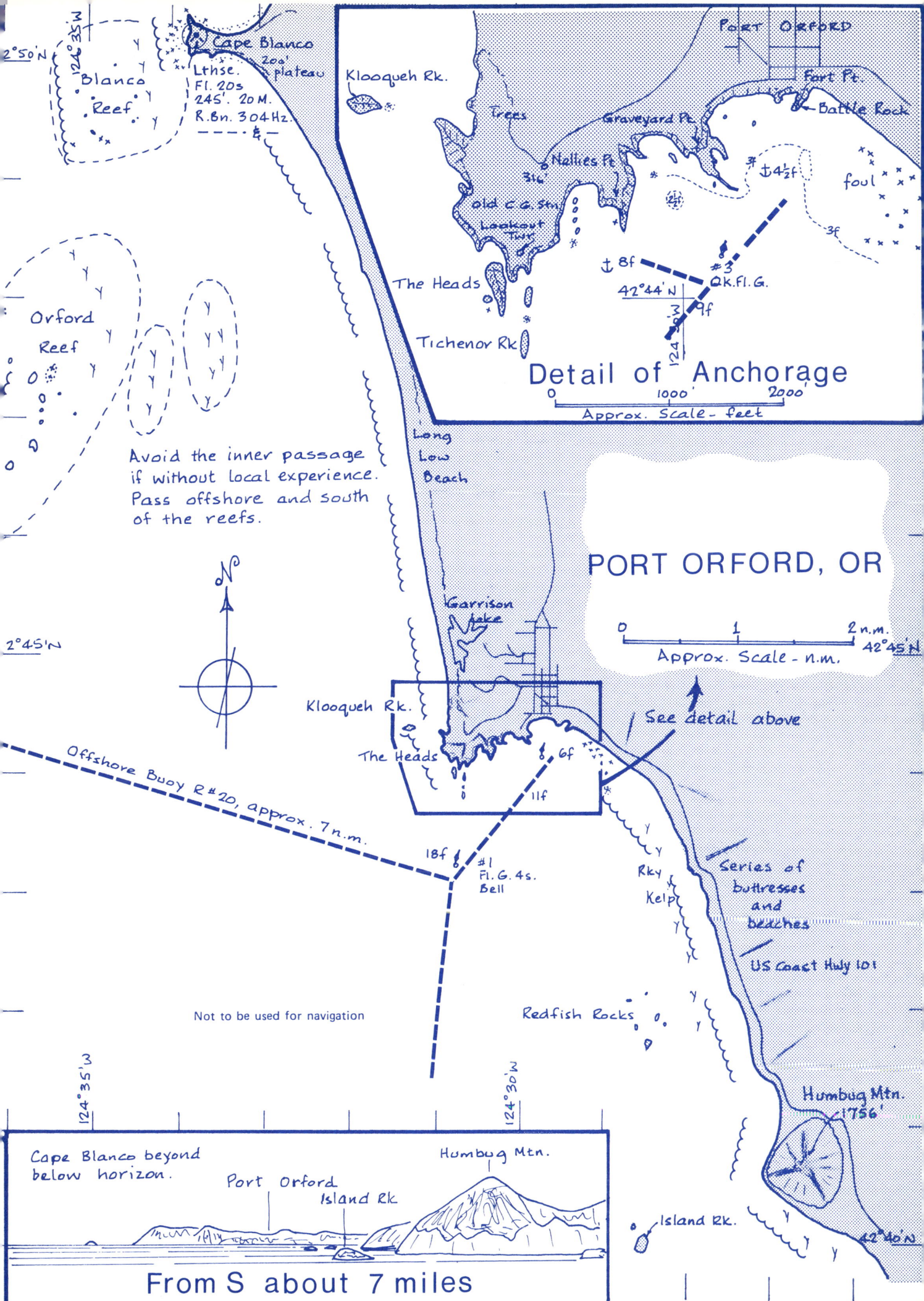

2°50'N
124°35'W

Cape Blanco
Lthse.
Fl. 20s
245'. 20M.
R.Bn. 304 Hz.

200' plateau

Blanco Reef

Klooqueh Rk.

Orford Reef

Avoid the inner passage
if without local experience.
Pass offshore and south
of the reefs.

N

2°45'N

Offshore Buoy R#20, approx. 7n.m.

18f

#1
Fl. G. 4s.
Bell

Not to be used for navigation

124°35'W

124°30'W

Detail of Anchorage

PORT ORFORD

Fort Pt.

Battle Rock

Graveyard Pt.

Trees

Nellies Pt.

316

old c.c. Stn.

Lookout Turt

The Heads

Tichenor Rk.

foul

‡4½f

⸸ 8f

42°44'N

124°30'W

9f

#3
Qk. Fl. G.

3f

0   1000'   2000'
Approx. Scale - feet

Long
Low
Beach

Garrison
Lake

Klooqueh Rk.

The Heads

6f

11f

PORT ORFORD, OR

0   1   2 n.m.
Approx. Scale - n.m.

42°45'N

See detail above

Rky

Kelp

Series of
buttresses
and
beaches

US Coast Hwy 101

Redfish Rocks

Humbug Mtn.
1756'

Island Rk.

42°40'N

Cape Blanco beyond
below horizon.

Port Orford
Island Rk

Humbug Mtn.

From S about 7 miles

64

ROGUE RIVER (GOLD BEACH)

This is not a recommended stop-over unless one has local knowledge. The Rogue River entrance is about 22 miles south of Port Orford and 27 miles north of Brookings. Rogue River is well known not only for its excellent sportfishing but also for its well publicized white-water rafting and jet boat trips.

The offshore whistle buoy "R" is a little over 2 miles southwest of the channel entrance; closer in is bell buoy "1". Two jetties extending in a southwesterly direction protect the entrance; a light and fog signal are at the seaward end of the northly one. Breakers are almost always present at the outer ends of the jetties, being especially dangerous when the sea is running from the west or southwest. Rogue waves may be experienced up to 1/4 mile off the ends of the jetties even on a calm day.

When approaching from the north take care to keep at least 5 miles off the coast to clear Rogue River Reef which extends 4 miles northwest of the entrance.

When entering the channel the vessel must wait for a period of lower seas and time the entrance carefully in order to get past the breakers. Depths over the bar are constantly changing and are often less than the 13 ft. project depth. At times, small boat traffic becomes quite congested just inside the bar where many trolling vessels congregate when the fish are running. Caution: a large gravel bar and shoal water are found on the southern side of the channel and three groins extend outward from this area.

A buoyed channel leads directly into the Gold Beach small craft harbor. Fuel, water, fishing tackle, and some marine supplies are available.

LOOKING S FROM ENTRANCE TO ROGUE RIVER

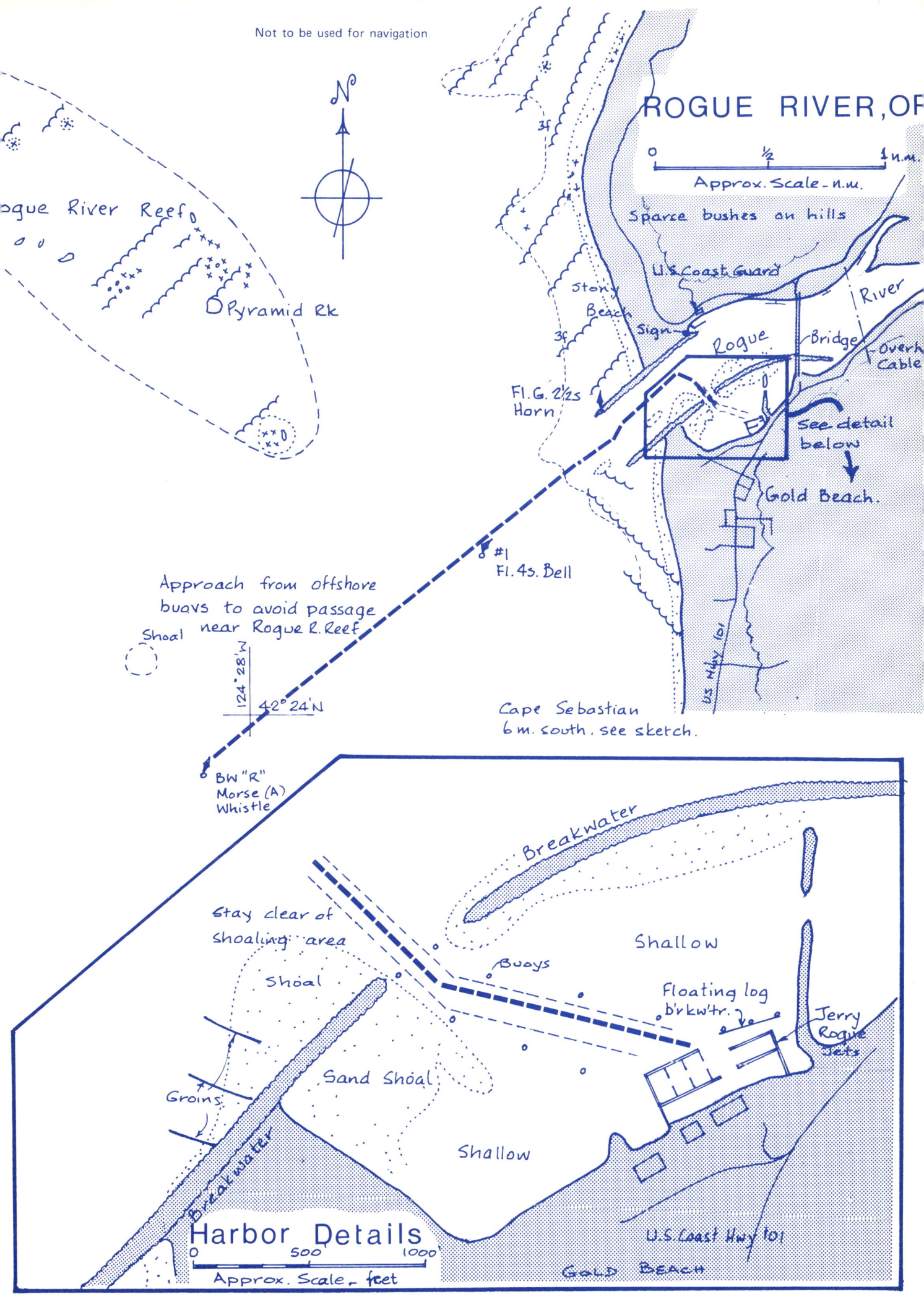

N

ROGUE RIVER, OF

0   ½   1 n.m.
Approx. Scale - n.m.

Sparce bushes on hills

U.S Coast Guard

ogue River Reef

Pyramid Rk

Stony Beach

Sign

3f

Rogue   Bridge

River

Overh Cable

Fl.G. 2½s Horn

See detail below

Gold Beach.

#1
Fl. 4s. Bell

Approach from offshore
buoys to avoid passage
near Rogue R. Reef

Shoal

124° 28' W

42° 24' N

Cape Sebastian
6 m. south. see sketch.

US Hwy 101

BW "R"
Morse (A)
Whistle

Breakwater

Stay clear of
shoaling area

Shallow

Buoys

Shoal

Floating log
b'rkw'tr.

Jerry
Rogue
Jets

Sand Shoal

Groins

Breakwater

Shallow

U.S.Coast Hwy 101

Gold Beach

Harbor Details

0   500   1000
Approx. Scale - feet

CHETCO RIVER (BROOKINGS)

The entrance to the Chetco River is about 26 miles south of Rogue River and 18 miles north of Crescent City, California. Avoid entering in southerly weather as the entrance can become difficult. This commercial fishing port also is a popular sportsfishing center for deep-sea and freshwater fishing.

The offshore whistle buoy "CR" is about 1 mile southwest of the entrance. A half mile closer in is bell buoy "2", followed by gong buoy "3". The smokestack of a plywood plant in Brookings is noticeable from some distance offshore.

The entrance is protected by two jetties. The West Jetty is the longer of the two, and it has a light and fog signal at the outer end. A lighted range marks the narrow (60 ft.) channel. Caution: depths in the channel are only 9 ft.; it is essential to stay within the channel because of the shoals and numerous rocks that are just alongside. The channel leads directly to a turning basin which is protected on the west by a 1,800 ft. dike.

Bar reports are given every hour during daylight hours on KURY (910 kHz). A rough bar advisory sign facing northwest is on the Coast Guard fuel dock. If in doubt, call the Coast Guard for current bar conditions.

There are two marinas, the southern one for commercial boats, the northern, for pleasure craft. Current rates are $8.50 per day for a 34-foot vessel. Fuel, water, and marine supplies are available at the northern basin where minor small craft repairs can be made. All facilities except showers are available. It's a nice walk up the road leading to the city level where a mall and many commercial establishments are located. Haran's Hardware is well worth a visit as it has an impressive inventory of anything one could hope for in a hardware store.

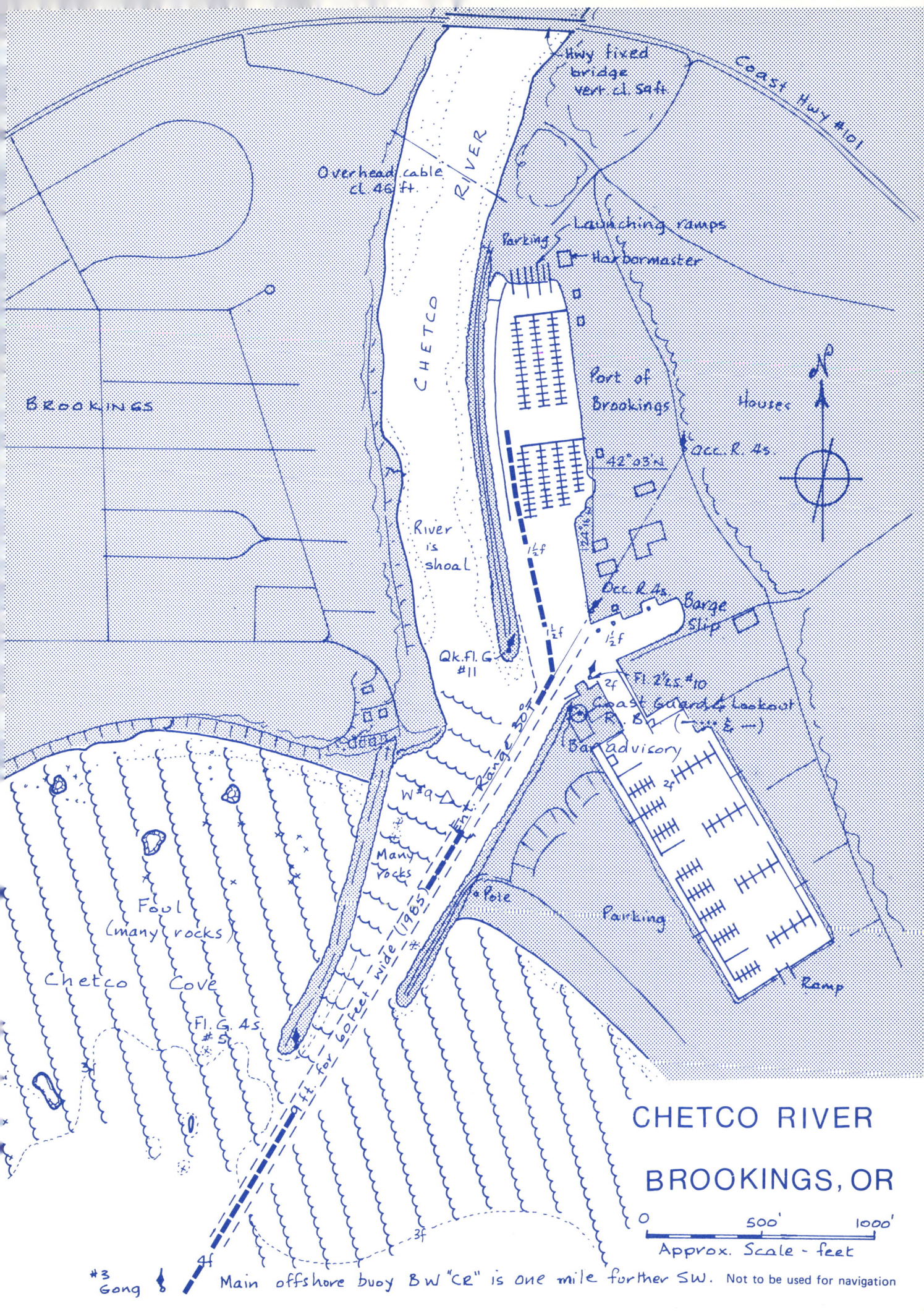

CHETCO RIVER

BROOKINGS, OR

CRESCENT CITY

Though this **harbor of refuge** is straightforward and easy to enter, strangers should not attempt an entrance at night.

Just 3 1/2 miles southeast of Point St. George, Crescent City is 18 miles south of Brookings and 45 miles north of Trinidad Head. For sailors from the north this initial moorage in Californian waters is often marked by the first sighting of pelicans as evidence of progress to warmer, southern waters. It is also the beginning of the famous California Redwood Forest. A trip inland to admire these awe-inspiring giants is a must.

Offshore whistle buoy "2" is a little over a mile WSW of the entrance to the harbor. Closer in is whistle buoy "4" followed in 1/2 mile by bell buoy "6". Extreme care must be taken when approaching the entrance because of the rocks and shoals that extend about a mile offshore to the northwest.

A breakwater protects the western side of the harbor, at the seaward end of which is Crescent City Entrance Light, a fog signal and radiobeacon. A private light is shown from an islet south of Battery Point. The entrance to the harbor lies between the end of the breakwater and bell buoy "6" and it is marked by a lighted range and buoys.

A dredged channel leads into the small craft harbor. Contact may be made with the harbormaster for berth allocation on Ch. 9 and 16 from 5 a.m. to 9 p.m. on weekdays or by checking in at the office. Transient vessels under 30 ft. may tie up at H dock; longer vessels must use end-ties. Moorage is about $7 per day. Sometimes the harbormaster directs incoming vessels to moorage using a loudspeaker.

Anchorage may be taken in the outer harbor where there is good protection from northwesterly winds but one is exposed to the south. More protected anchorage is available in Fishboat Harbor (labelled as Fishing Vessel Harbor on the sketch), though a vessel is subject to the wash from the many fishing boats offloading at the dock or taking on fuel or ice. Be sure the anchor is well set as strong local southeast winds known as "kick back" or "back draft" may start in the afternoon and last until midnight. These winds usually occur during periods of strong northwesterlies.

Two Chevron fuel docks are in the harbor while a pump-out station is in Fishboat Harbor. Repair facilities can handle vessels up to 110 ft. Groceries and other supplies are about a mile away in the downtown area on the north side of the bay. The only place showers can be taken is at the fish company. They are unisex, so ladies should bring a "guard."

There is still some evidence of the seismic sea wave which virtually wiped out the harbor in 1964. The devastation caused can only be appreciated by viewing the photographs on display.

It has been said of this town that it has more bars and churches per capita than any other U.S. city -- depending on your persuasion you may want to check this out!

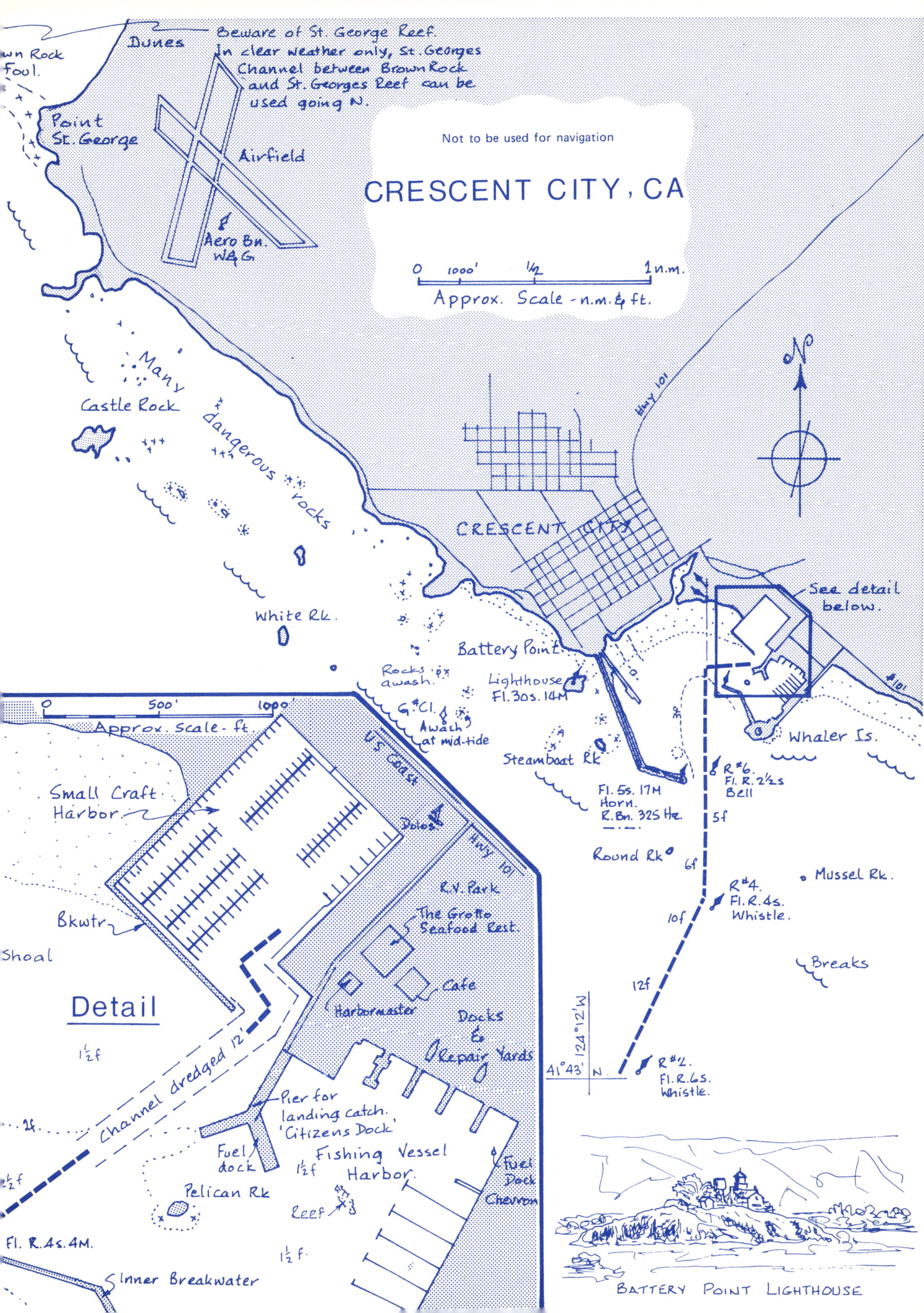

Beware of St. George Reef.
In clear weather only, St. Georges
Channel between Brown Rock
and St. Georges Reef can be
used going N.

Dunes

wn Rock
Foul.

Point
St. George

Airfield

Aero Bn.
W&G.

Not to be used for navigation

CRESCENT CITY, CA

0   1000'   ½   1 n.m.

Approx. Scale - n.m. & ft.

Many

Castle Rock

dangerous   rocks

Hwy 101

CRESCENT CITY

White Rk.

Rocks
awash.

Battery Point

G #Cl.
Awash
at mid-tide

Lighthouse
Fl.30s. 14M

See detail
below.

Whaler Is.

Steamboat Rk

Fl. 5s. 17M
Horn.
R.Bn. 325 Hz.

R #6.
Fl. R. 2½s
Bell

5f

Round Rk

6f

R #4.
Fl. R. 4s.
Whistle.

Mussel Rk.

10f

Breaks

0   500'   1000'

Approx. Scale - ft.

U.S. Coast

Small Craft
Harbor.

Pilot

Hwy 101

12f

124°12'W

Bkwtr

Shoal

R.V. Park

The Grotto
Seafood Rest.

Cafe

Docks
&
Repair Yards

41°43' N.

R #2.
Fl. R. 6s.
Whistle.

Detail

1½f

Harbormaster

Channel dredged 12'

2f

½f

Pier for
landing catch.
'Citizens Dock'

Fuel
dock

1½f

Fishing Vessel
Harbor.

Fuel
Dock
Chevron

Pelican Rk

Reef

1½ f

Fl. R. 4s. 4M.

Inner Breakwater

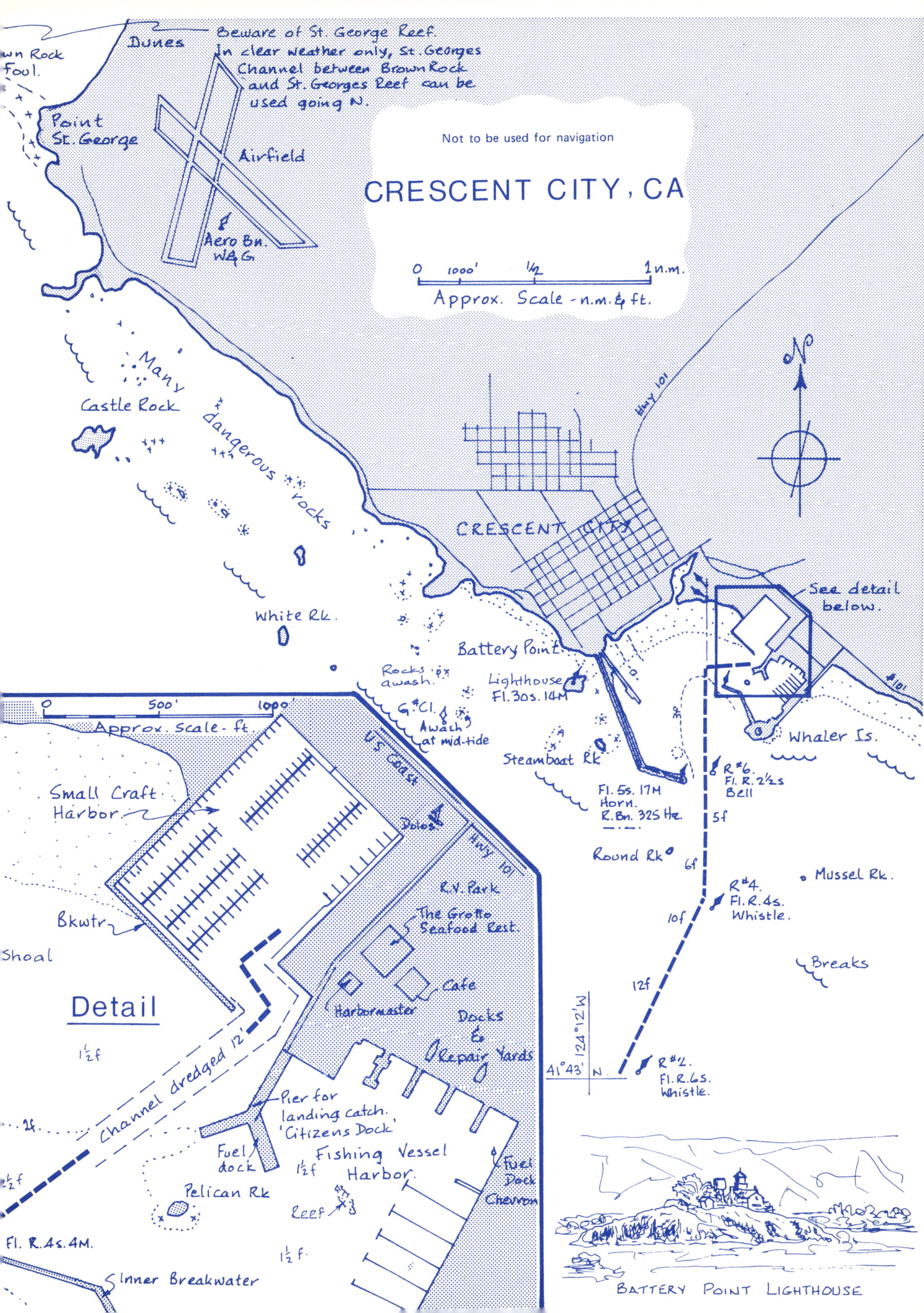
BATTERY POINT LIGHTHOUSE

TRINIDAD HEAD

TRINIDAD HEAD LIGHT.

This prominent coastal feature is almost 400 ft. high, though at a distance from either north or south it resembles a round-topped island. It is 45 miles south of Crescent City and almost 18 miles north of Humbolt Bay. Trinidad Head Light and a fog signal are on the southwestern side and another landmark is a prominent white cross northeast of the light.

When approaching from the north keep at least 2 miles offshore to clear rocks and reefs north of Trinidad Head. Offshore whistle buoy "26" lies about 1 mile west of Trinidad Head, followed by gong buoy "2" one mile to the southeast. When approaching from the south the coast is clear after passing Humbolt Bay (except for a wreck); the gong buoy is the first navigational aid to be picked up.

The anchorage is in a cove east of Trinidad Head. Since kelp and rocks extend off the northern shore the area for anchoring is somewhat limited. The best place to anchor is halfway between Prisoner Rock and Trinidad Head in 7 fathoms, mud. There is always some swell in the cove and holding is only fair; nevertheless, many fishing boats use this anchorage during the summer.

In a bight northeast of Trinidad Head is a small pier, which is used for offloading fish, and a marine railway used for launching boats. Gasoline and groceries are available in the "city" of Trinidad. Though the population is now only about 300 the city charter dating from 1852 is still in effect. At that time it had a population of 3,000. In its heyday, it was a busy lumbering port, then whaling station of which it was said, "You can smell it before you can see it."

A good walk can be taken on the trail which encircles Trinidad Head and leads to the granite cross. (The view is spectacular -- bring a camera.) A stroll into town can take one to the Holy Trinity Catholic Church built in 1873 which is now a U.S. Historical Landmark. Free tours and slide shows can be enjoyed at the Humboldt State University Marine Laboratory which is open Mon. to Fri. 8 a.m. to 5 p.m. or on weekends from 11 a.m. to 5 p.m.

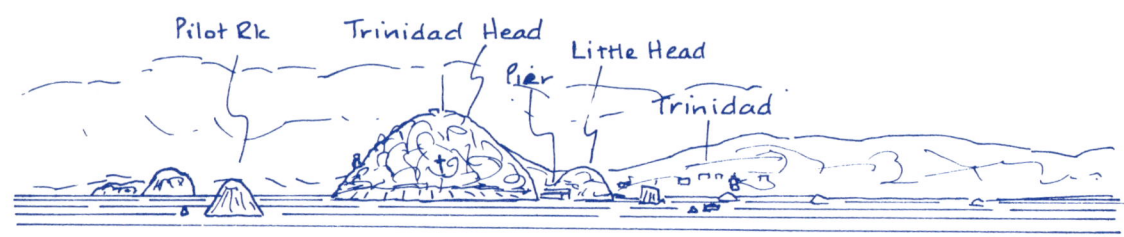

LOOKING N APPROACHING TRINIDAD HEAD.

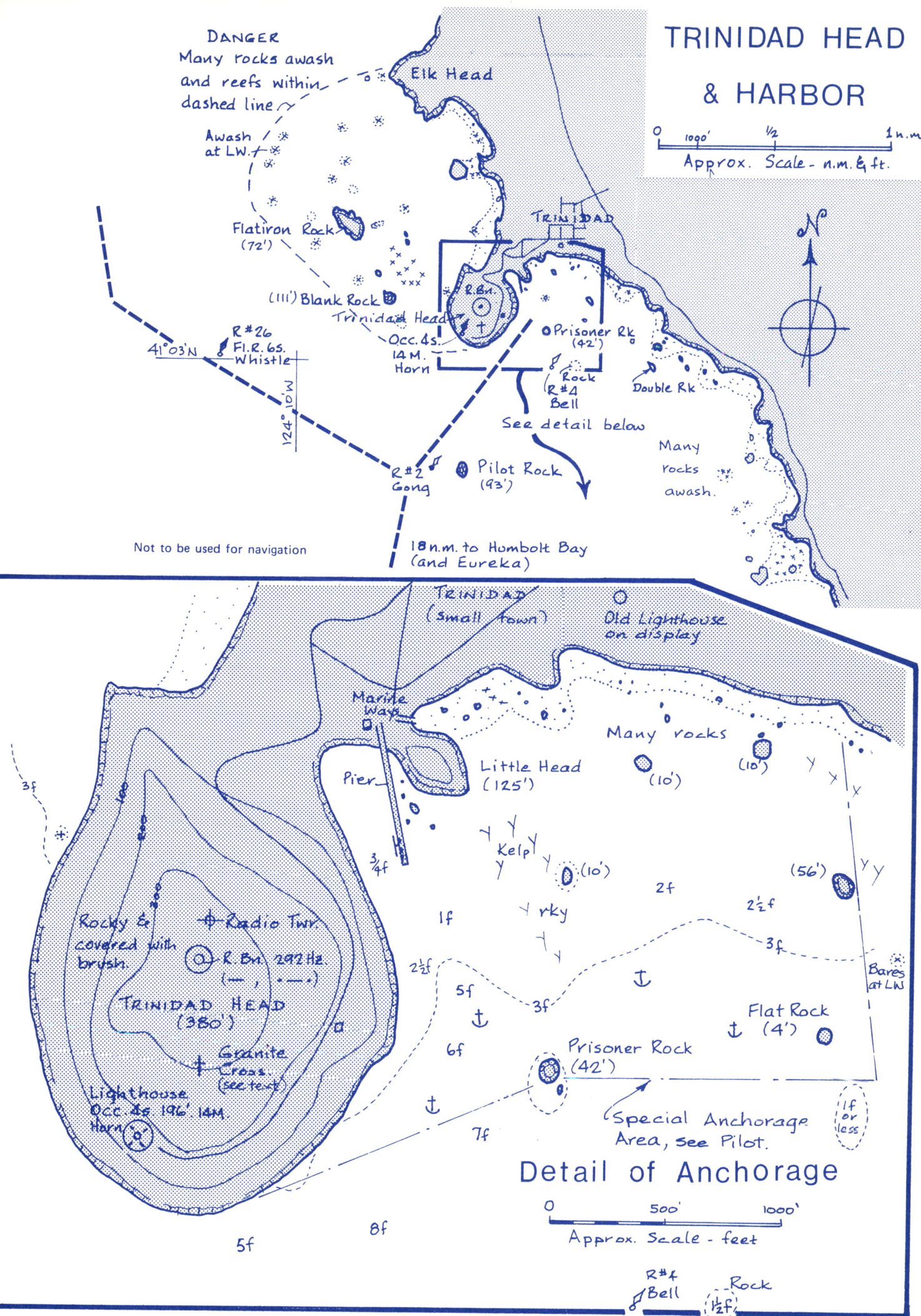

TRINIDAD HEAD & HARBOR

DANGER
Many rocks awash
and reefs within
dashed line

Elk Head

0 1000' ½ 1 n.m.
Approx. Scale - n.m. & ft.

Awash
at L.W.

TRINIDAD

Flatiron Rock
(72')

R. Bn.

N

(111') Blank Rock

Trinidad Head

Prisoner Rk
(42')

R #26
Fl.R. 6s.
Whistle

Occ. 4s.
14 M.
Horn

41°03'N

Rock
R #4
Bell

Double Rk

124°10'W

See detail below

Many
rocks
awash.

R #2
Gong

Pilot Rock
(93')

Not to be used for navigation

18 n.m. to Humbolt Bay
(and Eureka)

TRINIDAD
(small town)

Old Lighthouse
on display

Marine
Ways

Many rocks

Pier

Little Head
(125')

(10')

(10')

3f

Kelp

(10')

(56')

Rocky &
covered with
brush.

Radio Twr.

R. Bn. 292 Hz.
(—, •—•)

1f

rky

2f

2½f

3f

Bares
at LW

TRINIDAD HEAD
(380')

2½f

5f

3f

Flat Rock
(4')

Granite
Cross
(see text)

6f

Prisoner Rock
(42')

1f
or
less

Lighthouse
Occ. 4s 196' 14M
Horn

7f

Special Anchorage
Area, see Pilot.

Detail of Anchorage

0 500' 1000'
Approx. Scale - feet

5f

8f

R #4
Bell   Rock
(½f')

HUMBOLDT BAY (EUREKA)

This historic city is 17 miles south of Trinidad Head and 21 miles north of Cape Mendocino. It is a good place to recover from passing Cape Mendocino or to await the end of a storm prior to making the passage around this important turning point. Eureka is a Customs **Port of Entry.**

When there is good visibility Trinidad Head and Cape Mendocino are excellent landmarks to identify the general location of Humboldt Bay. The stacks and smoke from sawmills within the bay pinpoint the city of Eureka. There is an irregular southerly current in this area, so when coming from the north, sailing vessels should approach from off Trinidad Head to get a good slant to the Humboldt Bay entrance.

Offshore lighted whistle buoy "HB" is a little over a mile WNW of the entrance to the bay, followed by bell buoy "2" which is west of the southern jetty. Two jetties, each with lights at their seaward ends, form the channel entrance. Take care not to confuse the radio towers south of the entrance with a lighted range marking the entrance approach from the offshore buoy. Once over the bar another range indicates the entrance to the bay which is also marked by buoys. The turn is rather sharp when changing from the Approach Range to the Entrance Range -- don't carry either one past the beginning of the other when entering or leaving.

This can be a very dangerous bar - extreme caution is urged. Shoaling and strong currents in the channel can make it difficult to negotiate the entrance at times. It is advisable to call the Coast Guard for a current bar report.

Three towns are in the northern part of the bay: Bucksport 3 miles above the entrance, followed by Fairhaven and Eureka. Moorage is available at the **City Boat Basin** where people are very friendly. Check the depths -- dredging is done every five years or so. Moorage at 35 cents per foot is available at the classy Woodley Island Marina (showers and laundromats are extra). Transient berths are on D float (the westernmost, where a pump-out station is located). All services, repairs, and marine supplies are available in the marina and the city is a short dinghy ride across the channel.

Eureka owes its charm and fascination to the many Victorian homes which are a legacy of the lumber baron era. If a walking tour of Old Town is not for you then at least have a look at Carson Mansion, the most photographed of all. Celebrating the past are Clarke Museum (historical), Fort Humboldt State Historic Park (logging), and the Maritime Museum. The story of Indian Island (the site of a massacre of Indians at the hands of a band of white men) is well told in Barte Harte's book, The Northern Californian.

The many birds feeding in the mud at low tide give evidence as to why Humboldt Bay is a National Wildlife Refuge. The snowy egret nests in such numbers in the cypress trees on Indian Island that they resemble a blanket of snow.

A large fishing fleet is based in the bay. When southbound, the boats usually aim for the Cape Mendocino Buoy (5 miles offshore) and if it is windy, head for Punta Gorda Buoy (1 mile offshore) in order to avoid heavy winds and seas. But if there is no wind at Cape Mendocino Buoy they just proceed to their destination.

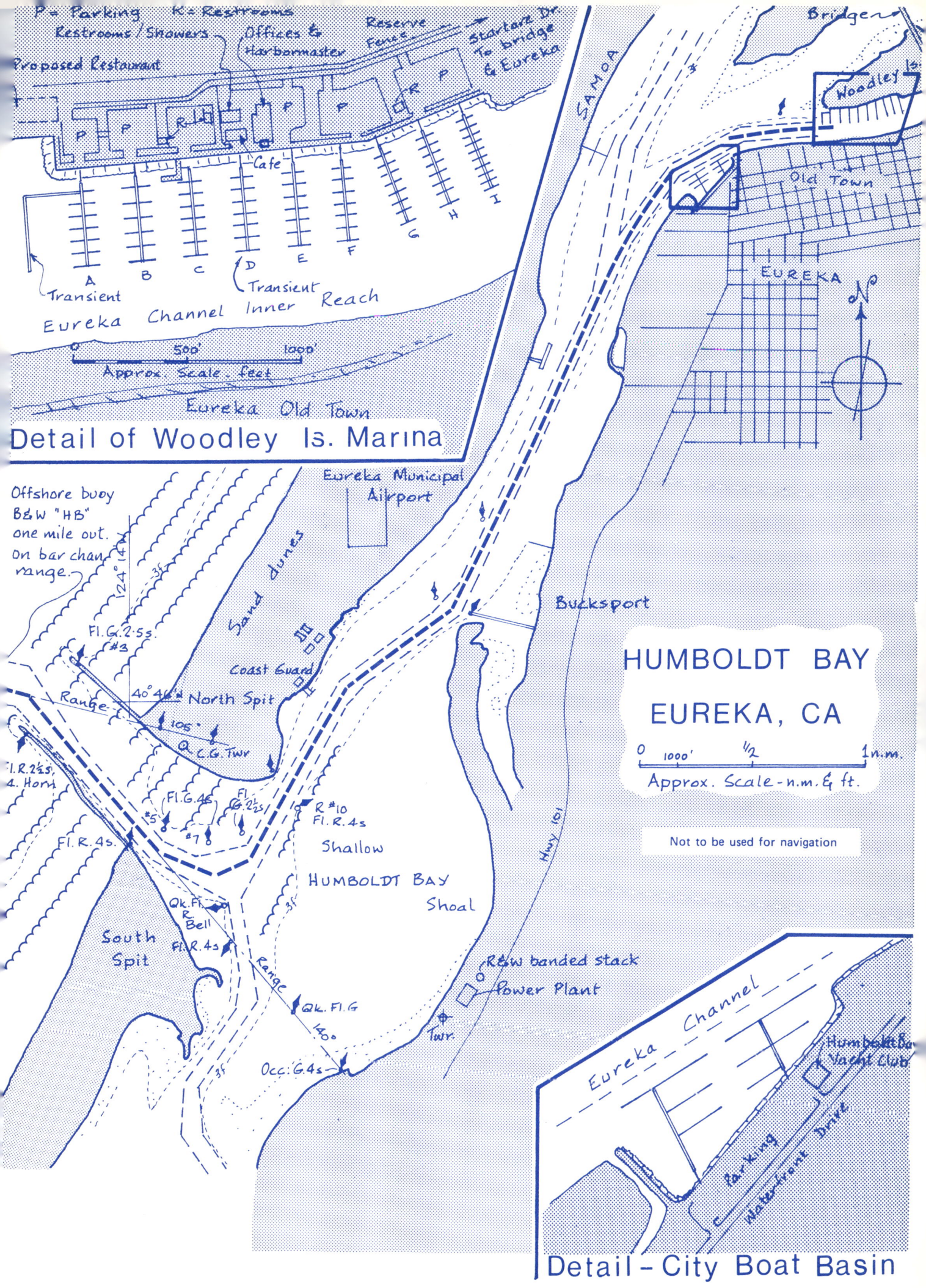

P = Parking **R** = Restrooms
Restrooms/Showers
Offices &
Harbormaster
Proposed Restaurant
Reserve Fence
Startare Dr. to bridge & Eureka
Bridge
SAMOA
Woodley Is.
Old Town
EUREKA
P
P
R
P
P
R
P
R
P
Cafe
N
A   B   C   D   E   F   G   H   I
Transient
Transient Inner Reach
Eureka Channel
Eureka Old Town

0   500   1000'
Approx. Scale - feet

Detail of Woodley Is. Marina

Offshore buoy
B&W "HB"
one mile out.
On bar chan.
range.

Eureka Municipal Airport

124° 14'

3f

Fl.G.2.5s.
#3

Sand dunes

40° 46' North Spit
Range
105°
Q. C.G. Twr

l.R.2.5s.
4. Horn

Fl.G.4s
*5

Fl.
G.2.5s
#7

R #10
Fl.R.4s

Coast Guard

Fl.R.4s.

Shallow

HUMBOLDT BAY
Shoal

Bucksport

HUMBOLDT BAY
EUREKA, CA

0   1000'   ½   1 n.m.
Approx. Scale - n.m. & ft.

Not to be used for navigation

Qk.Fl.
R. Bell

Fl.R.4s.

South
Spit

Range
1400

Qk.Fl.G

Occ:G.4s

Twr.

R&w banded stack
Power Plant

Hwy 101

Eureka Channel

Humboldt Bay Yacht Club

Parking
Waterfront Drive

Detail - City Boat Basin

SHELTER COVE

This popular anchorage tucked behind Point Delgada is about 60 miles south of Eureka and 37 miles north of Noyo River. Many small fishing vessels are launched off the beach to enjoy the excellent salmon, ling and rock cod, and red and black snapper found in local waters.

Point Delgada is a high plateau bordered by cliffs. It is easily recognized by its proximity to King Peak (over 4,000 ft.) which is almost 9 miles to the north. In clear weather it is visible to seaward for 75 miles. The King Range forms a mountainous backdrop for the miles of tidal beach bordering the anchorage.

Offshore whistle buoy "20" is about a mile southwest of Point Delgada. One mile in an ENE'ly direction is bell buoy "1" which marks the southern end of the rocks and kelp extending off the point. Keep to the south of both buoys in order to avoid shoals and rocks in this area. Anchorage may be taken in northwesterly weather although there is generally some surge in the cove.

This area is referred to as "California's Lost Coast" because of the 26-mile steep and narrow road separating it from Highway 101. In spite of its comparative isolation the community of Shelter cove has groceries, restaurants, a gift shop, and even a real estate office. Propane, gasoline, and diesel are available but it's a long trip back to the boat. A 2 1/2-mile hike up the hill takes one to the larger of the two grocery stores.

Of local interest is the archeological dig on Point Delgada plateau where Indian habitation is traced back several hundred years. A trail takes one to King Peak which is the highest point on the continental U.S. shoreline -- a great view. Seals and sea lions can be seen on the rocks below the Point as well as migrating Grey Whales just offshore during their semi-annual transit of the coast.

When northbound, picking up Punta Gorda buoy (1 mile offshore) before proceeding to Cape Mendocino Buoy (5 miles offshore) may enable a vessel to avoid the heavier winds and seas generally found off these points.

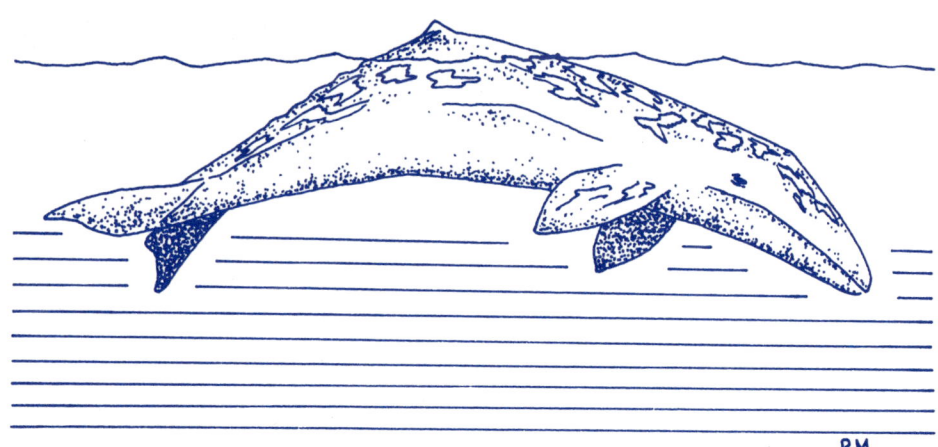

RM

Many boats find anchorage in Shelter Cove on California's "Lost Coast."

Dredging in a narrow channel can make passage very tight as at Noyo River.

California offers everything from the peace of a quiet anchorage such as San Simeon Bay to

the congestion of a city marina such as the Long Beach Municipal Downtown Marina.

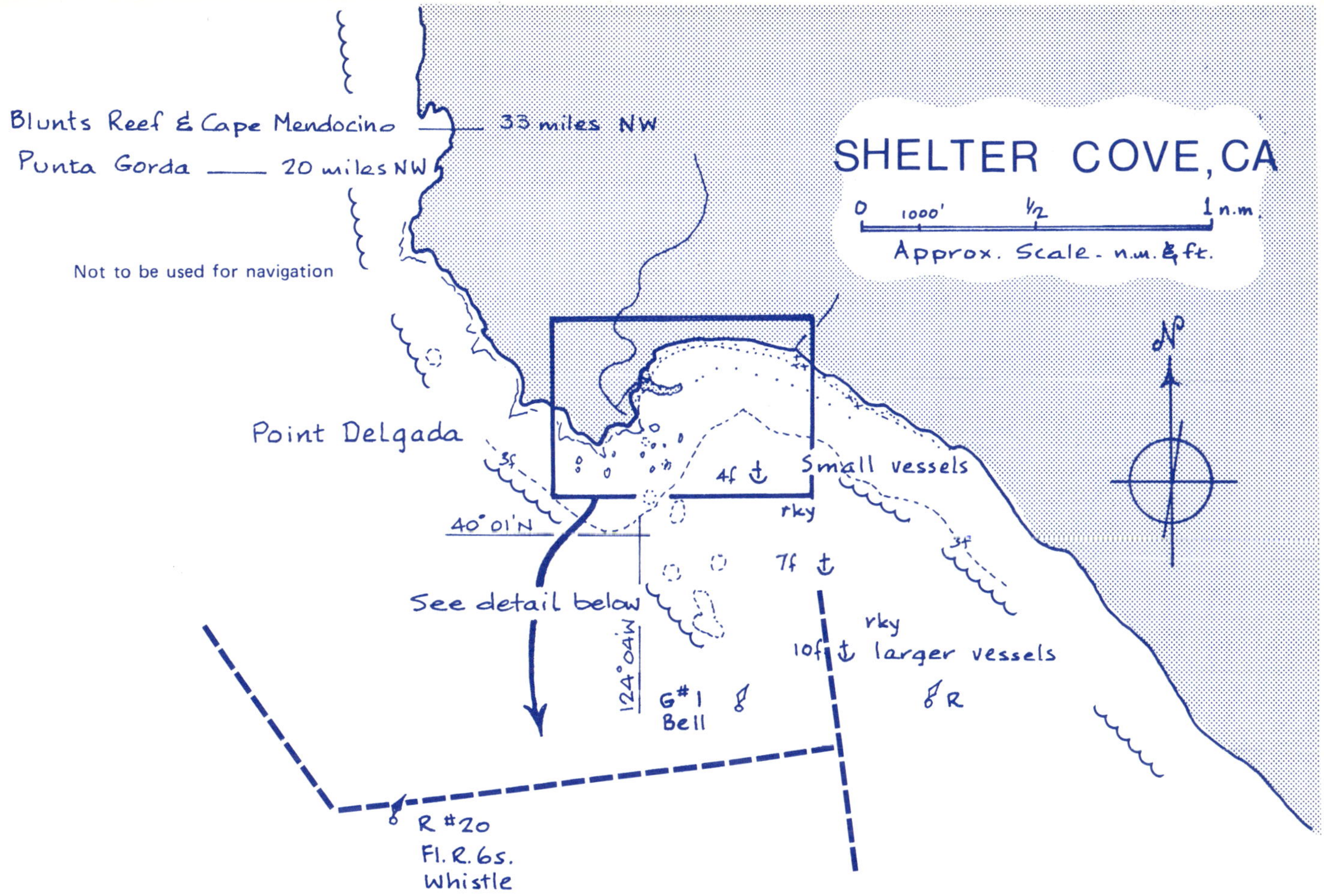

Blunts Reef & Cape Mendocino ——— 33 miles NW
Punta Gorda ——— 20 miles NW

Not to be used for navigation

SHELTER COVE, CA

0   1000'   ½   1 n.m.
Approx. Scale - n.m. & ft.

N

Point Delgada

40° 01'N

Small vessels

4f ⚓

rky

See detail below

124° 04'W

7f ⚓

rky
10f ⚓ larger vessels

⚓ R

G #1 ⚓
Bell

R #20
Fl. R. 6s.
Whistle

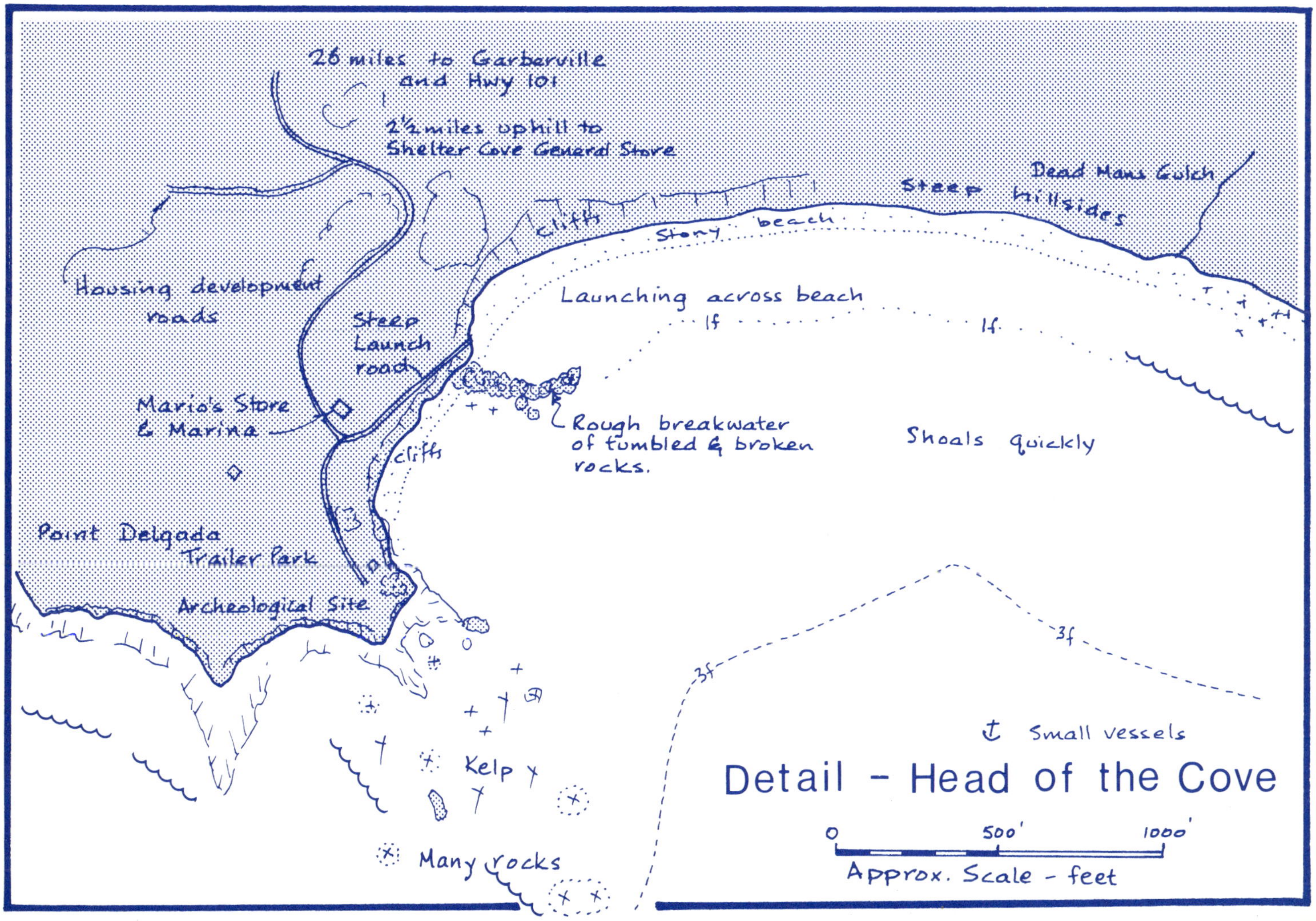

26 miles to Garberville
and Hwy 101

2½ miles uphill to
Shelter Cove General Store

Dead Mans Gulch

Steep hillsides

cliffs

Stony beach

Housing development
roads

Launching across beach

1f 1f

Steep
Launch
road

Mario's Store
& Marina

Rough breakwater
of tumbled & broken
rocks.

Shoals quickly

cliffs

Point Delgada
Trailer Park

Archeological Site

3f

3f

⚓ Small vessels

Kelp

Detail - Head of the Cove

Many rocks

0   500'   1000'
Approx. Scale - feet

NOYO ANCHORAGE (FORT BRAGG)

Pass by this stop-over if there is strong westerly weather or poor visibility, unless you have local knowledge. Noyo Anchorage is 37 miles south of Eureka and about 80 miles north of Bodega Bay. Noyo Anchorage refers to the bight into which the Noyo River flows; it should not be confused with the Noyo Boat Basin and the small craft anchorage in the Noyo River just off the entrance to the basin. The fishing community of Fort Bragg borders the shores of the Noyo River.

The offshore whistle buoy "NA" is a mile out from the entrance followed by bell buoy "2." The North Jetty has a light on its outer end and a fog signal closer inshore. A radiobeacon is a short distance NNE of the North Jetty light; the South Jetty has a daybeacon on its seaward end. The highway bridge spanning the river has a clearance of 80 ft. A dredged channel (8 ft.) leads to Noyo Basin which is protected from surge coming up the river by a breakwater.

When approaching the channel take care to clear the many rocks in the southern half of Noyo Anchorage. This is a very narrow channel in which fog and shoaling are common problems. Call the Coast Guard for a report on conditions at the entrance if you have concerns. Their station is on the south side near the entrance to the boat basin.

Report to the harbormaster for berth allocation -- the rate is a flat $7.50 per day. All facilities are available here - fuel, water, marine supplies, and a launching ramp. Boats up to 45' can be taken up for repairs. Two of the grocery stores will provide a ride back to the mooring basin -- Harvest Market (Ph. 964 - 7000) just west of the mooring basin in the Boatyard Shopping Center, and Brown's Market (Ph. 964 - 3647) on Main Street on the north side of the river. Otherwise, one may phone in an order which they will deliver since it is a long walk to the stores.

A laundromat is in the Boatyard Shopping Center and Polly Cleaners Coin Laundry will pick up and deliver if you call them at 964 - 3293. For showers ($1.50 for 10 minutes) one must go to Colombi's Laundromat which is about a 10-block walk on the north side to Oak Street. Propane is available at Force's Chevron Station at the north end of the Noyo Bridge. The people in Fort Bragg are very friendly and are always willing to help a visiting cruiser. What a pleasant change from communities that are oriented towards the tourist dollar!

Tiger rock fish

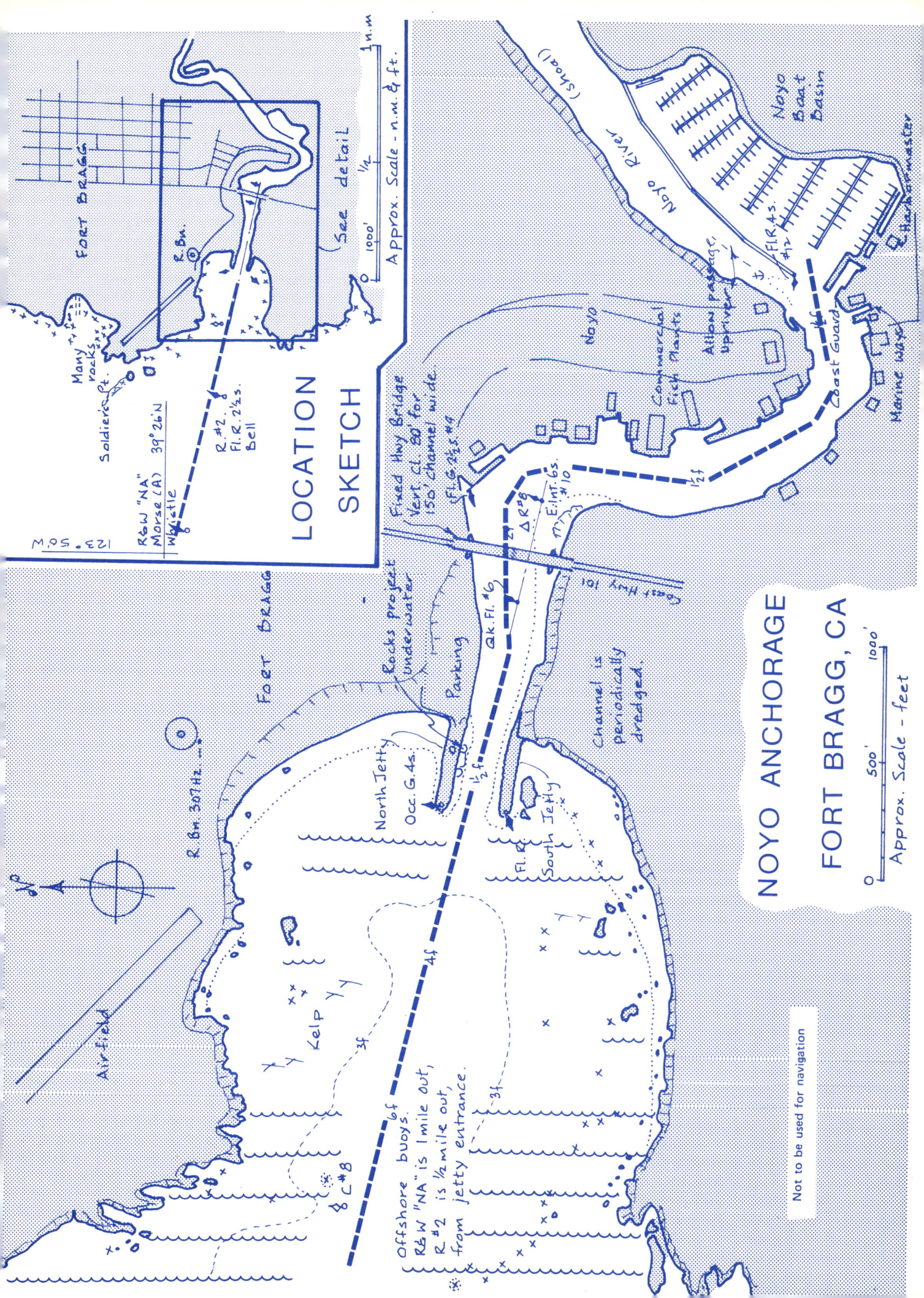

NOYO ANCHORAGE
FORT BRAGG, CA

LOCATION SKETCH

FORT BRAGG

123°50'W

R&W "NA" Morse (A) 39°26'N
Whistle

R.#2. Fl.R.2½s. Bell

Many rocks
Soldier's Pt.

(See detail)

0   1000'   ¼   ½   1 n.m
Approx. Scale - n.m. & ft.

R.Bn. 307 Hz.

Airfield

Kelp

3f

4f

6f

G C #8

Offshore buoys.
R&W "NA" is 1 mile out,
R. #2 is ½ mile out,
from jetty entrance.

North Jetty
Occ. G. 4s.

Parking

Rocks project underwater.

Fixed Hwy Bridge Vert. Cl. 80' for 150' channel wide.

Fl.G.4s #4

R #8
Qk.Fl. #6

E.Int. 6s. #10

Coast Hwy 101

South Jetty
Fl. R.

1½f

Channel is periodically dredged.

Noyo

Commercial Fish Plants

Allow passage Upriver

Coast Guard

Marine Ways

Fl.R. 4s. #12

Noyo Boat Basin

Harbormaster

Noyo River (Shoal)

0   500'   1000'
Approx. Scale - feet

Not to be used for navigation

BODEGA HARBOR

This is a major fishing and pleasure boating center where many Bay area sailors keep their boats. Located 80 miles south of Noyo River and 25 miles north of Drakes Bay, it features complete facilities to suit every taste.

In clear weather the 200 ft. cliffs which run for 2 miles north of Bodega Head help to identify this grass-covered landmark. Offshore whistle buoy "12" lies a little over a mile southwest of Bodega Head; 3 1/2 miles slightly north of east is gong buoy "BA".

When approaching the harbor a route should be taken as indicated on the sketch. Do not pass between Bodega Rock and Bodega Head unless calm conditions prevail. The entrance channel is protected by two jetties -- a light and fog horn are at the outer end of the southern jetty. Two lighted ranges lead a vessel through the entrance and beyond. The channel is clearly marked by a buoy, daybeacons, and lights to the turning basin at the north end of the harbor. When a strong wind is blowing the considerable fetch can kick up a fair chop in the channel. Do not be tempted to tack back and forth around the daybeacons, for outside the channel it IS shallow.

Bodega Bay marks the northern limit of the Gulf of the Farallones National Marine Sanctuary which includes the Farallones and offshore waters almost as far south as Muir Beach. Because of a fortuitous mix of salt and fresh water, ocean currents, shifting waters, and circulating nutrients, these waters are home to an abundant variety of marine life. Though fishing is allowed (provided of course, that one has a California Fishing Licence), as well as normal recreation, the restrictions are mainly related to oil and gas exploration, deep-sea ship discharge, and oil tanker traffic.

RM

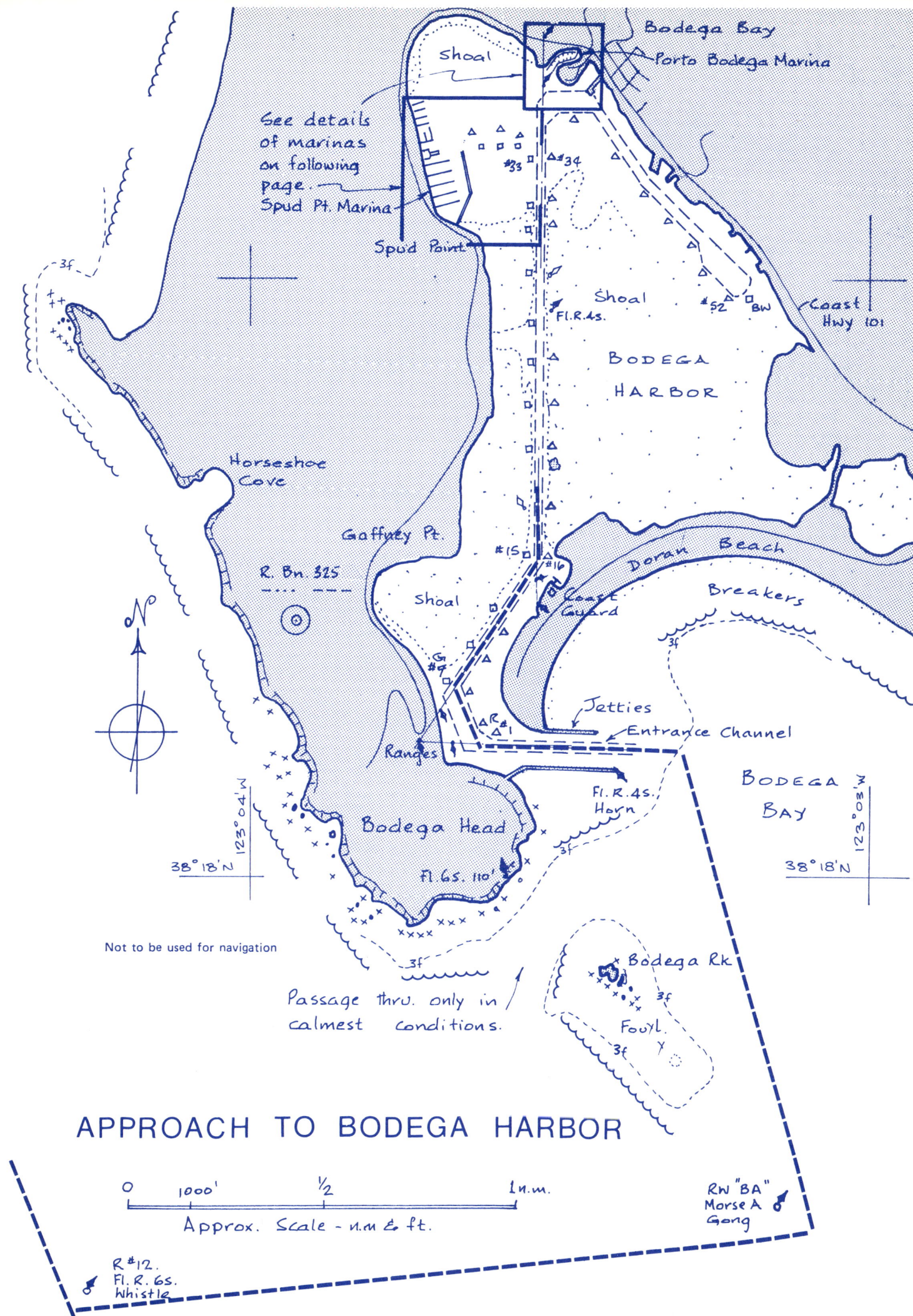

Bodega Bay
Porto Bodega Marina

Shoal

See details
of marinas
on following
page.
Spud Pt. Marina

Spud Point

#33   #34

Shoal
Fl.R.4s.

#52   BW

Coast
Hwy 101

BODEGA
HARBOR

Horseshoe
Cove

Gaffney Pt.

R. Bn. 325
- - - · · ·

N

Shoal

#15
#16

Doran   Beach

Breakers

Coast
Guard

3f

G
#7

Jetties
Entrance Channel

BODEGA
BAY

R #1

Ranges

38°18'N   123°04'W

Not to be used for navigation

Fl. R.4s.
Horn

3f

38°18'N   123°03'W

Bodega Head

Fl. 6s. 110'

3f

Passage thru. only in
calmest   conditions.

Bodega Rk

3f

Fowl.

3f

APPROACH TO BODEGA HARBOR

0   1000'   ½   1 n.m.

Approx. Scale - n.m & ft.

Rw "BA"
Morse A
Gong

R #12.
Fl. R. 6s.
Whistle

MARINAS IN BODEGA HARBOR

Spud Point Marina is the first facility seen as one proceeds north through the channel. To reach it, turn to port immediately after passing Buoy "33" and follow the marked side channel as shown on the sketch. This 244-berth marina can accommodate vessels up to 80 ft.; dredged to 12 ft., it is well protected by a breakwater.

Constructed in 1985, this multi-million-dollar facility has been designed to fill the needs and wants of the yachting set. It is operated by the Sonoma County Regional Parks Department. Fuel, water, restrooms, showers, a laundromat, public telephones, and even vending machines are available. Additional services are constantly being added such as a flake ice machine, waste oil disposal, bilge pumps, 70-ton Travelift, and welder receptacles. This is an official NOAA weather display station and the Marina Office has a Weatherfax machine where printouts of current weather conditions can be obtained. The marina office kindly posts messages for yachts in transit; from the number of messages seen, this is a popular spot for a rendezvous.

One may contact the harbormaster on Ch. 16 or by phone (707) 875 – 3535 for information on berthing or one may put into any berth showing a "T," prior to reporting to his office. A $25 fee is charged for failure to register, so don't "forget." Transient rates are calculated at 15 cents per foot per day plus $1 for electricity regardless of usage. A refundable deposit of $20 is charged for each key issued for washrooms.

Mason's Marina is just to the north of Spud Point Marina. It is used primarily by commercial craft and fishboats.

Porto Bodega Marina used to be the only place where exhausted cruisers could tie up for a rest or a chance to enjoy terra firma again after grappling with Cape Mendocino. Now it is known as the fisherman's marina. This is a snug little basin which gets congested with many vessels in the small berths while trailers, boat trailers, and campers crowd into the limited parking spaces. One may contact the harbormaster on Ch. 16 and 71 or by phoning (707) 875-2354 in order to arrange moorage; rates are about $8 per day. Marine supplies, tackle, groceries and almost any basic item can be obtained in the truly "general" general store.

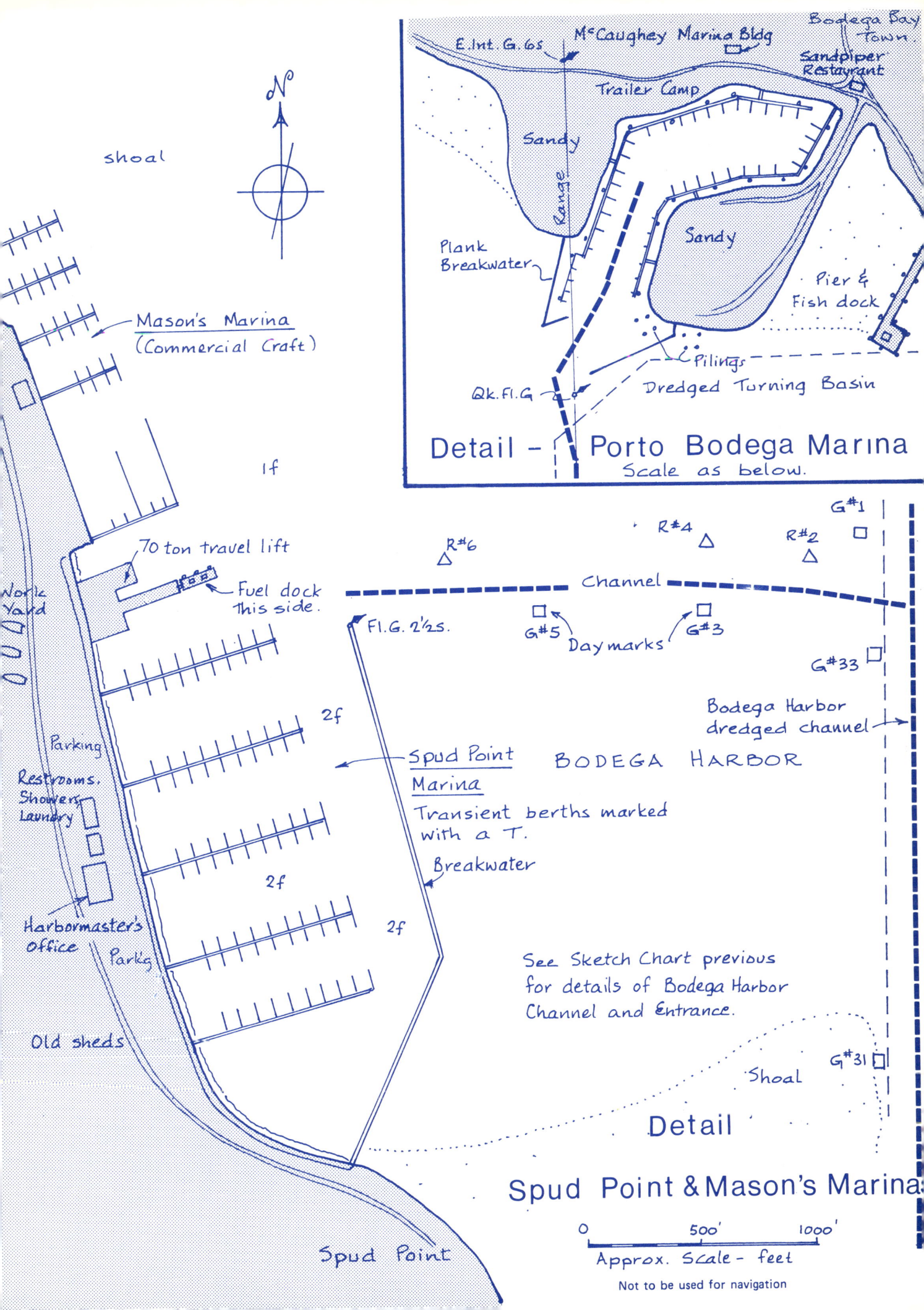

shoal

N

Mason's Marina
(Commercial Craft)

1f

70 ton travel lift

Fuel dock
This side.

Work
Yard

2f

Parking

Restrooms,
Showers,
Laundry

Harbormaster's
Office

Park'g

2f

2f

Old sheds

Spud Point

Detail — Porto Bodega Marina
Scale as below.

E. Int. G. 6s   McCaughey Marina Bldg   Bodega Bay Town

Sandpiper Restaurant

Trailer Camp

Sandy

Range

Sandy

Plank Breakwater

Pier & Fish dock

Qk. Fl. G

Pilings

Dredged Turning Basin

G #1

R #4

R #6   R #2

Channel

G #5   G #3

Fl.G. 2½s.   Daymarks

G #33

Bodega Harbor
dredged channel

Spud Point
Marina

BODEGA HARBOR

Transient berths marked
with a T.

Breakwater

See Sketch Chart previous
for details of Bodega Harbor
Channel and Entrance.

Shoal

G #31

Detail

Spud Point & Mason's Marina

0   500'   1000'

Approx. Scale - feet

Not to be used for navigation

DRAKES BAY

Drakes Bay was first visited by Sir Francis Drake in 1579. Its broad entrance and good protection from northwesterly winds made it an ideal anchorage for a heavy vessel under sail power alone. Nowadays it is a home port of numerous fishing vessels which operate from the bay during the season.

Drakes Bay is 25 miles south of Bodega Bay and 25 miles northwest of the Golden Gate Bridge. This rocky headland marks the northern edge of the Gulf of the Farallons; when seen at a distance in hazy weather it resembles an island. The Point Reyes Light is at the end of the point along with a fog signal and radiobeacon. After proceeding 3 miles east of the lighthouse and rounding lighted whistle buoy "1", one can enter the bay and take good anchorage in 4 – 6 fathoms, sand.

The Farallon Islands (23 miles west of Golden Gate) are a 7-mile chain extending in a northwesterly direction from the largest island, Southeast Farrallon. A lighthouse and radiobeacon are located here, while a whistle buoy "NR" is 1/2 mile west of Noonday Rock (the northern limit of the Farrallons).

APPROACHING SAN FRANCISCO

San Francisco is a normal port of call for vessels transiting this coast. Its large harbor and geographical location have made it a transportation center for seaborne traffic since 1775 when the Spaniards established their first settlement at Fort Point. Sailing one's own boat under the Golden Gate Bridge for the first time is a memorable experience for everyone aboard a cruising vessel. But to have this time of exhilaration there is a price to pay--and that price is thorough preparation for the entry and good seamanship. Preparation involves a careful study of the weather, tide and current tables, selection of one's entrance route, and knowledge of the hazards involved.

To reach the Golden Gate Bridge one must first cross the San Francisco Bar. It covers a large arc extending from 3 miles south of Point Lobos to within 1/2 mile of Point Bonita. The outer edge is about 5 miles WSW of the Bridge. The northern part of the bar is called Fourfathom Bank, part of which is the infamous Potato Patch Shoal (23'). The safest route over the bar is the Main Ship Channel, but should normally be avoided because of congested deep-sea commercial traffic. During a heavy swell or ebb tide it also can be dangerous. If weather or tide make conditions hazardous it is better to wait until seas moderate and the tide is right so that a safe passage can be made.

Because of the large volume of commercial traffic the Coast Guard has established a Vessel Traffic Service (VTS) to minimize collisons and aid in the smooth flow of traffic. Pleasure craft are not restricted to the traffic lanes but if using them a vessel must follow the established pattern and stay well to the right-hand side of the lane. If you must cross a lane do so at right angles and as quickly as possible. Right of way should always be given to any large vessel operating in the channel. Information on major shipping traffic can be obtained by monitoring Ch. 16 VHF-FM or by contacting VTS on this channel.

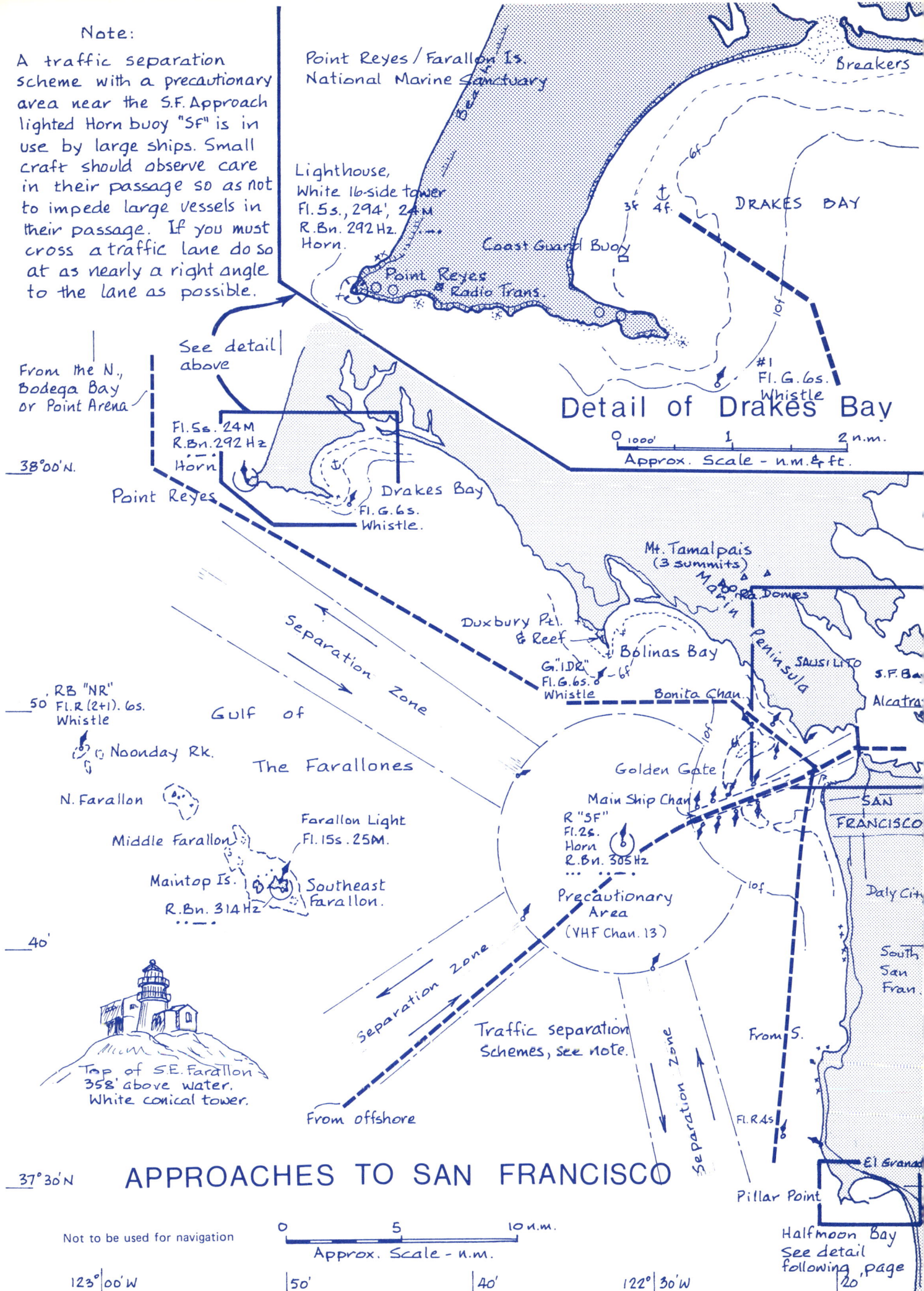

Hazards which may be encountered while entering or leaving the Bay may include one or all of the following: strong currents, high winds, choppy seas, fog, and congested traffic.

Currents are a major consideration since about 1/6 of the Bay's entire water volume flows in and out twice a day through Golden Gate. Refer to Tidal Current Charts, San Francisco Bay for direction and velocity of daily currents.

The well known Bay **winds** always live up to their gear- and crew-testing reputation. In summer the normal northwesterlies may blow up to 10 knots in the morning, increasing to 20 - 25 in the afternoon, creating choppy waters. Winter winds are unpredictable, ranging from calms to 75-knots during storms. On average, spring is the windiest season, generally in the 20 - 30 knot range.

Fog is common from July to September. Fog signals in the Gulf of the Farrallons operate 40 - 50% of the time during August. Offshore fog usually rolls over Golden Gate by noon and can be seen boiling over the western hills. Having radar is a distinct advantage, though ghost echoes occurring in the vicinity of the Bridge sometimes make identification of radar targets difficult.

APPROACHES TO SAN FRANCISCO

When approaching from the north, cruising vessels may enter the Bay by rounding Point Reyes and proceeding to whistle buoy "DR" which marks the end of Duxbury Reef before entering via Bonita Channel. A lighted range and buoys mark this channel. Alertness at the helm is essential as there is a dangerous rip off Point Bonita, while on the ebb there is a set towards Potato Patch Shoal which must be countered. Enter only on a flood tide, and if seas are very rough it may be advisable to enter via the main ship channel or await calmer conditions.

When approaching from offshore, a vessel should identify San Francisco Approach Lighted Horn Buoy "SF" which is 14 miles southwest of the Bridge and about 8 miles south of Duxbury Reef whistle buoy "DR". A circular precautionary area having a radius of 6 miles around the "SF" buoy should be avoided by small craft. This area may have large ocean-going vessels converging as a result of routing maneuvers, changing from the Main Ship Channel to offshore lanes and/or taking on or dropping off Pilots. Keep clear of traffic while proceeding to the Main Ship Channel which is indicated by four pairs of lighted buoys. Keep well to the right side of the channel to leave a maximum amount of space for large commercial vessels, which are slow to respond to the helm and need a considerable space to decelerate.

Vessels approaching from the south may follow the coast after clearing gong buoy "1" which marks the end of the dangerous reefs and shoals southwest of Pillar Point. By using unbuoyed South Channel until Seal Rocks have been safely cleared, one may then approach the Golden Gate.

On a rare day one can see the Golden Gate Bridge and San Francisco from Drakes Bay.

Approaching the Golden Gate is always exciting for coastal cruisers.

Seen from the St. Francis Yacht Club, the fog is just beginning to enter San Francisco Bay.

Looking across from San Francisco's Aquatic Park, one sees Alcatraz with Angel Island beyond.

Sausilito is an area often preferred by coastal cruisers because of its clean air, lack of congestion, and quiet pace. Originally an artists' colony, its spectacular homes clinging to steep cliffs are a sharp contrast to the cheek-by-jowl houses of San Francisco. Located 2 miles north of the Bridge it is reached by way of a channel marked by lights and buoys.

This is a pleasure boat haven where every possible boating need can be met. Anchorage can be taken in the southern part of Richardson Bay but watch your depth sounder when looking for a place to drop the hook as it is very shallow outside of the anchoring area.

The largest marina development is **Clipper Yacht Harbor** which has accommodation for 700 berths. The newest development is **Kappas Marina,** located a short distance past the Clipper complex. On the opposite side of the channel from the platform is **Schoonmaker Point Marina.** Transient berths are usually available; rates vary with the length of the vessel, a 34-ft. boat costing about $12 per day in 1988.

This is the northern home port of the cadet training tallship, "Californian," which is sponsored by the Nautical Heritage Society. Other home ports where she can be seen at various times are Ventura and Chula Vista.

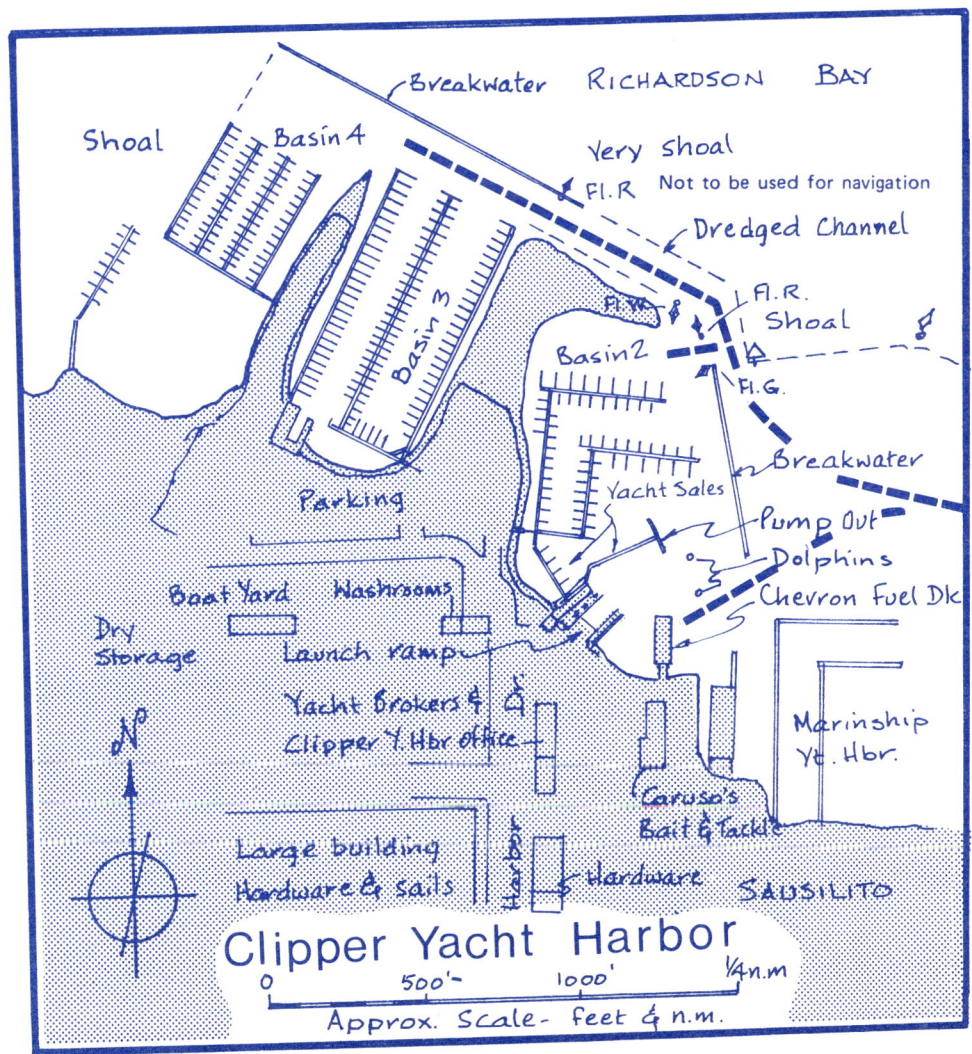

Clipper Yacht Harbor

It is important to remember that the VTS traffic patterns continue into the Bay. Extreme caution is essential in the precautionary zone where large vessels converge to cross and join diverging traffic lanes. Great care must be taken to watch for other vessels of every size and shape and to follow the rules of the road.

San Francisco Bay is a large body of water covering some 400 square miles. Cities which border this extensive bay include San Francisco, Oakland, Emeryville, Richmond, Berkeley, San Leandro, Sausilito, Redwood City, and South San Francisco. San Francisco/Oakland is a **Port of Entry.** To report in, call Customs at 556-2844 during the day or 876-2812 at night; vessels making a landfall from a foreign country must also call Immigration at 876-2876 days, or 495-6667 after hours.

Flowing into the Bay are the San Joaquin and Sacramento Rivers which are navigable all the way up to Stockton and Sacramento respectively. The tributaries, canals, and deltas of these two rivers compose what is known as the Delta Region. There are many miles of navigable waters which provide protected cruising; if one is planning to visit these waters reference should be made to one of several guides devoted solely to the Delta and Bay areas. As this guide is intended for sailors transiting the coast, attention is limited to marina facilities closest to the Golden Gate Bridge, though municipal marinas are also found at **Oyster Point** and **Coyote Point.**

Marina Yacht Harbor is almost 2 miles east of the Bridge. A breakwater with a light at the eastern end gives protection to the docks of the Saint Francis Yacht Club and the San Francisco Municipal Yacht Harbor. Another part of the Municipal Yacht Harbor is just to the east. A few transient berths are available; check with the harbormaster for berth allocation. Rates are reasonable -- $8 for a 40-ft. vessel. Transportation by bus or taxi is required to reach the nearest laundromat or grocery store while the only supply of propane is in Sausalito.

Aquatic Park is located about 1/2 mile east of Marina Yacht Harbor. A pier curves out from the western side, giving protection from the winds sweeping in from Golden Gate. Good anchorage for a few days may be taken in 1 1/2 - 2 fathoms, mud. Fuel, water, and marine supplies are available at Fisherman's Wharf just to the east.

Pier 39 has moorage for pleasure craft but reservations are required for transient vessels wishing to tie up.

One could spend many days visiting the varied attractions in the Bay and surrounding areas. The downtown points of interest include Fisherman's Wharf, Chinatown, the Palace of Fine Arts, the Cannery, Alcatraz, Coit Tower, Ghiradelli Square, the shops and restaurants of Pier 39, Cable Cars, and even the unique architecture of the houses of San Francisco. By travelling further afield interesting day trips can be taken to the wine country in Napa Valley, Sausilito, and Muir Woods Park, and to the state capital at Sacramento where many museums and historic buildings are found.

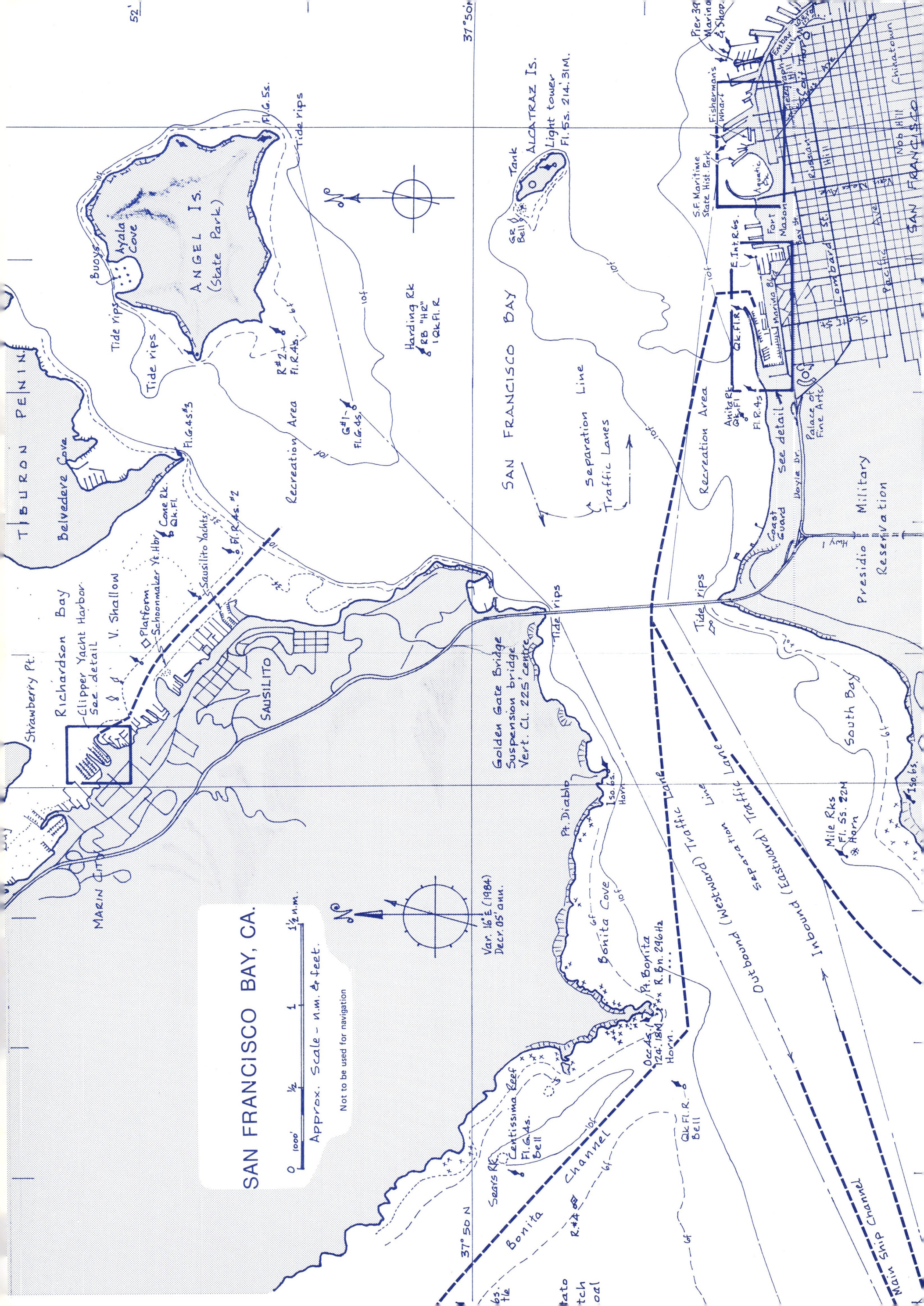

52'

37°50'

Tide rips
Fl.G.5s.

ANGEL IS.
(State Park)

Ayala Cove

Buoys

Tide rips

Tide rips

Tide rips

10f

6f

R#2
Fl.R.4s.

Recreation Area

G#1
Fl.G.4s.

10f

Harding Rk
RB "H2"
1Qk.Fl.R.

Tank

Gr
Bell

ALCATRAZ IS.
Light tower
Fl.5s. 214.'31M.

SAN FRANCISCO BAY

Pier 39
Marina
& Shop.

Fisherman's
Wharf

S.F. Maritime
State Hist. Park

Aquatic

Fort
Mason

TIBURON PENINSULA

Belvedere Cove

Fl.G.4s#3

Cone Rk.
Qk.Fl.

Platform
Schoonmaker Yt Hbr

Sausilito Yachts

Fl.R.4s.#2

Fl.R.4s.#3

10f

Separation Line
Traffic Lanes

Recreation Area

Anita Rk
Qk.Fl.
Fl.R.4s

E.Int.R.6s.

St. Francis
Marina
Qk.Fl.R.

See detail

Strawberry Pt.

Richardson Bay

Clipper Yacht Harbor.
See detail.

V. Shallow

Marin C.

SAUSILITO

35'

10f

Golden Gate Bridge
Suspension bridge
Vert. Cl. 225' centre

Tide rips

10f

Tide rips

Coast Guard

Doyle Dr.

Palace of
Fine Arts

Presidio Military
Reservation

Hwy 1

Pt. Diablo
Iso.6s.
Horn

Bonita Cove

6f

10f

Var. 16°E (1984)
Decr. 05' ann.

Pt. Bonita
12A.'18M. 2×× R.Bn. 296Hz.
Horn.

Centissima Reef
Fl.G.4s.
Bell

Qk.Fl.R.
Bell

Occ.4s.
12A.'18M.2××
Horn.

Sears Rk.

R.#4

Bonita Channel

6f

65'

10f

Mile Rks
Fl. 5s. 22M
& Horn

South Bay

Iso.6s.

10f

Outbound (Westward) Traffic Lane

Separation Traffic Line

Inbound (Eastward) Traffic Lane

37° 50 N

Main Ship Channel

Bonita Channel

Sausilito is an area often preferred by coastal cruisers because of its clean air, lack of congestion, and quiet pace. Originally an artists' colony, its spectacular homes clinging to steep cliffs are a sharp contrast to the cheek-by-jowl houses of San Francisco. Located 2 miles north of the Bridge it is reached by way of a channel marked by lights and buoys.

This is a pleasure boat haven where every possible boating need can be met. Anchorage can be taken in the southern part of Richardson Bay but watch your depth sounder when looking for a place to drop the hook as it is very shallow outside of the anchoring area.

The largest marina development is **Clipper Yacht Harbor** which has accommodation for 700 berths. The newest development is **Kappas Marina**, located a short distance past the Clipper complex. On the opposite side of the channel from the platform is **Schoonmaker Point Marina.** Transient berths are usually available; rates vary with the length of the vessel, a 34-ft. boat costing about $12 per day in 1988.

This is the northern home port of the cadet training tallship, "Californian," which is sponsored by the Nautical Heritage Society. Other home ports where she can be seen at various times are Ventura and Chula Vista.

It is important to remember that the VTS traffic patterns continue into the Bay. Extreme caution is essential in the precautionary zone where large vessels converge to cross and join diverging traffic lanes. Great care must be taken to watch for other vessels of every size and shape and to follow the rules of the road.

San Francisco Bay is a large body of water covering some 400 square miles. Cities which border this extensive bay include San Francisco, Oakland, Emeryville, Richmond, Berkeley, San Leandro, Sausilito, Redwood City, and South San Francisco. San Francisco/Oakland is a **Port of Entry.** To report in, call Customs at 556-2844 during the day or 876-2812 at night; vessels making a landfall from a foreign country must also call Immigration at 876-2876 days, or 495-6667 after hours.

Flowing into the Bay are the San Joaquin and Sacramento Rivers which are navigable all the way up to Stockton and Sacramento respectively. The tributaries, canals, and deltas of these two rivers compose what is known as the Delta Region. There are many miles of navigable waters which provide protected cruising; if one is planning to visit these waters reference should be made to one of several guides devoted solely to the Delta and Bay areas. As this guide is intended for sailors transiting the coast, attention is limited to marina facilities closest to the Golden Gate Bridge, though municipal marinas are also found at **Oyster Point** and **Coyote Point.**

Marina Yacht Harbor is almost 2 miles east of the Bridge. A breakwater with a light at the eastern end gives protection to the docks of the Saint Francis Yacht Club and the San Francisco Municipal Yacht Harbor. Another part of the Municipal Yacht Harbor is just to the east. A few transient berths are available; check with the harbormaster for berth allocation. Rates are reasonable -- $3 for a 40-ft. vessel. Transportation by bus or taxi is required to reach the nearest laundromat or grocery store while the only supply of propane is in Sausilito.

Aquatic Park is located about 1/2 mile east of Marina Yacht Harbor. A pier curves out from the western side, giving protection from the winds sweeping in from Golden Gate. Good anchorage for a few days may be taken in 1 1/2 - 2 fathoms, mud. Fuel, water, and marine supplies are available at Fisherman's Wharf just to the east.

Pier 39 has moorage for pleasure craft but reservations are required for transient vessels wishing to tie up.

One could spend many days visiting the varied attractions in the Bay and surrounding areas. The downtown points of interest include Fisherman's Wharf, Chinatown, the Palace of Fine Arts, the Cannery, Alcatraz, Coit Tower, Ghiradelli Square, the shops and restaurants of Pier 39, Cable Cars, and even the unique architecture of the houses of San Francisco. By travelling further afield interesting day trips can be taken to the wine country in Napa Valley, Sausilito, and Muir Woods Park, and to the state capital at Sacramento where many museums and historic buildings are found.

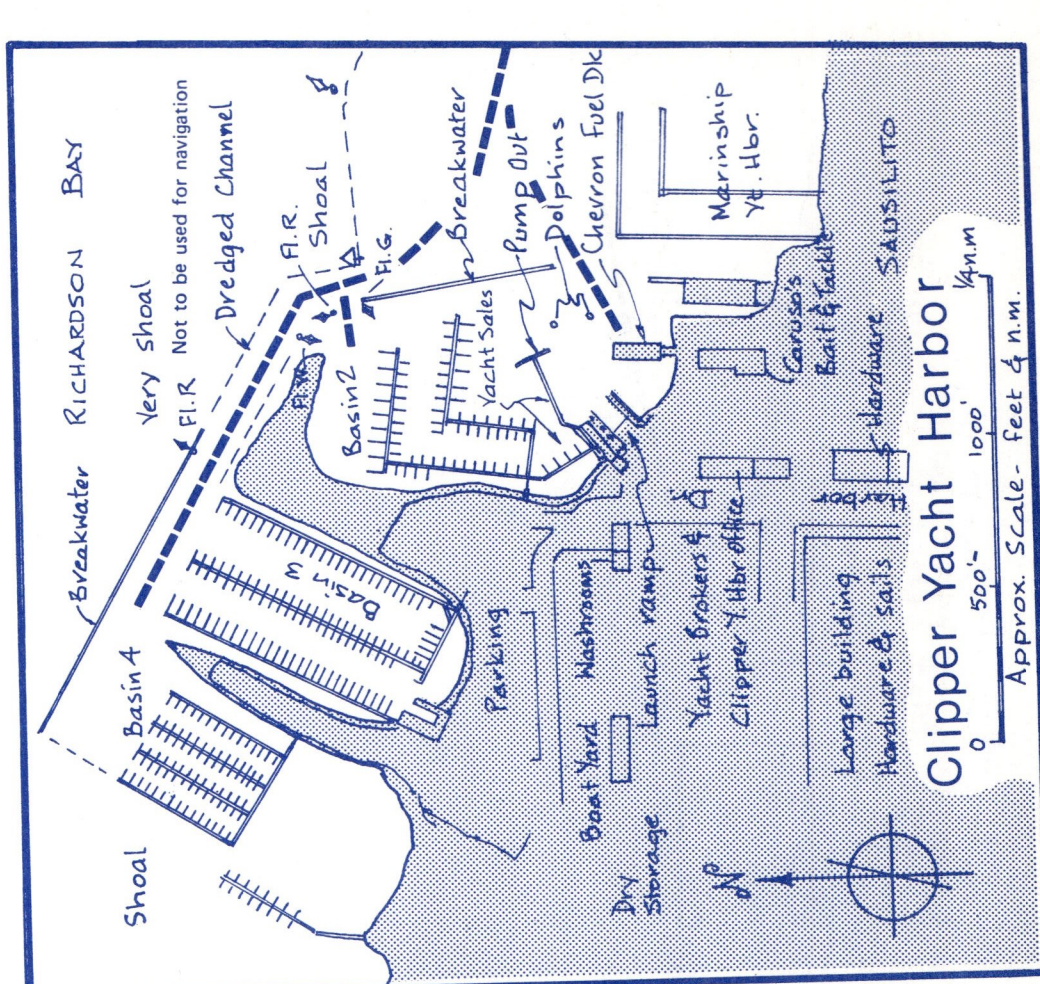

Clipper Yacht Harbor
Approx. Scale - Feet & n.m.
0   500'   1000'   ¼ n.m.

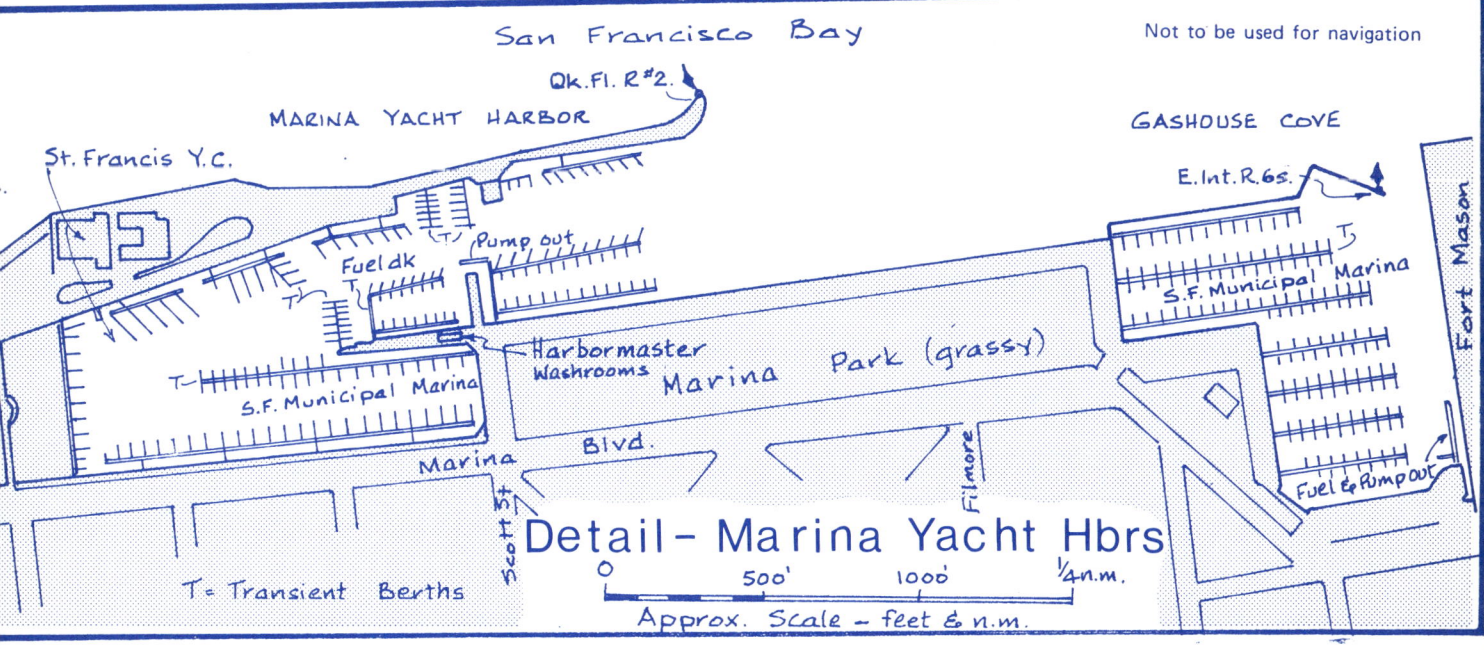

Detail- Marina Yacht Hbrs

San Francisco Bay

Not to be used for navigation

Qk.Fl. R #2.

MARINA YACHT HARBOR

GASHOUSE COVE

St. Francis Y.C.

E. Int. R. 6s.

Fort Mason

Pump out

T

S.F. Municipal Marina

Fuel dk

T

T

Harbormaster
Washrooms

Marina Park (grassy)

T

S.F. Municipal Marina

Filmore

Marina   Blvd.

Scott St.

Fuel & Pumpout

T = Transient Berths

0   500'   1000'   ¼ n.m.

Approx. Scale - feet & n.m.

Detail- S.F. Maritime Pk

N

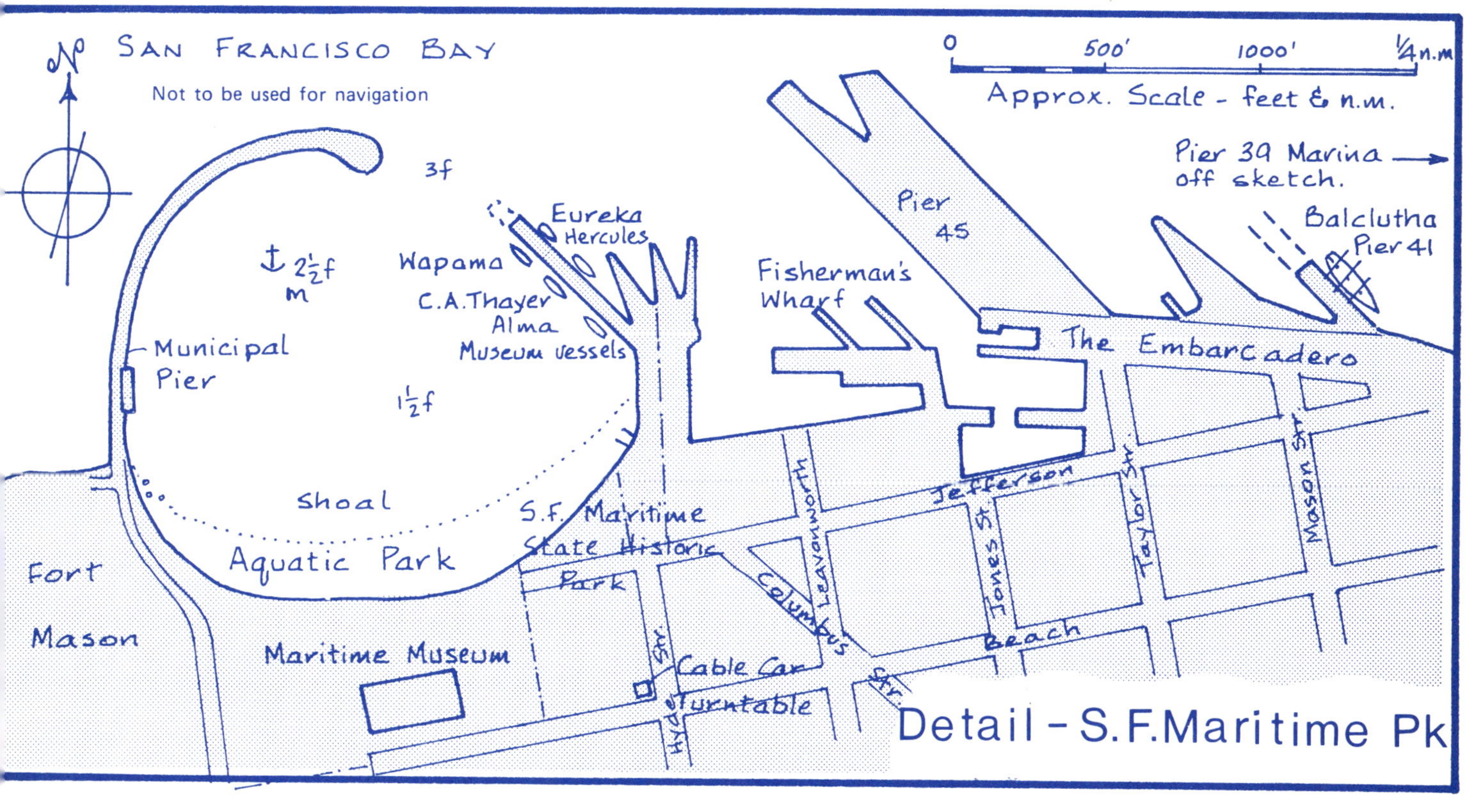

SAN FRANCISCO BAY

Not to be used for navigation

0   500'   1000'   ¼ n.m.

Approx. Scale - feet & n.m.

3f

Pier 45

Pier 39 Marina →
off sketch.

Eureka
Hercules

Wapama

⚓ 2½f
m

Balclutha
Pier 41

C.A.Thayer
Alma
Museum vessels

Fisherman's
Wharf

1½f

Municipal
Pier

The Embarcadero

Shoal

Jefferson

Mason Str.

S.F. Maritime
State Historic
Park

Taylor Str.

Jones Str.

Aquatic Park

Leavenworth

Columbus Str.

Fort
Mason

Beach

Maritime Museum

Hyde Str.

Cable Car
Turntable

HALF MOON BAY (PILLAR POINT HARBOR)

This is a popular stop-over for southbound boats wanting to return to the cruising mode after the excitement of San Francisco, and for northbound vessels wishing to have a short trip prior to entry at the Golden Gate. Adding to its activity during summer months are many pleasure and fishing vessels from the Bay. Half Moon Bay is about 20 miles south of San Francisco and 46 miles north of Santa Cruz. This well protected harbor lies in a bight east of Pillar Point; the coast then curves in a southeasterly direction in a long beach backed by sand dunes.

Pillar Point is easy to recognize by the pair of conspicuous radar towers near the tip. By giving the point a clearance of 1 1/4 miles one can avoid the numerous rocks and kelp which lie in an arc from southwest to southeast of the point. Buoys "1" and "3" mark the seaward edge of this dangerous area. About 1/1/2 miles SSE of the point is lighted buoy "2" which marks the northern extremity of Southeast Reef. This 1-mile long area of submerged and exposed rocks lies to the southeast and is marked at its southern end by lighted gong buoy "1" (6 sec.). Do not confuse this gong buoy "1" with the buoy mentioned in a following paragraph which has a 2 1/2 sec. light.

The harbor is protected by two outer angular breakwaters: the west break-water extending out from Pillar Point, has a light and fog signal at the end, while the east breakwater, built out from the beach, is marked by a light at the seaward end. The inner harbor is protected by two more breakwaters reaching out from the shore and a detached breakwater which lies across the southern side. There is a light at each end of the detached breakwater.

When approaching from the north pick up lighted gong buoy "1" (2 1/2 sec.) which is about 3/4 mile southeast of Pillar Point. Proceed in an ESE direction for about 1 mile to bell buoy "3" before turning north to the harbor entrance. On making an approach from the south a vessel must identify and clear Southeast Reef before picking up bell buoy "3" and continuing north to the entrance.

Dense fog can appear quickly in this area and can make entrance to the harbor hazardous, especially if one's navigation is rather approximate. Take care to update the vessel's position frequently and if your navigation is not accurate it would be better to pass by rather than attempt a first entrance in foggy conditions.

Pillar Point Harbor is a pleasant place which has fuel, showers, restrooms, and restaurants. Contact the harbormaster for authorization to use a buoy or slip. The end ties on all except Docks D and E are available to transients at 30 cents per foot per day.

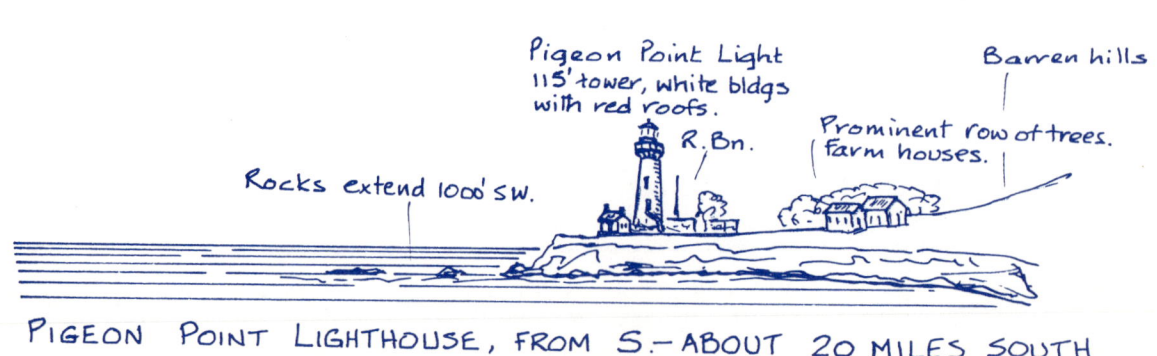

PIGEON POINT LIGHTHOUSE, FROM S.—ABOUT 20 MILES SOUTH OF HALFMOON BAY

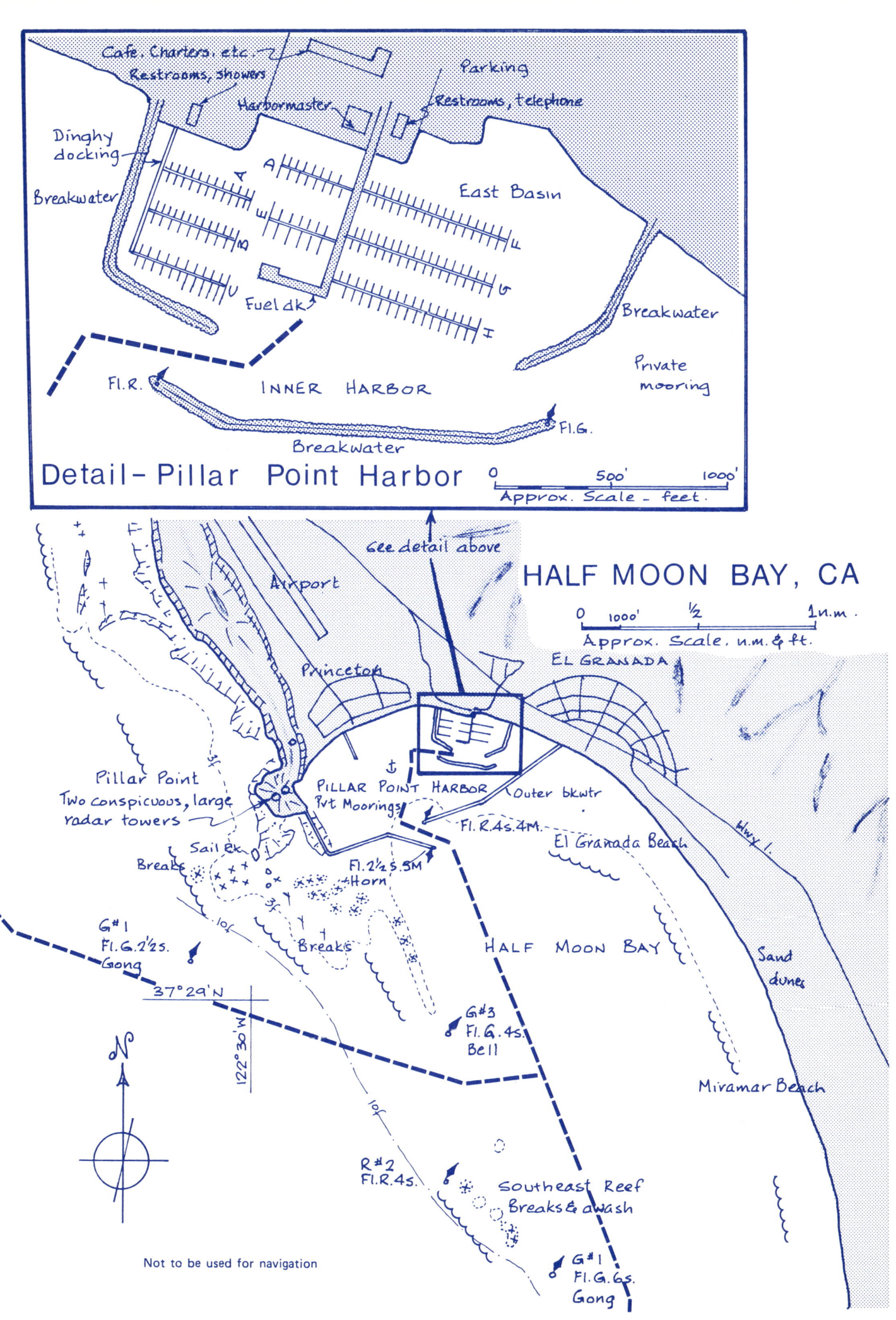

Detail- Pillar Point Harbor

Cafe, Charters, etc.
Restrooms, showers
Parking
Harbormaster
Restrooms, telephone
Dinghy docking
Breakwater
A A
East Basin
B
U
Fuel dk
Breakwater
Private mooring
Fl. R.
INNER HARBOR
Fl. G.
Breakwater

0   500'   1000'
Approx. Scale - feet.

See detail above

HALF MOON BAY, CA

0   1000'   ½   1 n.m.
Approx. Scale. n.m. & ft.

Airport
Princeton
EL GRANADA
Pillar Point
Two conspicuous, large radar towers
PILLAR POINT HARBOR
Pvt Moorings
Outer bkwtr
Fl. R. 4s. 4M.
El Granada Beach
Sail bk
Breaks
Fl. 2½ s. 5M
Horn
Breaks
HALF MOON BAY
hwy 1
Sand dunes
G #1
Fl. G. 2½ s.
Gong
37° 29' N
G #3
Fl. G. 4s.
Bell
Miramar Beach
R #2
Fl. R. 4s.
Southeast Reef
Breaks & awash
G #1
Fl. G. 6s.
Gong

Not to be used for navigation

SANTA CRUZ

This year-long summer vacation spot owes its popularity to magnificent beaches and a climate that is made for enjoyment of water sports and beach activities. Founded in 1791 by the Franciscans, Santa Cruz became one of the series of 21 missions linking San Francisco to San Diego. Another note of historical interest is that in 1881 loganberries originated here, in the garden of Judge J. Logan.

Santa Cruz lies at the northern end of Monterey Bay between Point Santa Cruz on the west and Black Point on the east. It is about 46 miles south of Half Moon Bay and 18 miles distant from Moss Landing when one has bypassed the Naval Operating Area. Easily identifiable landmarks are the Casino, amusement park, and the .4 mile long pier. A maximum speed of 5 knots within the harbor limits is closely patrolled. Boats are prohibited from the outermost 100 yards of the pier and the swimming areas which are clearly marked by City buoys.

Entry into the **Small Craft Harbor (Woods Lagoon)** is made by way of a channel between two jetties. The shorter, eastern jetty extends outward from Twin Lakes Beach. The longer, western jetty turns southeastward near the tip where a light, fog signal and radiobeacon are located. A bridge separating the lower basin from the upper basin has a clearance of 18 ft. Do not enter if a heavy swell is running as the shoaling in the vicinity of the entrance causes dangerous breakers. (Shoaling during the winter storms of 1969-70 completely blocked the entrance causing the boats within the harbor to be land-locked. In 1977 major shoaling extended about 3/4 of the way across the entrance.) For advice on entering one may call the Port Director who monitors Ch. 9, 12, and 16. Also monitoring the same channels is a patrol boat which will guide vessels into the harbor on request.

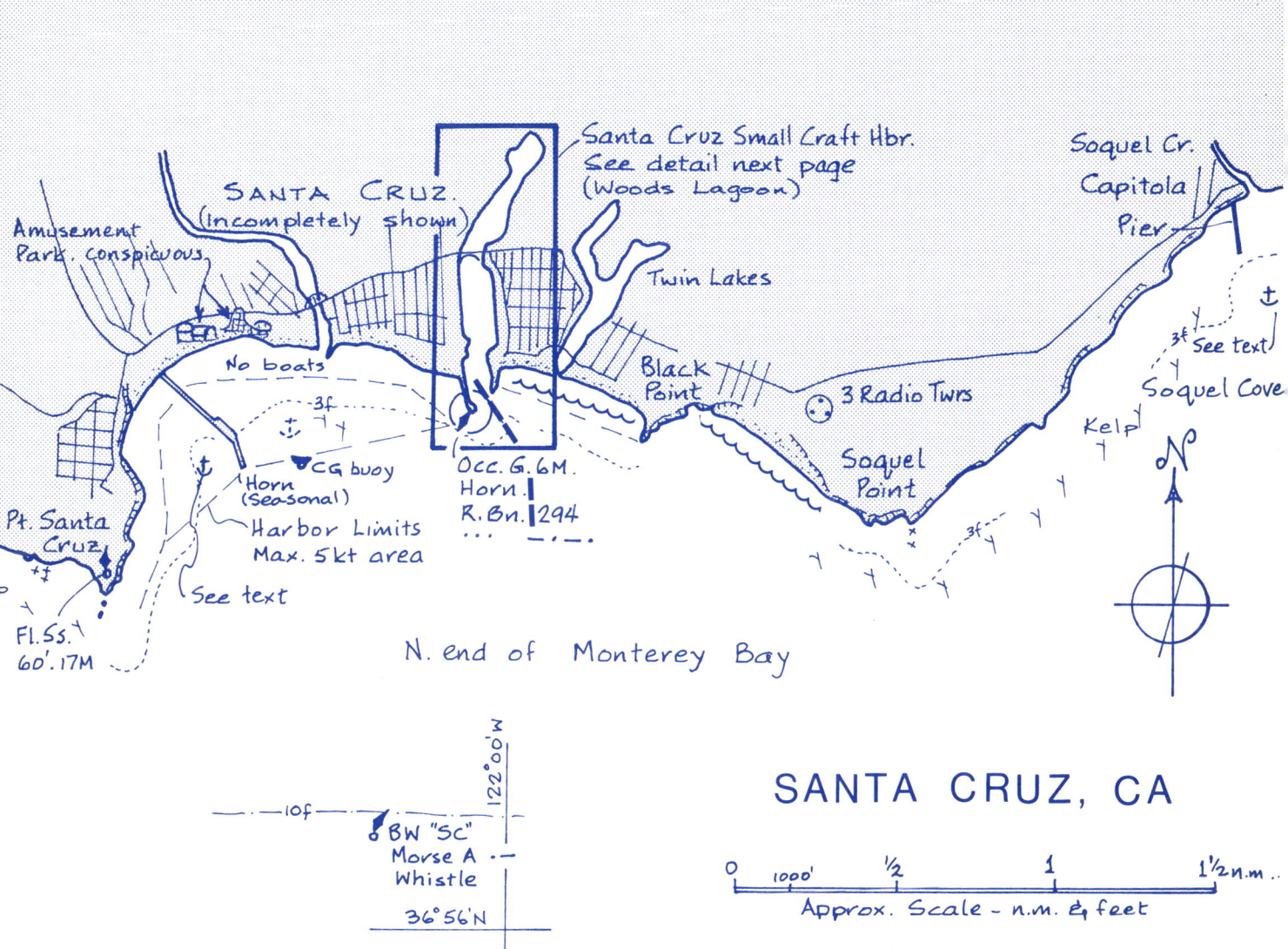

Amusement Park. Conspicuous.

SANTA CRUZ.
(Incompletely shown)

Santa Cruz Small Craft Hbr.
See detail next page
(Woods Lagoon)

Soquel Cr.
Capitola
Pier

Twin Lakes

No boats

Black Point

3 Radio Twrs

3f See text

Soquel Cove

-3f-

Soquel Point

Kelp

CG buoy

Horn (Seasonal)

Occ. G. 6M.
Horn.
R. Bn. 294

3f

Harbor Limits
Max. 5kt area

Pt. Santa Cruz.

See text

P

Fl.5s.
60'. 17M

N. end of Monterey Bay

122°00'W

10f

BW "SC"
Morse A
Whistle

36°56'N

SANTA CRUZ, CA

0   1000'   ½   1   1½n.m.

Approx. Scale - n.m. & feet

Not to be used for navigation

The Small Craft Harbor can accommodate 950 wet berths and 275 in dry storage. On average there are about 50 coastal travellers per day passing through this area. The end ties are reserved for transients, but as a result of heavy traffic no reservations can be made for these berths, which are filled on a first-come first-serve basis. Weekends and holidays often find transient boats rafted up, daily rates being about $12 for a 34 ft. vessel. Contact the Harbormaster for instructions regarding moorage; he monitors Ch. 16 from 8:30 to 5:00.

With the exception of swimming and pier areas mentioned above, anchorage may be taken anywhere within the harbor limits in 6 fathoms, sand, though in northwesterly weather the surge is uncomfortable. Alternatively, one may drop the hook in **Soquel Cove,** the best spot being southeast of Soquel Creek.

A fuel dock, laundromat, showers, restaurants, restrooms, and the Harbormaster's Office are all conveniently located as shown. Marine repairs and supplies are available from a number of shops in the vicinity of the Harbor.

For a change of pace your crew might enjoy a day at the beachside amusement park which was established in 1907. It isn't every day that one can take a ride on a landmark, in this case the roller coaster that was so conspicuous from sea. Surfers find Twin Lakes Beach a good place to catch a wave.

Detail of

Santa Cruz

Small Craft Harbor

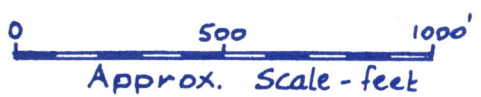

0   500   1000'

Approx. Scale - feet

Not to be used for navigation

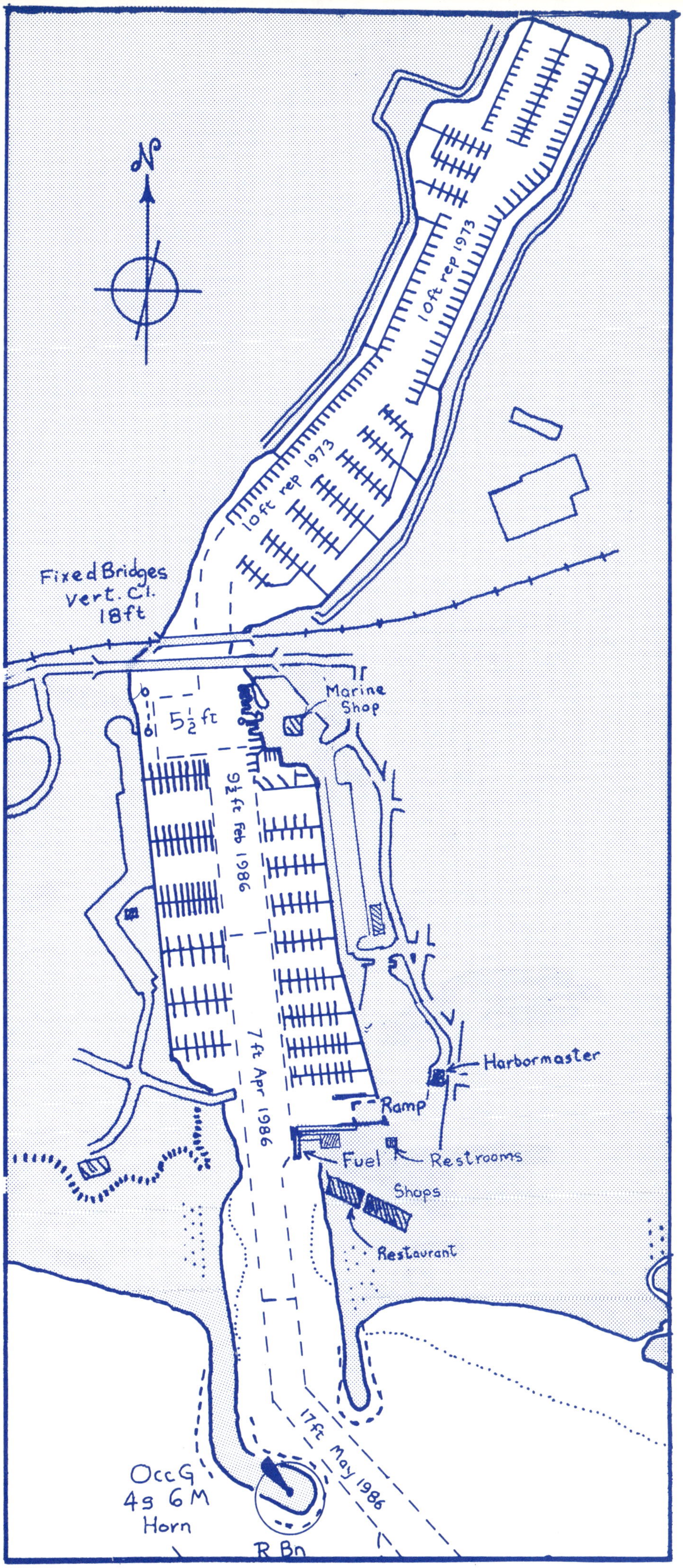

N°

10 ft rep 1973

10 ft rep 1973

10 ft rep 1973

Fixed Bridges
Vert. Cl.
18 ft

Marine Shop

5½ ft

9½ ft Feb 1986

7 ft Apr 1986

Harbormaster

Ramp

Fuel

Restrooms

Shops

Restaurant

17 ft May 1986

Occ G
4s 6M
Horn

R Bn

MOSS LANDING

This **harbor of refuge** is located approximately mid-way on the east side of Monterey Bay. Moss Landing is about 18 miles distant from Santa Cruz and 15 miles northeast of Monterey. Both destinations involve clearance being given to the Naval Operating Area, and Restricted and Prohibited zones in the vicinity.

There are several prominent features which easily iden- tify Moss Landing: two huge powerplant stacks (528 ft. high), other stacks in the vicinity, and a white water tank on the southern side of town. In addition, two radio towers are located 4 miles north of the town.

When approaching, pick up lighted bell buoy "MLA" which is about 3/4 mile southwest of the entrance to the channel. Two private buoys are in the vicinity: one which is 250 ft. southwest of the south jetty marks the dis- charge from the power plant, and a second one almost a mile northwest of the harbor entrance marks a submerged pipline which supplies fuel to the power- plant. A short distance northeast of the south jetty is a fog signal and radiobeacon.

Two lighted, short (15 ft.) jetties protect the entrance to the channel which leads to a turning basin within the harbor. When entering, favor the north side of the channel as shoaling is more evident on the south side. Once inside, there is a buoyed channel to the North Harbor which is maintained by the Elkhorn Yacht Club. A clubhouse and slips are located at the far end. Entry without local knowledge is inadvisable. The dredged channel to the harbor facilities in the South Harbor is well marked with lights, buoys, and a daybeacon.

The Harbormaster monitors Ch. 16 and it is advisable to contact him prior to entering the harbor. Rates are reasonable, moorage for a 34 ft. vessel was $6.80 in 1987. Fuel, water, and marine repairs are available. For showers and laundromats one must go to Castroville which is 3 miles away on Hwy. 1. Propane is available at Moss Landing Boat Works.

The numerous marshes in this region make it a haven for birds. Because of the profusion and variety of shore birds Elkhorn Slough is an ecological reserve. A walk near any of the local marshes (even along the road bordering North Harbor) is indeed enjoyable whether or not one is a bird-watcher.

NOTE: When travelling south from Moss Landing be sure to check Chart #18685 to identify the prohibited and restricted areas located on a direct line to Monterey. Do NOT enter the prohibited area as it is part of the firing range used by the army stationed at Fort Ord. From August 1 to February 15 avoid also the Restricted Area which is used for mine warfare training. When travelling north, one may check as to whether or not Naval Operations are taking place, but it's simpler just to avoid the area so marked.

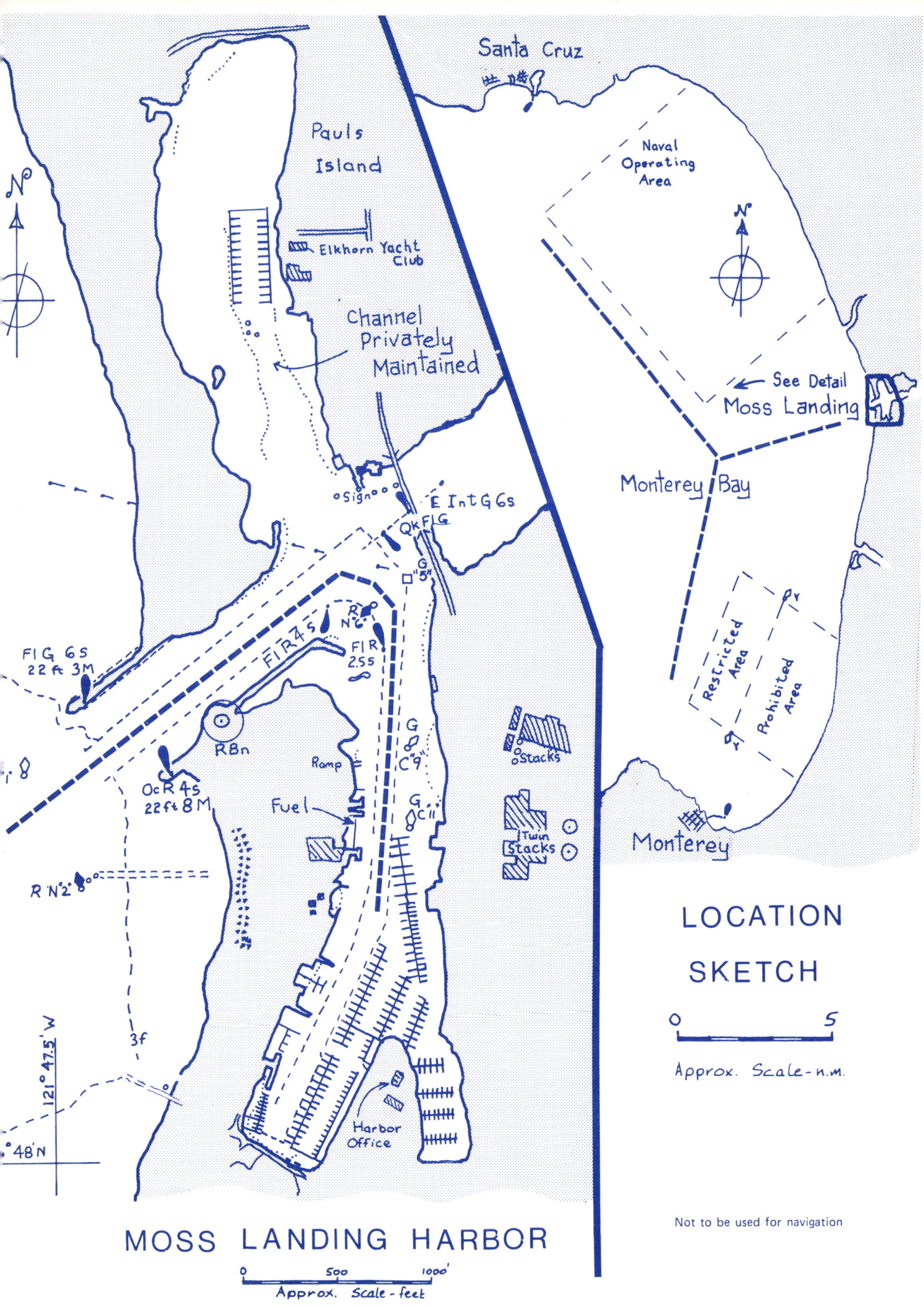

N

Santa Cruz

Pauls
Island

Naval
Operating
Area

N

Elkhorn Yacht
Club

See Detail
Moss Landing

Channel
Privately
Maintained

Monterey Bay

Sign

E Int G 6s

Qk Fl G

G "5"

Restricted
Area

Prohibited
Area

R
N "6"

Fl R 4s

Fl R
2.5s

Fl G 6s
22 ft 3M

G
C "9"

Stacks

RBn

Ramp

G
C "11"

Twin
Stacks

Monterey

Oc R 4s
22 ft 8M

Fuel

R N "2"

3f

Harbor
Office

LOCATION

SKETCH

0   5

Approx. Scale-n.m.

Not to be used for navigation

121° 47.5' W

48' N

MOSS LANDING HARBOR

0   500   1000'

Approx. Scale-feet

MONTEREY

    From a historical stand-point alone, this is a stop-over of major significance; in addition, entry is straightforward and people are friendly. Located within the hook at the southern end of Monterey Bay this historic city is 15 miles around the Prohibited and Restricted areas from Moss Landing and about 90 miles from San Simeon anchorage. It was discovered in 1602 by Vizcaino; while under Mexican rule until 1846, Monterey was the capital of California. Monterey is now a treasure trove of historical buildings, landmarks, museums, and art galleries.

    The entrance to Monterey Harbor is 3 miles southeast of Point Pinos. Pick up lighted bell buoy "4" which is 1/2 mile off Point Cabrillo and proceed another mile to the southeast, where the 1,700 ft. rock breakwater (Coast Guard Pier) marks the entrance to the harbor. A light and fog signal are at the tip of the breakwater, while at the inner end is the Coast Guard office. Built out from the southern shore is Municipal Wharf #2 which forms the eastern boundary of the harbor. Within the harbor is Municipal Wharf #1 (Fishermans Wharf) on which are located many small shops, cafes, and boat charters.

    Good but rolly anchorage, sand and clay, may be taken in the area south of the Coast Guard Pier. To enter the small craft harbor, a vessel must proceed through the gap between the end of Fishermans Wharf and the frontal seawall, which extends out from about the half-way point on Municipal Wharf #2. The outer section of this wharf is used for commercial purposes.

    Prior to entering, call the Harbormaster (Ch. 16). Pier H, just inside the seawall, is for transients; there is a flat rate of $9 per day. A refundable deposit of $20 is required for each key needed for washrooms. Laundry, restrooms, and showers are in the main building, fuel is handy, while propane can be obtained at Kim's Propane. If one prefers to be near the activity, closer to Fisherman's Wharf, Breakwater Cove Marina has transient berths where reservations can be made (Ph. 373-7857)

    One should spend at least a day visiting the various original and reconstructed buildings which relate to Monterey's colorful past. In addition, numerous art galleries feature local artists, many of whom have world-wide reputations. The aquarium is noteworthy as it features the largest underwater viewing gallery of any facility of its kind in the world. A cultural highlight of the year is the Bach Festival. The much publicized 17-Mile Drive which commences in Pacific Grove and follows the coast (via Cypress Point and the Pebble Beach Golf Course) to Carmel is worth a day-trip if time permits.

    The presence of the military is quite evident. This is a result of three factors: the Presidio of Monterey is the home of the U.S. Army Language School, a few miles to the east is the Fort Ord Army Training Center, and the U.S. Naval Postgraduate School is within the city limits.

    NOTE: When travelling to Moss Landing be sure to check Chart #18685 to identify the Prohibited and Restricted Areas which lie on the direct route. Do NOT enter the Prohibited Area as it is part of the firing range used by the army stationed at Fort Ord. From August 1 to February 15 avoid the Restricted Area which is used for mine warfare training.

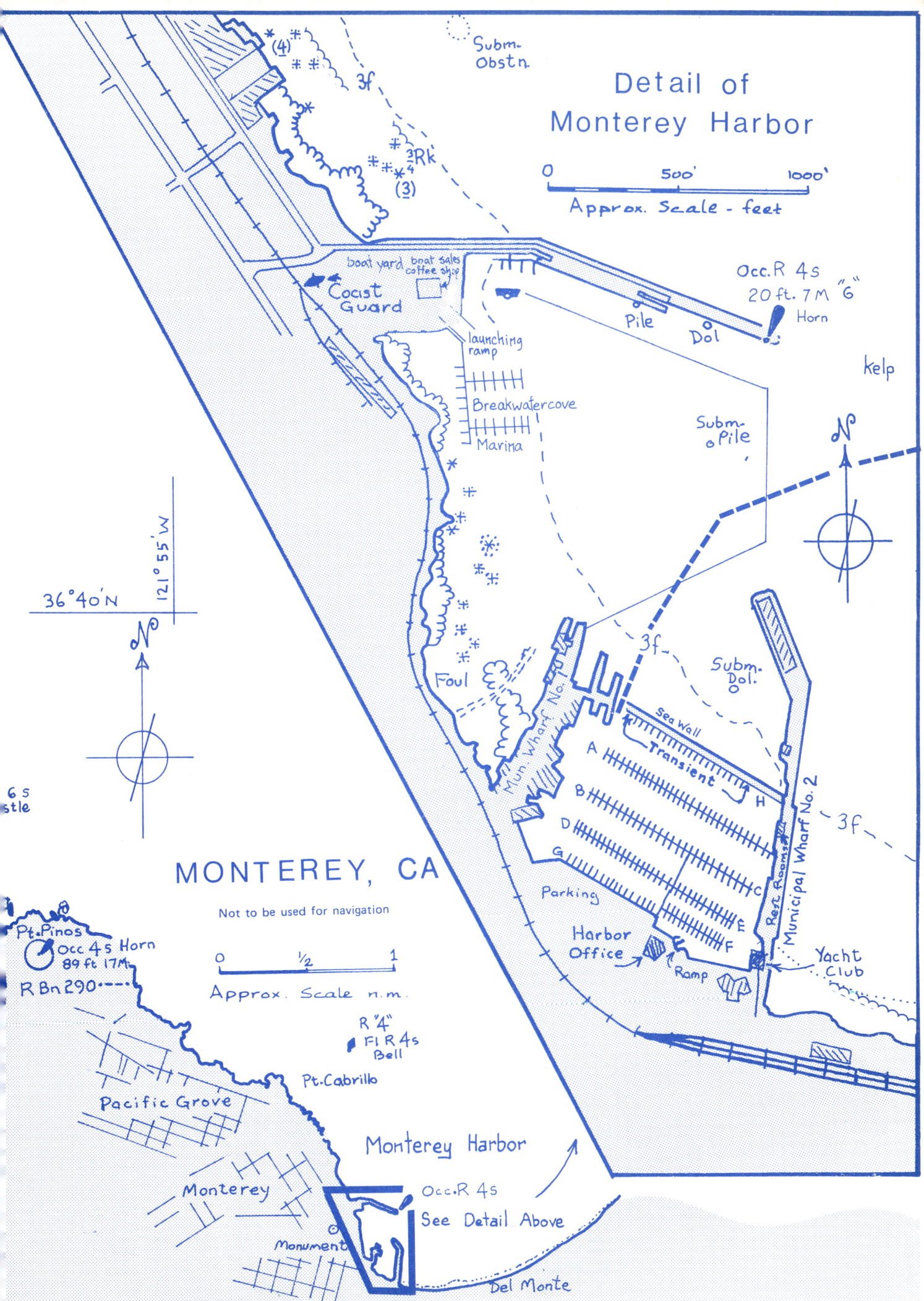

Detail of Monterey Harbor

Subm. Obstn.

(4)

3f

3Rk
3/4

(3)

0   500'   1000'
Approx. Scale - feet

boat yard   boat sales
coffee shop

Coast Guard

launching ramp

Breakwater cove

Marina

Pile   Dol

Occ.R 4s
20 ft. 7M "6"
Horn

kelp

Subm. o Pile

N

Foul

3f

Subm. Dol.

Mun Wharf No.

Sea Wall

Transient

A

B

D

G

H

C

E

F

Municipal Wharf No. 2

Rest. Rooms

3f

Parking

Harbor Office

Ramp

Yacht Club

36°40'N

121°55'W

N

6 s
stle

MONTEREY, CA

Not to be used for navigation

0   1/2   1
Approx. Scale n.m.

Pt. Pinos
Occ 4s Horn
89 ft 17M
R Bn 290 ----

R "4"
Fl R 4s
Bell

Pt. Cabrillo

Pacific Grove

Monterey

Monument

Monterey Harbor
Occ.R 4s
See Detail Above

Del Monte

SAN SIMEON BAY

For cruisers interested in visiting the unique Hearst San Simeon State Historical Monument, the anchorage at San Simeon Bay is ideally located. It is about 90 miles southeast of Monterey and 45 miles northwest of Morrow Bay. The bay is a circular bight northeast of San Simeon Point.

When approaching from the north, one passes Point Piedras Blancas which has a lighthouse, radio beacon, and lighted whistle buoy 1 1/2 miles to the southwest. Five miles southeast of Point Piedras Blancas is San Simeon Point. When approaching from the south, San Simeon Bay is about 23 miles northwest of Point Buchon. The bay can be readily identified by the many conspicuous buildings of Hearst Castle perched high on the hill.

When approaching the bay, pick up lighted bell buoy "1" which is about 1/2 mile southeast of Point San Simeon and proceed into the bay. Because rocks and kelp reach out from the point almost to the buoy, it must be passed to port. Anchorage may be taken in the middle of the bight in 5 to 8 fathoms, sand. There is good protection from northwesterlies, though there is some surge and it is open to the south.

A sportfishing pier extends out from the northern shore of the bay. It is best to go ashore by way of the pier and climb up the ladder though the northwesterlies sometimes kick up quite a chop in the bay and may give one a wet return trip to the boat. The village of San Simeon has a general store dating from 1852 where one can obtain a few groceries and souvenirs; an open-air eating establishment is nearby. Fuel and kerosene may be obtained from the gas station which is operated by the store.

Hearst Castle is prominently located on high ground about 3 miles northeast of the town. During the summer it is advisable to make reservations if one wishes to take any of the four different tours of the castle. Reservations may be made from 9:00 to 6:00 within California by calling MISTIX at 1 - 800 - 446 - PARK, or from outside California at 619-452-1950. Tour buses leave throughout the day from the parking lot near the store. Even if one doesn't take a tour, the interesting displays in the Visitor Center can make one aware of what opulence could mean in the 1920s and 1930s.

RM

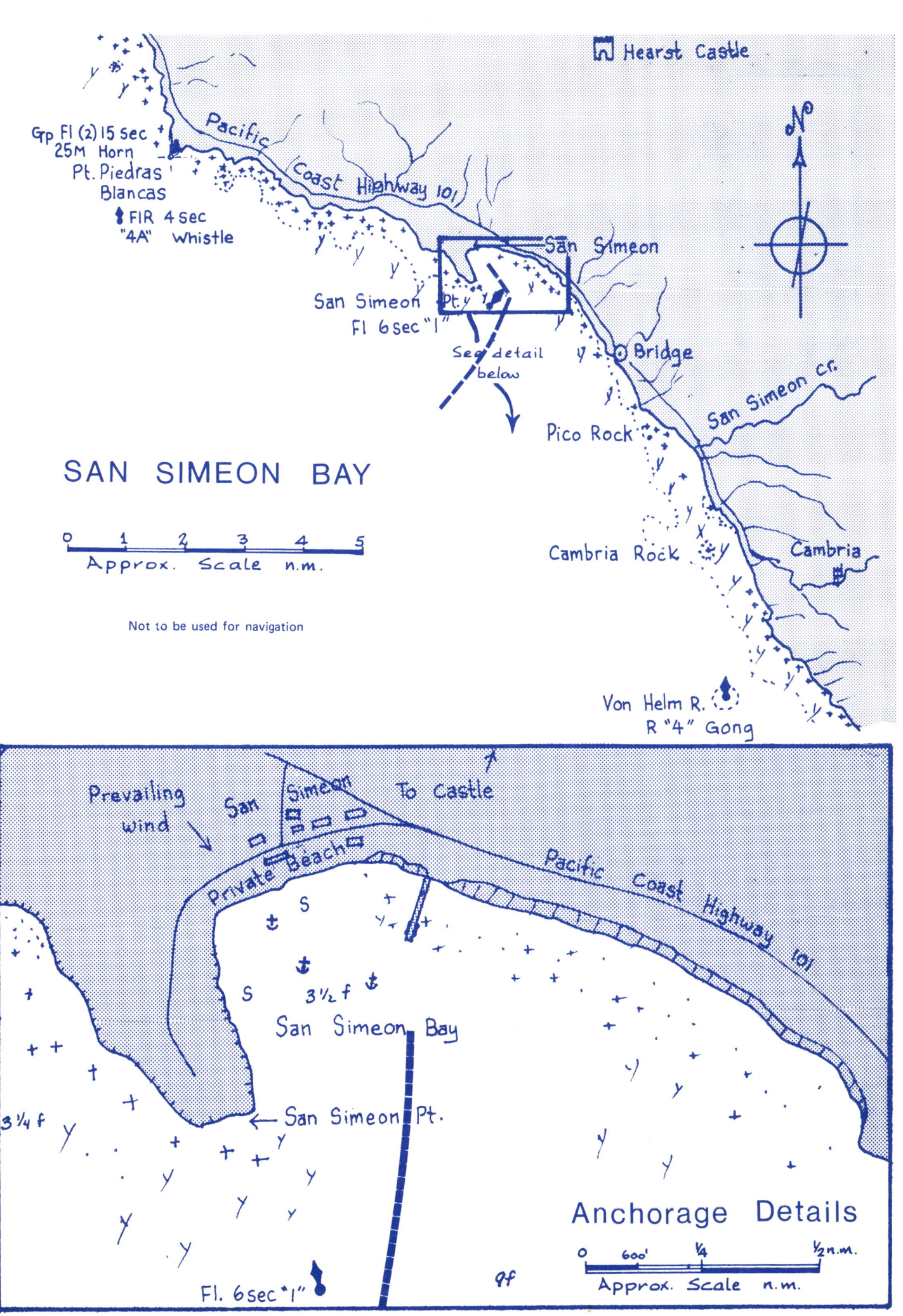

Hearst Castle

Gp Fl (2) 15 sec
25M Horn
Pt. Piedras
Blancas

Fl R 4 sec
"4A" Whistle

Pacific Coast Highway 101

San Simeon

San Simeon
Fl 6 sec "1"

Pt.

See detail
below

Bridge

San Simeon Cr.

Pico Rock

SAN SIMEON BAY

0   1   2   3   4   5
Approx. Scale n.m.

Not to be used for navigation

Cambria Rock

Cambria

Von Helm R.
R "4" Gong

N

Prevailing
wind

San Simeon

To Castle

Private Beach

Pacific Coast Highway 101

S

S

3½ f

San Simeon Bay

3¼ f

San Simeon Pt.

Fl. 6 sec "1"

9f

Anchorage Details

0   600'   ¼   ½ n.m.
Approx. Scale n.m.

MORRO BAY

Located 45 miles south of San Simeon Bay and about 20 miles from Port San Luis, Morrow Bay is a convenient stop-over. This area has two remarkable features: of dubious distinction is the Pilot report that this is one of the foggiest areas of the Pacific Coast, and the other is the unforgettable "Rock." Guarding the entrance to the bay, Morro Rock, is an eye-catching 580-ft. cone which is a symbol of the city.

On a clear day Morro Rock and three nearby 450-ft. powerstacks are excellent landmarks which can be seen well at sea. Two 1,800 ft. breakwaters protect the entrance channel. The west breakwater extends south of Morro Rock and has a light, radio beacon, and foghorn at its tip; the south breakwater is built out from the sand dunes which form the peninsula protecting Morro Bay.

When entering, approach from the southwest as currents in the channel can be strong at times. Vessels should favor the west side of the channel as shoaling occurs on the eastern side. During flood tides, currents in the north end of the bay set towards the city T-pier.

The bar can be dangerous when west or southwesterly swells are running, especially at low water or when a considerable time has elapsed since the last dredging was done. Do not enter when breakers are seen across the entrance. If conditions look rough, contact the Coast Guard for current channel and entrance conditions. Special weather broadcasts are given on Ch. 16 and 22 A. Twenty-four hour weather reports are available by calling (805) 772 - 4141. Accurate navigation is essential when travelling in this area known for its dense and frequent fog.

Good anchorage may be taken off the channel opposite the city west of buoy #12. Take care to set the anchor securely and use plenty of scope as tidal currents are quite strong. One can tie to the 50 ft. floating dock near buoy #12 for up to 30 days. The Morro Bay Yacht Club allows authorized club members to side tie at the dock and at the first row of buoys opposite the Yacht Club. Contact the Club harbormaster who monitors Ch. 16 or 68 from 4:30 to 6:00 p.m.

All basic cruising needs can be met on the waterfront and on the first major street inshore where there are some interesting arts and crafts shops. Propane is available at the Shell Station at 41st. and Main, or at the RV Center at Preston and Main (about 1 mile away). A Dial-a-Ride Bus Service operates here; there is about a half-hour wait. The Coast Guard and harbormaster's office are located in the low buildings on the T-pier across the street from the powerstacks. A pleasant walk on the sand dunes on the west side of the bay is sometimes rewarded with a few good shells.

The State Park operates a marina east of White Point, though as the slips are filled with permanent tenants no transient berths are available; in any case, it's a long distance out of the way.

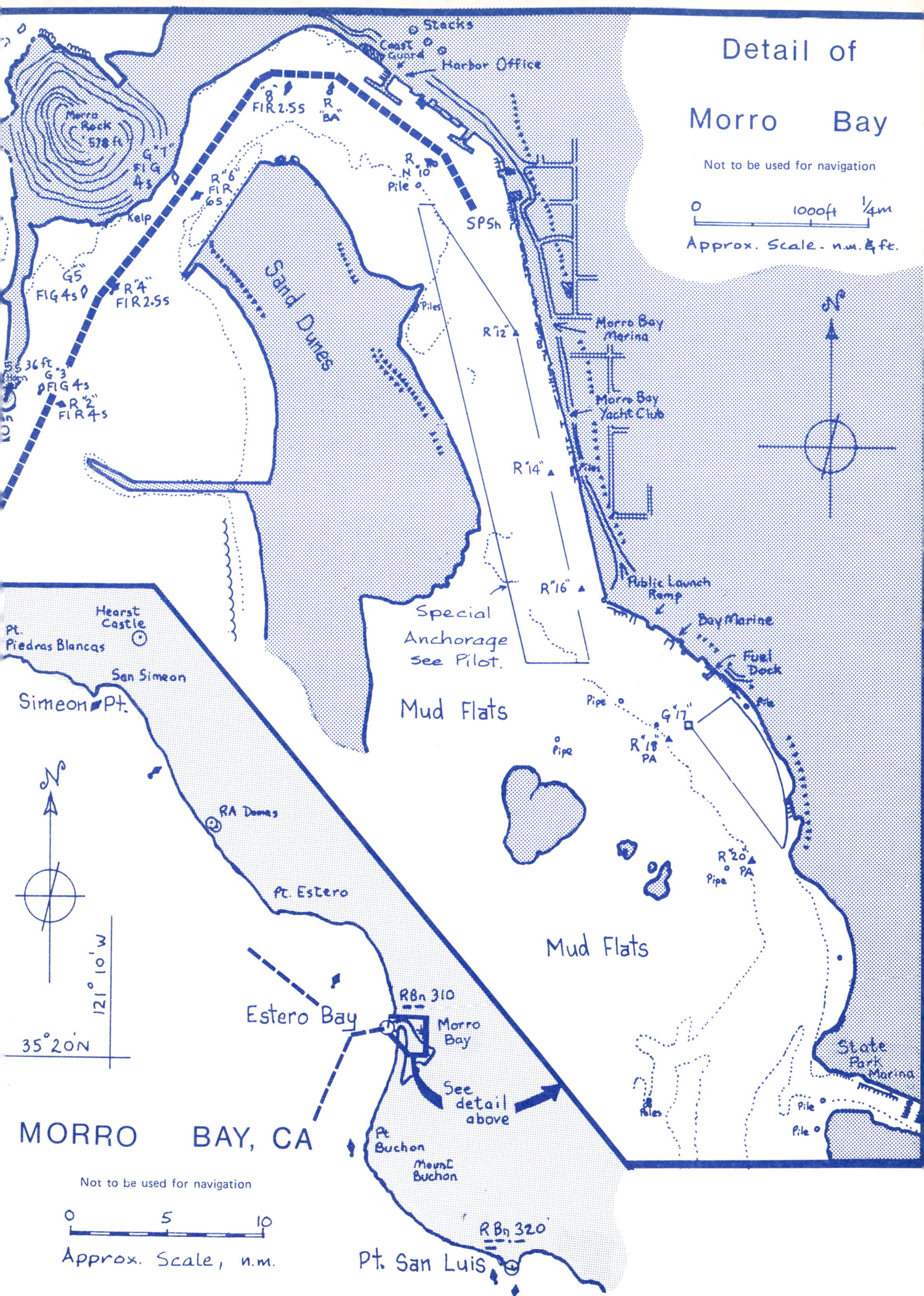

Detail of Morro Bay

Not to be used for navigation

0   1000ft   1/4m

Approx. Scale - n.m. & ft.

Morro Rock 578 ft

Kelp

Sand Dunes

G"1" Fl G 4s
R"6" Fl R 6s
Fl R 2.5s
R"BA"
"B"
"8"
Coast Guard
Stacks
Harbor Office

R"N 10" Pile
SP Sh

R"12"
R"14"
R"16"

Special Anchorage see Pilot.

Mud Flats

Morro Bay Marina
Morro Bay Yacht Club
Public Launch Ramp
Bay Marine
Fuel Dock
Pile

G"17"
R"18" PA
R"20" PA
Pipe
Pipe

G5 Fl G 4s
R"4" Fl R 2.5s
S 36 ft Horn
G"3" Fl G 4s
R"2" Fl R 4s

Mud Flats

State Park Marina
Pile
Pile

N°

Hearst Castle
Pt. Piedras Blancas
San Simeon
Simeon Pt.

RA Domes

Pt. Estero

N

121° 10' W
35° 20' N

Estero Bay

R Bn 310
Morro Bay
See detail above

MORRO   BAY, CA

Not to be used for navigation

0   5   10

Approx. Scale, n.m.

Pt. Buchon
Mount Buchon

R Bn 320

Pt. San Luis

PORT SAN LUIS

This popular haven for pleasure and fishing boats is about 20 miles (around Point Buchon) from Morro Bay, and over 100 miles (around Points Arguello and Conception) distant from Santa Barbara. San Luis Obispo Bay is a wide bight east of Point San Luis. This bold headland has a fog signal, radio beacon and light. The town of Port San Luis is tucked beyond the point on the west shore of the bay. The loading terminal for Union Oil is to the northeast.

There are a number of rocks in the vicinity which must be identified. Westdahl Rock, about 1 1/3 miles southwest of the San Luis Obispo Light is marked by lighted bell buoy. Souza Rock, about 2 miles southeast of the light is identified by lighted gong buoy. Howell Rock, about 1/2 miles east of the light is marked by a buoy. Landsing Rock (covered 18 ft.) and Atlas Rock (covered 13 ft.) are about 7/10 and 1/2 mile east of the light, respectively. Avoid the east part of the bay where there are many rocks and much kelp.

When approaching from the north, a vessel must clear the buoy marking Westdahl Rock and the lighted whistle buoy of the Point San Luis breakwater before proceeding into the anchorage. On entering from the south the vessel should pass about 100 yards west of the buoy marking Souza Rock, proceed about 2 miles until past Lansing Rock and then to the anchorage or wharves. The Port San Luis breakwater is 2,400 ft. long. The wharf 1/2 mile to the north of Point San Luis is used by fishermen.

Contact the Harbormaster on Ch. 16 for use of one of the mooring buoys at $4 per day. Because of increased week-end activity one should make reservations if you hope to have a buoy. The anchorage is under the jurisdiction of the harbormaster and he may tell you where to anchor. Shore facilities include washrooms, showers, a boatyard, hoist, launching ramp, and fuel dock.

This is a beautiful spot to rest, for the hills form a peaceful backdrop to the anchorage, which affords good protection in northerly or westerly weather. At the end of the old dock, originally built in the 1800's, is a restaurant which can provide a change from eating on the boat.

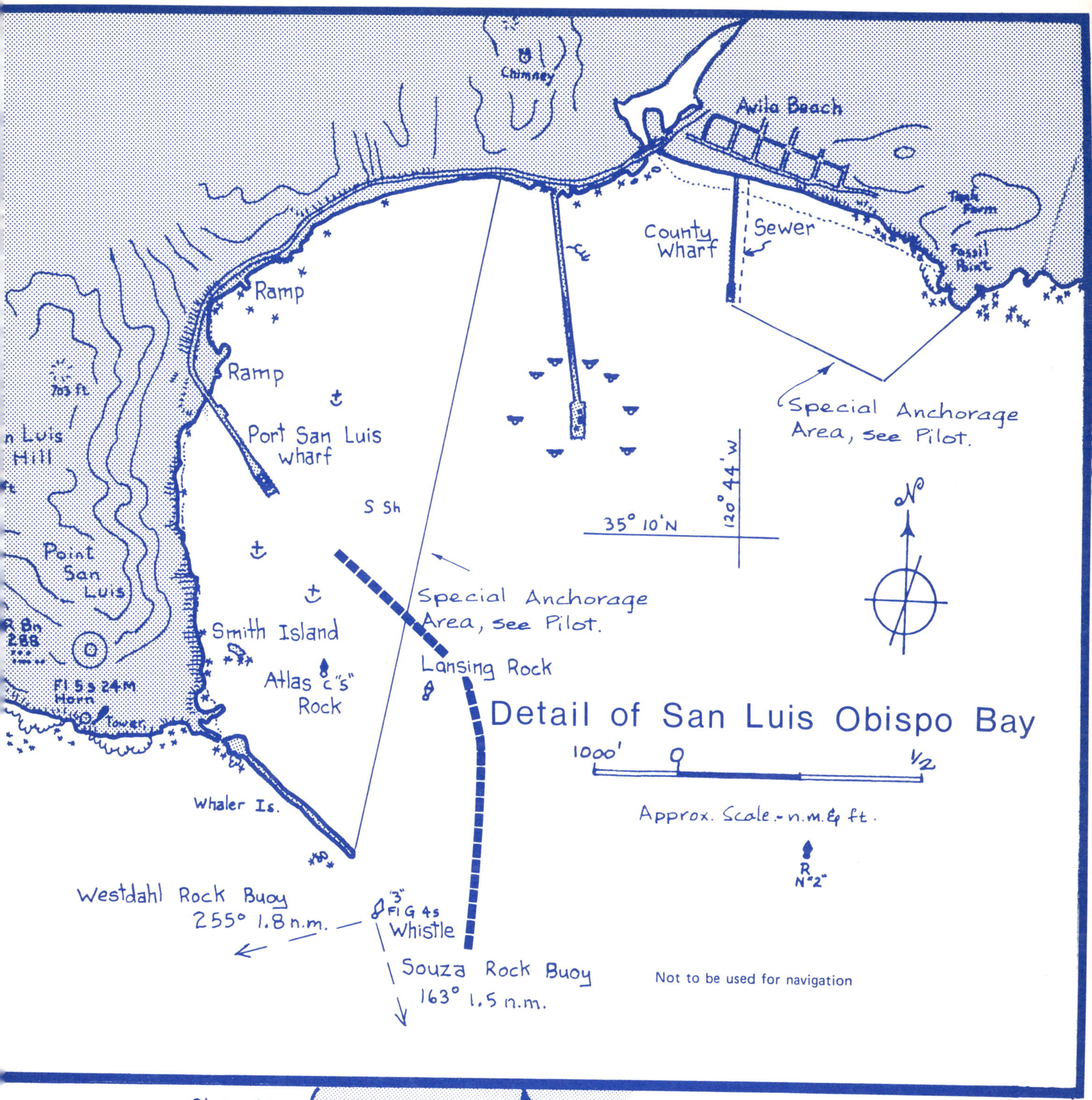

Chimney

Avila Beach

County Wharf

Sewer

Ramp

Ramp

Port San Luis wharf

S Sh

703 ft

n Luis Hill

Point San Luis

R Bn 288

Fl 5 s 24 M Horn

Tower

Smith Island

Atlas c "s" Rock

Whaler Is.

Lansing Rock

Special Anchorage Area, see Pilot.

Special Anchorage Area, see Pilot.

35° 10'N

120° 44'W

N

Detail of San Luis Obispo Bay

1000'   0   ½

Approx. Scale - n.m. & ft.

R N "2"

Westdahl Rock Buoy
255° 1.8 n.m.

"3"
Fl G 4s
Whistle

Souza Rock Buoy
163° 1.5 n.m.

Not to be used for navigation

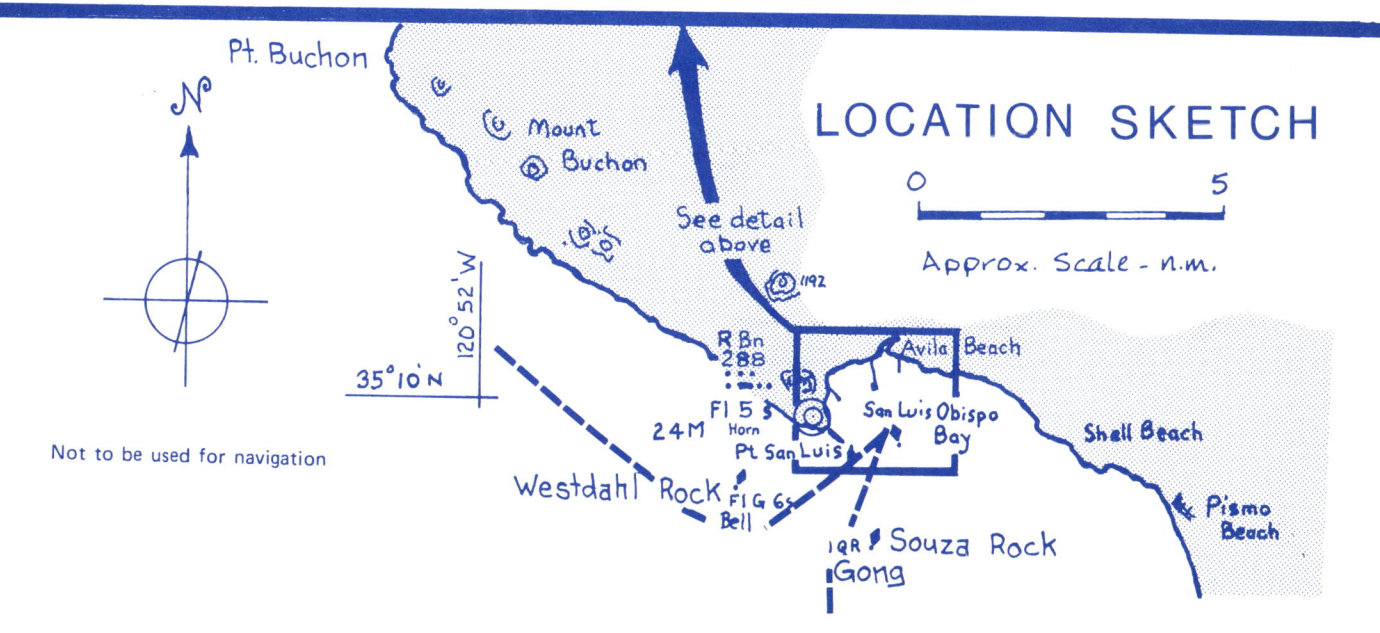

Pt. Buchon

N

Mount Buchon

See detail above

1192

R Bn 288

Fl 5 s
24M Horn

Pt San Luis

Westdahl Rock

Fl G 6s
Bell

IQR Souza Rock
Gong

Avila Beach

San Luis Obispo Bay

Shell Beach

Pismo Beach

LOCATION SKETCH

0   5

Approx. Scale - n.m.

35° 10'N

120° 52'W

Not to be used for navigation

PASSAGE AROUND POINTS ARGUELLO AND CONCEPTION & COJO ANCHORAGE

   A glance at a chart shows an abrupt change in the trend of the coastline
which is somewhat northwesterly-southeasterly north of Point Arguello and
easterly south of Point Conception. Partly as a result of the Venturi effect,
such geographic turning points normally experience accelerated winds and rough
seas in the area adjacent to the land prominence, turbulence often extending a
considerable distance offshore. This effect, along with the funnelling effect
caused by the offshore Channel Islands also influences the winds in and near
the Santa Barbara Channel, which lies to the south of Point Conception.

   With the foregoing generalization in mind a look at the peculiarities of
the two points is revealing. Point Conception is referred to in the Pilot as
the "Cape Horn of the Pacific." It seems to be a point of extremes; there is
either little or no wind or there is a great deal of it. Then again, the winds
may be exceptionally strong over a large area yet within a relatively short
distance one may pass into calm and -- when travelling south -- markedly warmer
air. Point Arguello has an unenviable record for fog: visibility is less than
1/2 mile on 12 to 20 days per month, July and August having the worst records.
In addition, this area marks a surprisingly clear line between the cool,
invigorating air to the north and warm (often hot) air to the south. It's the
area where south-bound sailors can discard their heavy sweaters and don swim
suits. Thus, the rounding of this "turn in the road" is a crucial passage in
the transit of the U. S. Pacific Coast.

   Passage of this area is often easier when done at night. It can seem like
a long over-night trip when the fog is dense but by keeping a sharp look-out
and constant monitoring of the radar it can be safely accomplished. Care in
plotting one's position regularly is essential and good seamanship is crucial.

   Cojo Anchorage, just 1 1/2 miles east of Point Conception is convenient for
recovering from the passage when southbound or waiting for the right time to
start when northbound. You must work your way through the kelp beds and though
it can be very windy here, the water remains calm. It is difficult not to be
terrified by the night-time roar of trains, for they sound so close. The best
place to anchor is opposite a culvert under the railroad tracks in 5 fathoms,
hard sand. The large mooring buoys are for oil platform tenders which may
arrive at any hour. Little Old Cojo Cove, just over 3 miles east of Point
Conception should not be entered as it is foul.

   The first time we made the passage from Morro Bay to Santa Barbara we were
treated to one of nature's rare displays when passing through this area. The
fog was very dense but for several hours during the night our limited range of
visibility was lit by broad bands of underwater "sea-lights." The bands of
light were about 50 feet wide and were separated by unlit bands of about the
same width. Several dolphins which were zig-zagging across our bows ignored
the lights in their enthusiasm and added their own trail of phosphorescence to
the all-night show. On researching this unique display it was found that,
though rare, this light is produced under proper conditions by certain organ-
isms (dinoflagellates). This unforgettable experience was not repeated in any
of our other cruises nor have we heard of others who have enjoyed this awesome
display in this area. Yes, this part of the coast is full of surprises!

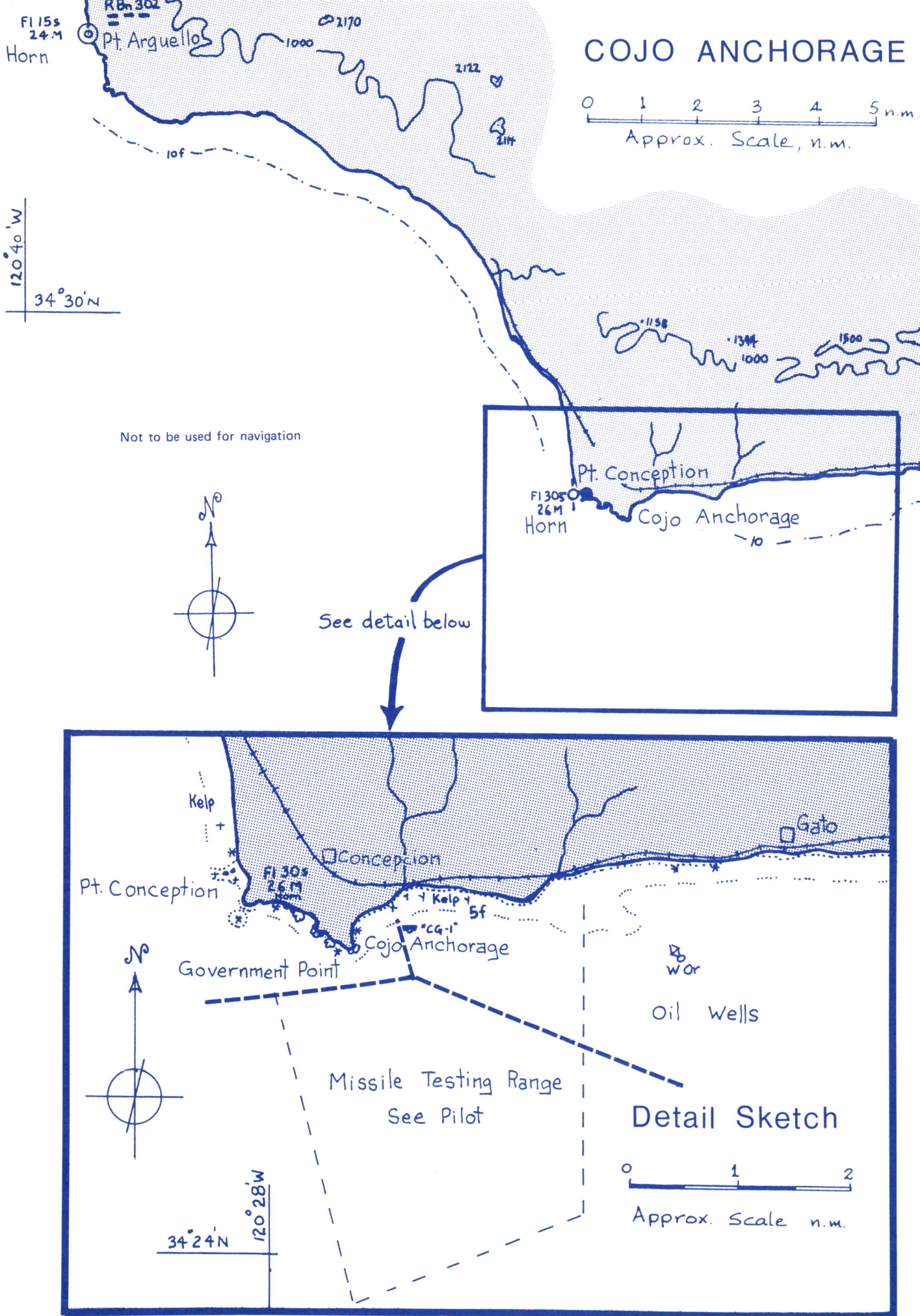

COJO ANCHORAGE

Fl 15s 24 M
Horn

R Bn 302

Pt. Arguello

2170

2122

1000

2114

10f

0 1 2 3 4 5 n.m.
Approx. Scale, n.m.

120°40'W

34°30'N

Not to be used for navigation

N

See detail below

Pt. Conception

Fl 30s 26 M
Horn

Cojo Anchorage

1158   1344   1500
1000

10

Kelp

+

Concepcion

Gato

Pt. Conception

Fl 30s 26 M

Kelp

5f

"CG-1"
Cojo Anchorage

N

Government Point

Wor

Oil Wells

Missile Testing Range
See Pilot

Detail Sketch

120°28'W

34°24'N

0   1   2
Approx. Scale   n.m.

SANTA BARBARA

   This attractive, affluent city marks the northern boundary of the Southern
California Coastal region. Over 200,000 pleasure boats are berthed in this
warm, sunny part of the state. The congestion in and near marinas and the
heavy boat traffic (especially on weekends) is normal for boaters in this area
but takes some getting used to for cruising vessels from elsewhere.

   Santa Barbara is 40 miles east of Cojo Anchorage and about 22 miles WNW of
Ventura. Santa Barbara Light is about 2 miles east of the harbor entrance.
Prominent from any direction are a hill about 1/2 mile NE of the light and the
many buildings of the city. This man-made harbor fights a continual battle
against the constant shoaling that occurs at the entrance to the harbor.

   A 500-yard rock breakwater built out from the shore joins a jetty across a
sand bar to protect the harbor from southerly weather. A light marks the
junction of the breakwater and jetty. Along the breakwater are over 100
flagpoles which make a colorful and distinctive honor guard for the harbor.
Stearns Wharf forms the northeast side of the harbor. A number of shops are
located on the wharf and a light, radiobeacon, and fog signal are at its
sseaward end. A 150 ft. groin extending south from the mid-northern shore has
a light at its tip.

   When entering follow the buoyed channel which passes between the sand bar
and Stearns Wharf before turning southwest into the harbor. The channel buoys
are not shown on the sketch as they are frequently altered to mark the changing
channel. Fog is a hazard especially from August to November. It is inadvisable to enter at night as the many city lights and masts within the harbor can
be confusing for a first-time visitor. Be sure to identify all lights and
follow the buoyed channel carefully. For current channel conditions contact
the harbormaster on Ch. 16; assistance on entering the harbor is given by a
Patrol Boat on request.

   Transient berths may be obtained by contacting the harbormaster; a hot-
berthing system is used so no reservations may be made. Rates are 40 cents per
foot per day and it doubles after 14 days. Showers, restrooms, chandlers, and
boat brokers are found on the breakwater. Fuel is available at Stearns Wharf
but propane is about 12 blocks away at a U-Haul Rental on Milpas Street or at
Van Gas.

   Anchorage may be taken east of Stearns Wharf (no closer than 300 ft.).
There is some surge but the area affords good protection from northwesterlies.
However, if Santana winds are predicted move to the marina.

   A very interesting stop-over can be enjoyed in Santa Barbara. Points of
interest include beautiful Mission Santa Barbara, the Museum of Natural History
(first-class in presentation and variety of exhibits), the Museum of Art,
Carriage Museum and the Botanical Gardens. The efficient bus system makes
travel easy in this clean city.

SANTA BARBARA, CA

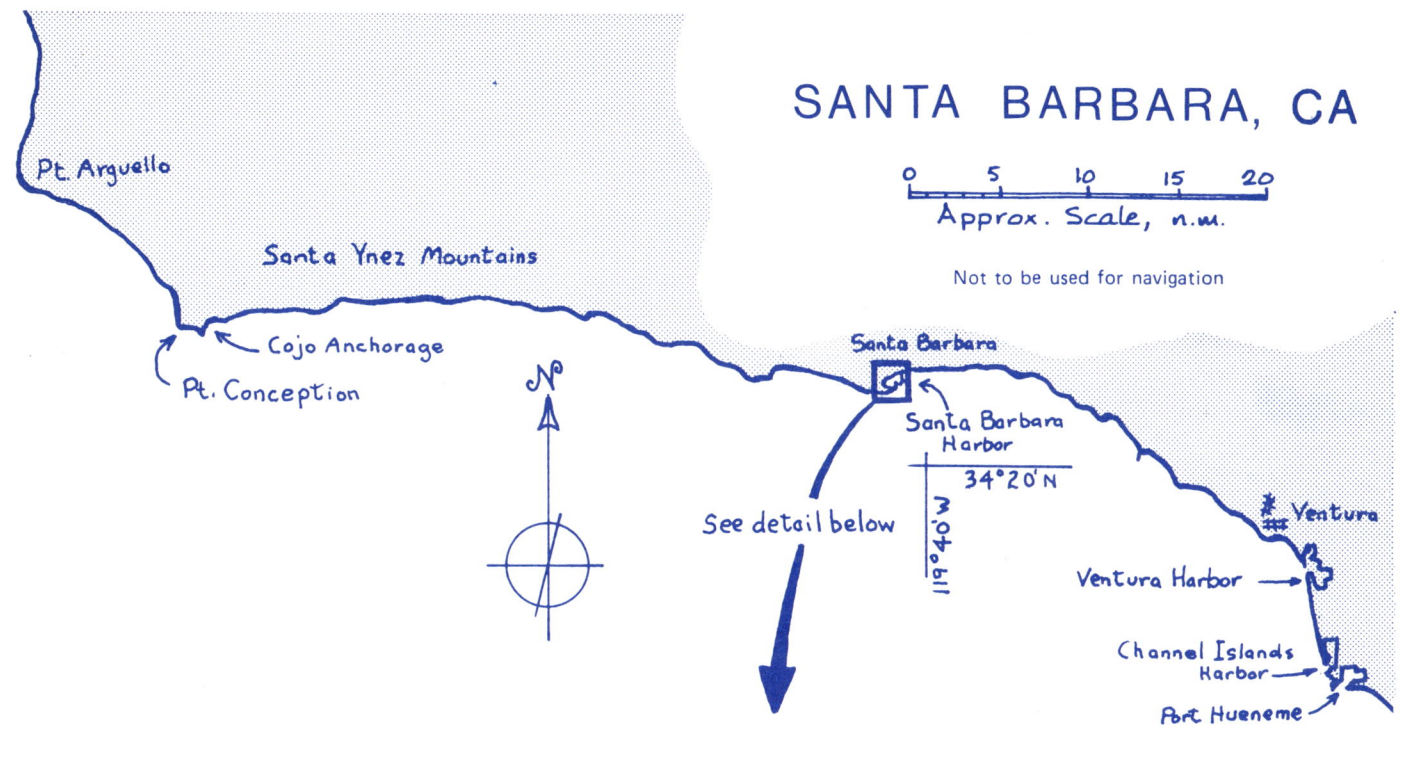

0   5   10   15   20
Approx. Scale, n.m.

Not to be used for navigation

Pt. Arguello

Santa Ynez Mountains

Cojo Anchorage

Pt. Conception

N

Santa Barbara

Santa Barbara Harbor

34°20'N

119°40'W

See detail below

Ventura

Ventura Harbor

Channel Islands Harbor

Port Hueneme

Harbor Details

0   500'   1000'
Approx. Scale - ft

Not to be used for navigation

Launching Ramp

Restrooms

Showers

Fuel Dock & Pumpout

Cafe

Naval Armory

Cafe & Restrooms

Harbormaster

Yacht Club

Restrooms & Showers

Qk Fl 5M "12"

Pile

E Int 6s 9 M

3f

G "3" Fl G 2.5s

RBn 294

Stearns Wharf

3f

3f

Fl R 6 7 M

3f

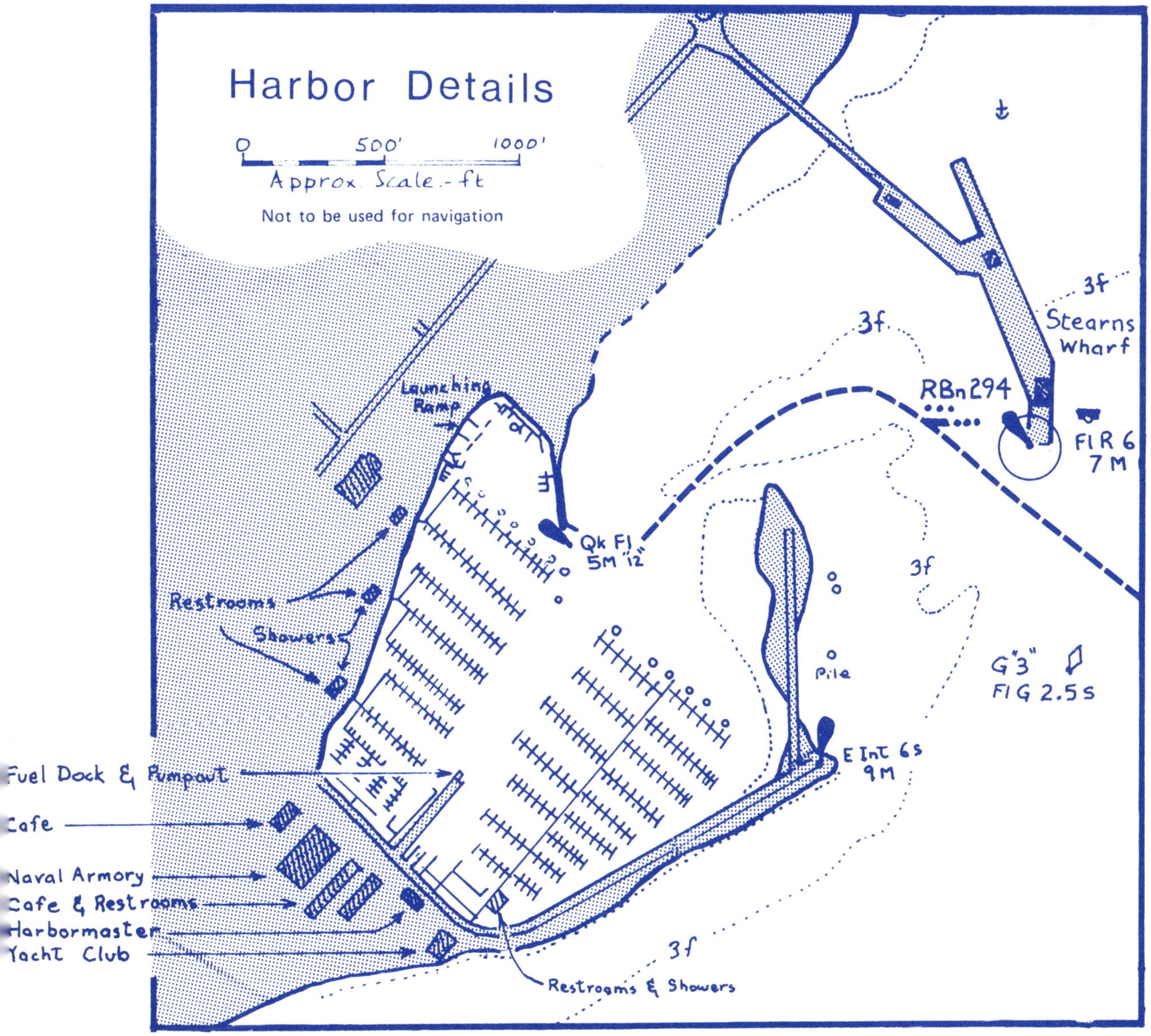

VENTURA

Avoid this harbor if strong westerlies are blowing as they may cause hazardous conditions and breakers at the entrance.

Ventura, just 13 miles east of Santa Barbara and 7 miles from Oxnard's Channel Islands Harbor is a well developed man-made harbor which along with its entrance, is dredged frequently to counter the effects of constant shoaling. It has commercial fish-handling facilities and also caters to pleasure craft, having accommodation for about 2,000 vessels. Weekend and summer traffic to the nearby Channel Islands of Santa Cruz and Anacapa is heavy. Seven miles to the SSE lies the deep-sea commercial terminal of Port Hueneme (Y-nee-mee) which has no small craft facilities.

Two landmarks of note are the large white cross on a hill northwest of the town and a large Holiday Inn Motel sign west of the pier. The entrance to the harbor lies between two lit jetties, the southern one also having a fog signal and radio beacon. A 1,500 ft. detached breakwater (lit only at the southern end) lies about 250 yards off the ends of the jetties.

When approaching the harbor, pick up Ventura Harbor Entrance lighted whistle buoy "2" which is about 3/4 miles southwest of the entrance. Proceed directly to the entrance, passing to the south of the detached breakwater before following the buoyed channel. Do NOT approach the entrance from the north as shoals prohibit passage in this area. Buoys marking the channel are frequently moved to mark the best part of the channel and so are not shown on the sketch.

Do not take chances here. Contact the harbormaster on Ch. 12, 16, or 73 for current entrance and harbor conditions. A patrol boat is on call 24 hours per day.

No transient berths are available from the harbormaster but one may tie up at his dock while making arrangements for moorage at one of the three large marinas in the harbor. Rates are about $15 per day with refundable deposits of about $25 for electronic cards or keys for use of restrooms, dock entry etc. All have first-class facilities, and marine supplies, repairs, fishing gear and hoists are available from the many boating businesses in the vicinity of the harbor. There are two fuel docks as shown on the sketch. See Appendix 2 for a keyed list of marina telephone numbers.

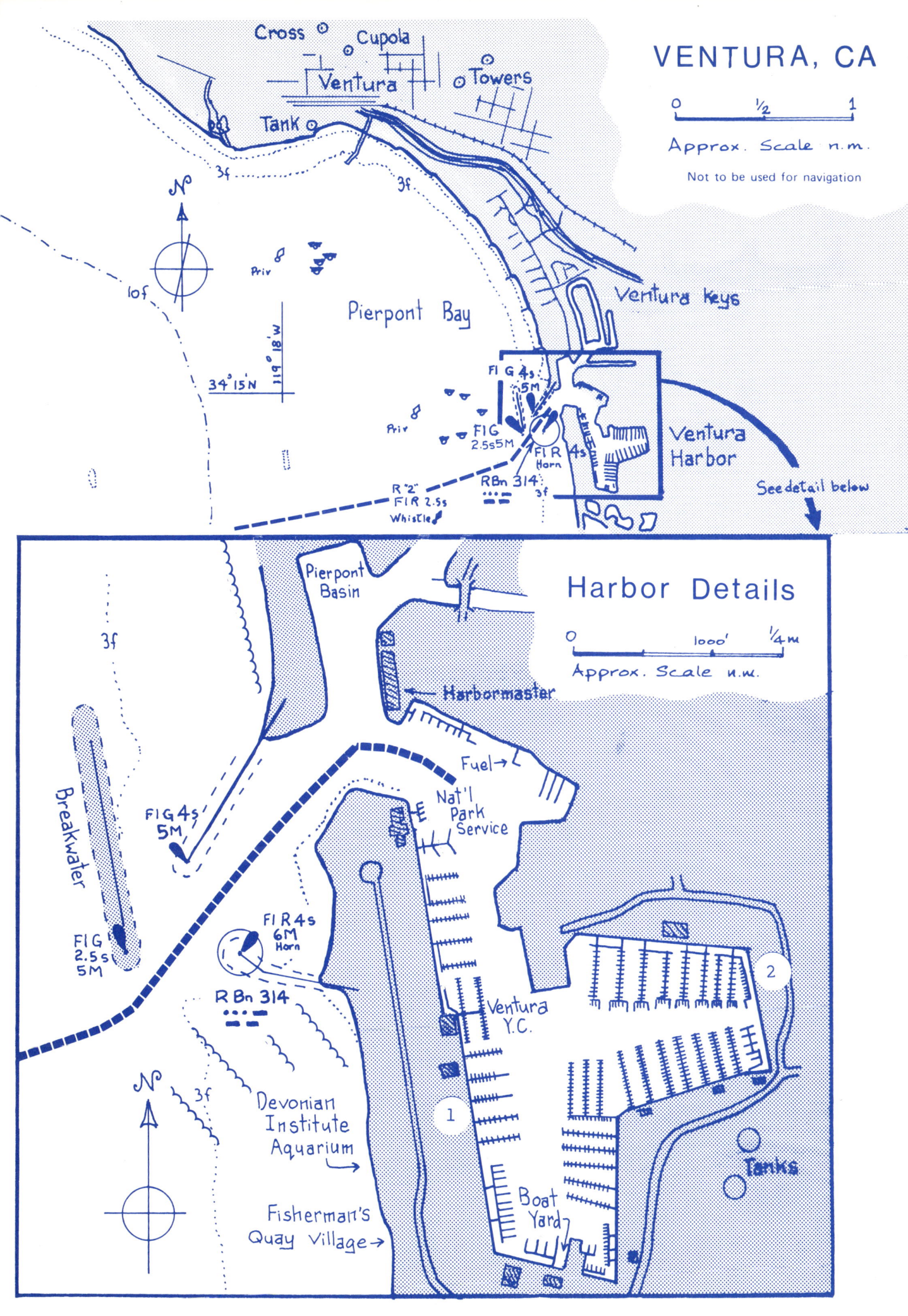

VENTURA, CA

0   ½   1

Approx. Scale n.m.

Not to be used for navigation

Cross ⊙
Cupola ⊙
⊙ Towers
Ventura
Tank
3f
3f

N

Priv

lof

Pierpont Bay

119°18'W

34°15'N

Ventura Keys

Fl G 4s
5M

Fl G
2.5s 5M

Priv

Fl R 4s
Horn

Ventura Harbor

R "2"
Fl R 2.5s
Whistle

R Bn 314

3f

See detail below

Harbor Details

0   1000'   ¼ m

Approx. Scale n.m.

Pierpont Basin

3f

← Harbormaster

Fuel →

Breakwater

Fl G 4s
5M

Nat'l Park Service

Fl R 4s
6M
Horn

Fl G
2.5s
5M

R Bn 314

2

N

3f

Ventura Y.C.

Devonian Institute Aquarium →

1

Tanks

Fisherman's Quay Village →

Boat Yard

OXNARD (CHANNEL ISLANDS HARBOR)

Aptly named because of its close proximity to the beautiful Channel Islands which are just across Santa Barbara Channel, Oxnard's Channel Islands Harbor is home to over 2,000 pleasure craft. It is devoted to the yachting and sportsfishing community -- five yacht clubs are based here: Channel Islands, Anacapa, Bahai, Cabrillo, Pacific Corinthian, and Islander. The harbor is almost 8 miles southeast of Ventura and about 42 miles northwest of Marina del Rey.

One mile to the SSE lies the deep-sea commercial terminal of Port Hueneme (y-nee-mee) which has no small craft facilities. Only in the event of an extreme emergency should a cruising vessel enter this port.

Two jetties extending southwesterly from the beach protect the entrance channel of **Channel Islands Harbor.** A detached breakwater is seaward of the ends of the jetties. The ends of both jetties and each end of the breakwater are marked by lights. The seaward end of the south jetty also has a fog signal and a radiobeacon. To enter go around either end of the breakwater before following the buoys through the channel. Shoaling occurs southeast of the entrance; caution is advised when entering.

Contact the Coast Guard for advice on channel entrance information if this is your first entry. Fog can be a problem from July to October so be sure your navigation is accurate.

Having 40 slips available for transients this is a popular stop-over for cruising sailors. Contact the harbormaster on Ch. 12 or 16 for berth assignment. In addition, the private marinas usually have transient slips for $8 to $10 (or more) per night depending on size and availability. Fuel, repairs, and all boating needs can easily be met by the many nautical businesses in the harbor.

Oxnard is the central California home port of the state tallship, "Californian," an awesome replica of the 1849 Revenue Cutter, "Lawrence." Sponsored by the Nautical Heritage Society, this beautiful boat is used as a training ship for young people.

The "Californian"

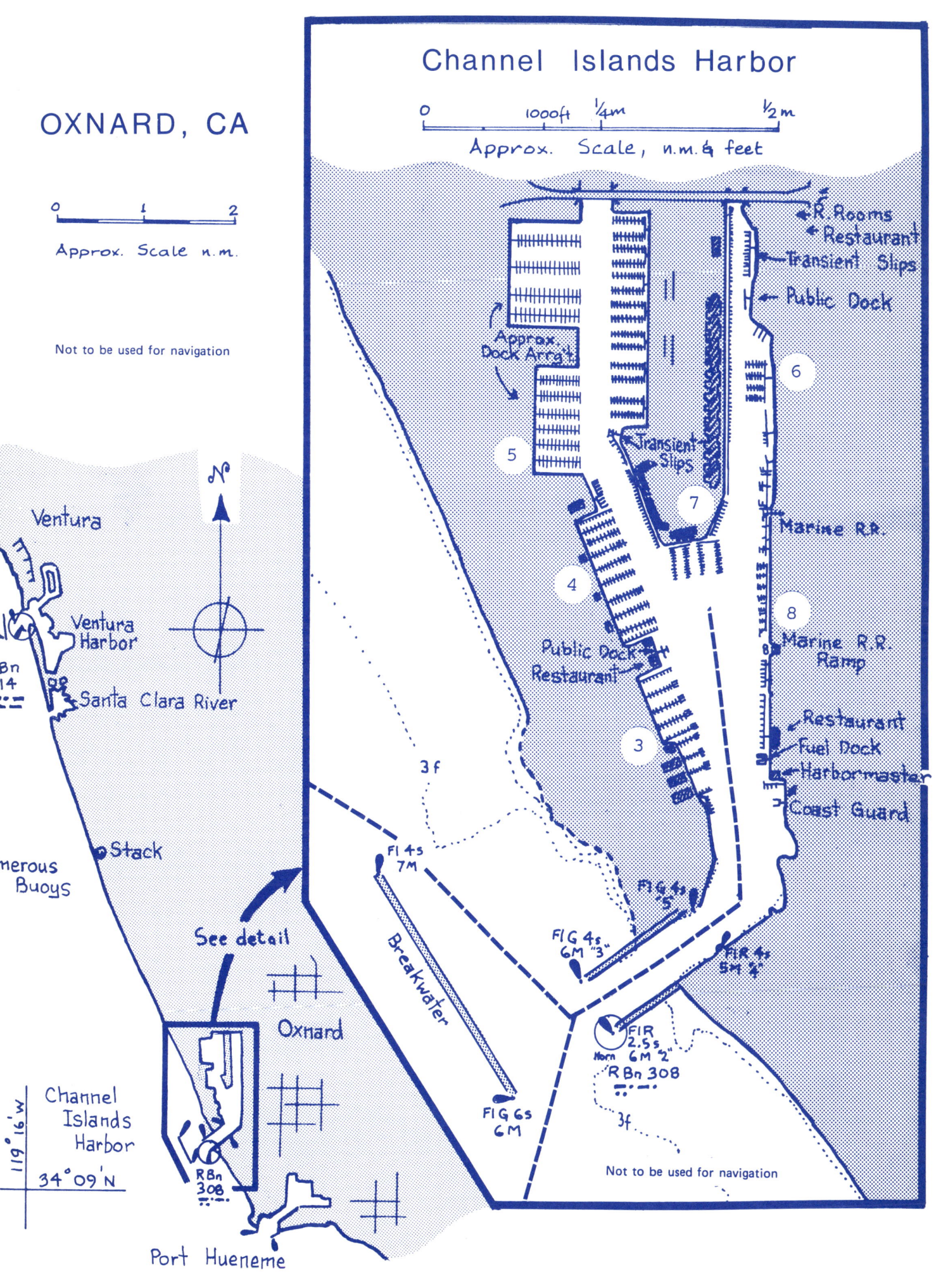

OXNARD, CA

0   1   2
Approx. Scale n.m.

Not to be used for navigation

Channel Islands Harbor

0   1000ft   1/4m   1/2m
Approx. Scale, n.m. & feet

R.Rooms
Restaurant
Transient Slips
Public Dock

6

Approx.
Dock Arr'g't

5

Transient
Slips

7

4

Marine R.R.

8

Public Dock
Restaurant

Marine R.R.
Ramp

3

Restaurant
Fuel Dock
Harbormaster
Coast Guard

Ventura

Ventura Harbor

Bn
14

Santa Clara River

Stack

merous
Buoys

See detail

Oxnard

Breakwater

Channel
Islands
Harbor

34°09'N

119°16'W

R Bn
308

Port Hueneme

3 f

Fl 4s
7M

Fl G 4s
"5"

Fl G 4s
6M "3"

Fl R 4s
5M "4"

Fl R
2.5s
6M "2"
Horn
R Bn 308

3 f

Not to be used for navigation

Fl G 6s
6M

LOS ANGELES AND LONG BEACH

The combination of Los Angeles and Long Beach forms the densest and largest population and commercial concentration on the Pacific Coast. Within this 35 miles of coastline are found two of the largest deep-sea ports on the Pacific Coast: Los Angeles has over 100 cargo-sized piers and wharves while Long Beach has 70.

Because of the heavy international and intercoastal traffic extreme caution must be exercised when transiting this area. Take note of the Traffic Separation Scheme in effect and don't linger in the busy lanes and Precautionary Zones. When crossing traffic lanes do so quickly and at a right angle. Always give way to large ocean-going vessels as they have difficulty maneuvering in the confined traffic lanes and need a great distance to stop. For them the many pleasure craft hereabouts are an annoying blip on the radar screen which may not be noticed.

In addition to heavy commercial traffic a large number of recreational vessels are headquartered in this area. Weekend traffic of small craft is aptly referred to as the LA Marine Freeway. To satisfy the needs of such a large number of boaters, small craft facilities have been developed in every possible space. Accommodation in over 20,000 wet berths is to be found at Marina del Rey, Redondo Beach (King Harbor), San Pedro, Los Angeles Harbor, Long Beach Harbor, and Alamitos Bay.

Because of the demands of a large and steadily increasing boating population, moorage is expensive, sometimes $10 or more per foot per month, and the waiting period may be as much as 4 or 5 years for certain sizes of boats. Such pressure from boaters wanting permanent moorage makes it easy to understand the very limited number of slips that are set aside for transients. Municipal docks vary in their allotment of space for transients, though temporary moorage may be obtained from most private marinas on a hot-berthing basis.

This guide will cover public marina facilities but will not give rates and details related to the many private marinas, since they change so quickly. A marina in Marina del Rey increased its rates three times in one year, so it is impossible for a guide such as this to keep up to date. A list of marinas along with their current telephone number is given in Appendix 2. This list is probably already out of date at the time of printing, but it does give a possible starting point for a cruiser wanting temporary moorage.

In addition to congested commercial and pleasure boat traffic the weather deserves some comment. Though fog is more common during the fall and winter months, visibility is often reduced during summer months by a greyish-brown haze. Another concern is the short warning period that weather forecasts can give of the onset of Santa Ana winds. These offshore desert winds may reach 50 knots or more in a very short time and may extend as much as 50 miles offshore.

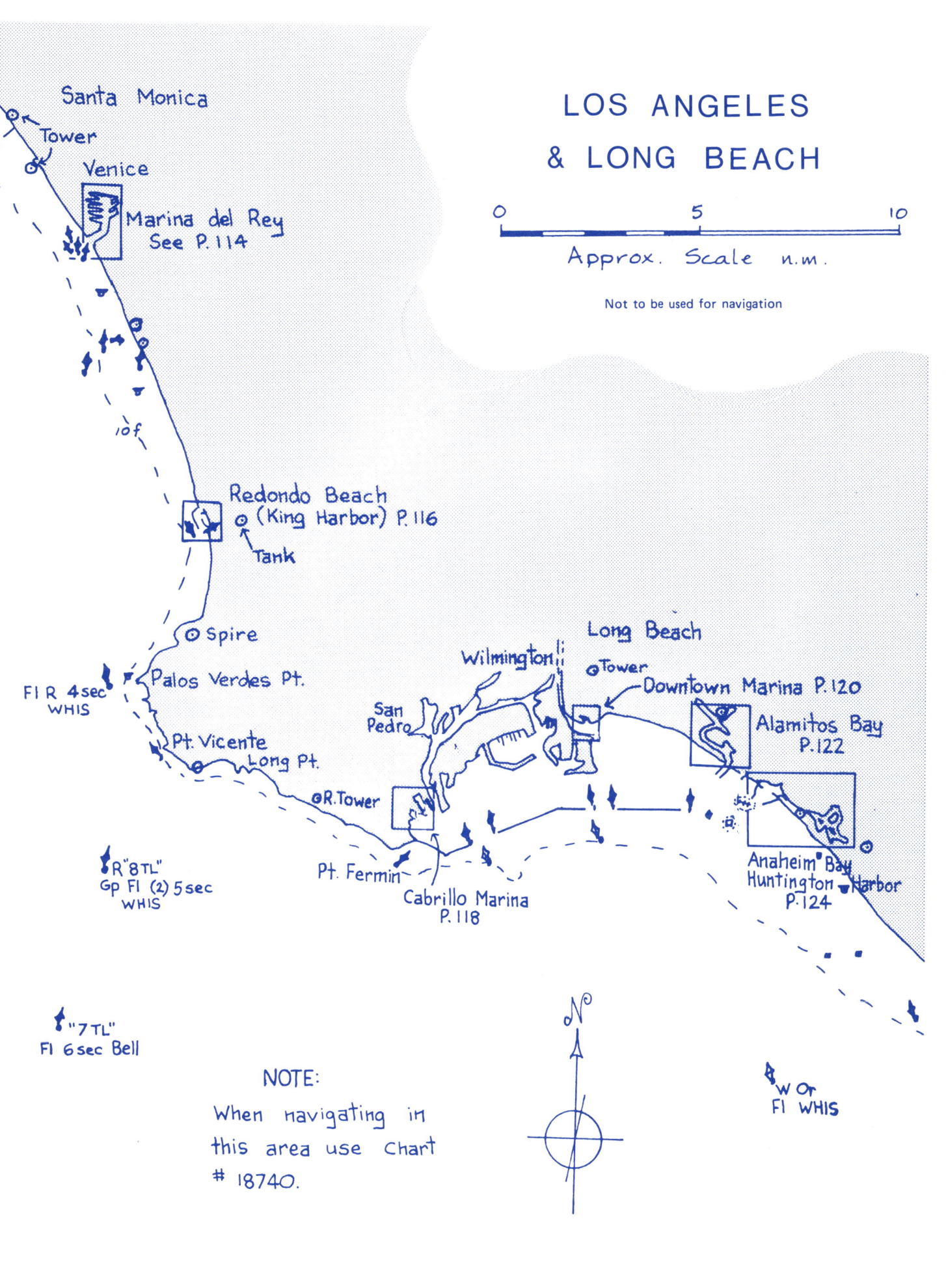

LOS ANGELES
& LONG BEACH

Approx. Scale n.m.

Not to be used for navigation

Santa Monica
Tower
Venice
Marina del Rey
See P. 114

10 f

Redondo Beach
(King Harbor) P. 116
Tank

Spire
Palos Verdes Pt.
FI R 4 sec
WHIS
Pt. Vicente
Long Pt.

R "8TL"
Gp Fl (2) 5 sec
WHIS

"7 TL"
Fl 6 sec Bell

Wilmington
Long Beach
Tower
Downtown Marina P. 120
San Pedro
Alamitos Bay
P. 122

R. Tower

Pt. Fermin
Cabrillo Marina
P. 118

Anaheim Bay
Huntington Harbor
P. 124

N

W Or
Fl WHIS

NOTE:
When navigating in
this area use Chart
18740.

MARINA DEL REY

Home port to over 6,000 pleasure boats, this is the ultimate marine basin. Administered by the County of Los Angeles, it is an immense center devoted to yachting with 9 yacht clubs and 16 marinas based here. It is favorably located some distance from the activity of commercial traffic in the Los Angeles/Long Beach Harbor area while being conveniently close to the cruising offered in the offshore islands. It is about 42 miles ESE of Channel Islands Harbor and 8 miles NNW of Redondo Beach (King Harbor).

Landmarks in the area include the long Santa Monica pier 3 1/2 miles to the northwest, and the shorter Venice pier 1 mile to the north. Three miles south of the entrance are two prominent stacks at El Segundo, and lighted bell buoy "2ES" which is about 2 miles offshore. Two jetties with lights at their seaward ends protect the channel entrance; a fog signal and radiobeacon are also found at the end of the northern jetty. A detached breakwater having lights at both ends is seaward of the ends of the jetties.

When approaching, a vessel must use the northern entrance as there is shoaling between the south jetty and the end of the breakwater. No anchoring is allowed in the restricted area shoreward of the offshore breakwater and the most seaward 1,000 ft. of the entrance channel. A dredged channel between the two jetties leads into the basin. Traffic separation lanes have been established in the entrance channel where lanes are marked by buoys labelled, "No Sail." The center lane between the buoys is used by vessels under sail power alone, both entering and leaving the harbor, while the outer lanes are used by vessels under power or motorsailing.

A pergola and an impressive statue of a helmsman are seen at Chace Park where moorage is available for about 30 transient boats. Contact the harbormaster (Ch. 16) for berth allocation. Rates are 40 cents per foot per day from November 1 to April 30, and 50 cents per foot per day from May 1 to October 31. A refundable $5 deposit is required for the key to showers and restrooms. The closest laundromat is 4 blocks away at Villa Marina Shopping Center, 13175 Mindanao Way.

In an emergency, anchorage can be taken in the northern part of the main channel. Permission must be obtained from the harbormaster and fore and aft anchors are required.

Two fuel docks in the basin and all boating needs can be met by the many boat-oriented businesses hereabouts. Propane is available at Marina Boat and RV Storage (823-7979). A 24-hour grocery store is in the Marina Shopping Center at Mindanao and Admiralty. Many restaurants and specialty shops line the harbor and make shore trips rather interesting.

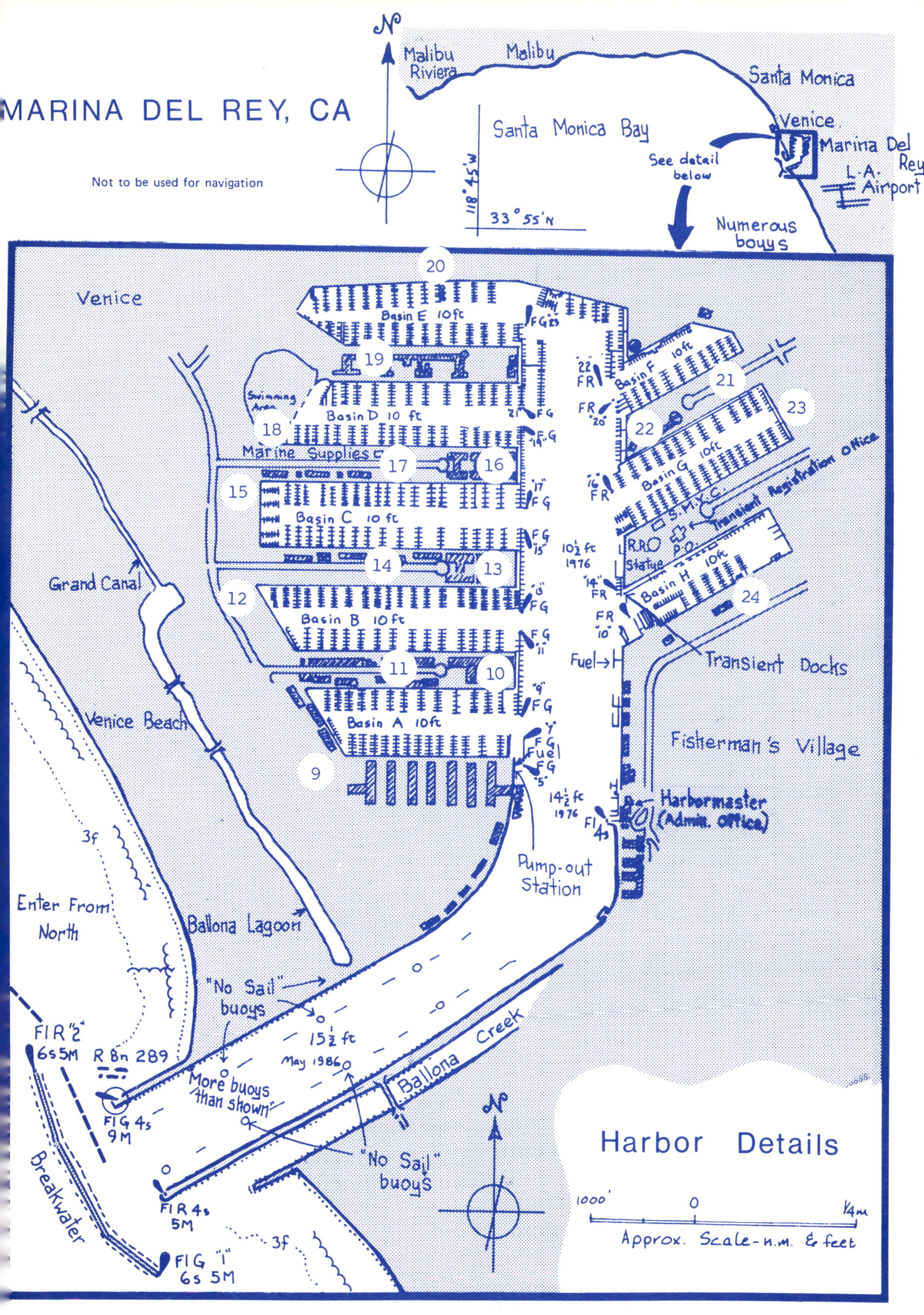

MARINA DEL REY, CA

Not to be used for navigation

N

Malibu Riviera
Malibu
Santa Monica
Santa Monica Bay
See detail below
Venice
Marina Del Rey
L.A. Airport
Numerous bouys

118° 45' W

33° 55' N

Venice

20

Basin E 10ft
F G "23"
19
Swimming Area
Basin D 10 ft
18
Marine Supplies
17   16
Basin F 10ft
22 FR
FR "20"
21
23
22
Basin G 10ft
"16" FR
Transient Registration Office

15
Basin C 10 ft
14   13
12
Basin B 10 ft
11   10
Basin A 10ft
9
"21" F G
"19" F G
"17" F G
F G "15"
"13" F G
F G "11"
"9" F G
"7" F G
Fuel F G "5"

10½ ft 1976
R.R.O P.O.
S.M.C.
Statue
Basin H 10ft
24
"14" FR
FR "10"
Fuel→

Transient Docks
Fisherman's Village

Grand Canal

Venice Beach

Ballona Lagoon

Enter From North

3f

"No Sail" buoys

15½ ft May 1986

More buoys than shown

"No Sail" buoys

Ballona Creek

14½ ft 1976
Fl 4s
Harbormaster (Adm. Office)

Pump-out Station

Fl R "2" 6s 5M
R Bn 289
Fl G 4s 9M
Fl R 4s 5M
Breakwater
Fl G "1" 6s 5M
3f

N

Harbor Details

1000'   0   ¼ m
Approx. Scale - n.m. & feet

REDONDO BEACH (KING HARBOR)

This man-made harbor was widely televised in January, 1988 as it suffered millions of dollars worth of damage in the violent storm which struck the Californian coast. The breakwater protecting the harbor was breached in several places, boats were sunk, and 200 ft. of the pier were destroyed. Repairs now being made will return the harbor to its normal status. However, under normal weather conditions there are no problems in entering or using this harbor.

Just 8 miles south of Marina del Rey and about 20 miles around Palos Verdes Point from Los Angeles Harbor, King Harbor is a moorage devoted to pleasure craft. Eight large powerplant smokestacks at the north end of the harbor make this an easy spot to identify. A private light is shown from the top of the powerplant.

Two breakwaters having lights at their tips protect the entrance to the harbor; the eastern breakwater also has a radiobeacon and fog signal at the light. The western breakwater is about 1,200 ft. long and curves from the north end of the harbor in a roughly SSE direction to give protection to the three basins.

Some areas to avoid: When approaching from the north do not pass within the 9-fathom line as there are underwater hazards in this area. The areas to the south of the eastern breakwater should also be avoided as shoaling occurs in that location. The sports fishing barges anchored up to 2 miles offshore during summer months should also be given a wide berth. However, the restricted area shown offshore and to the south of Marina del Rey does not apply to recreational craft.

When approaching from any direction pick up lighted bell buoy "1" which is about 230 yards SSW of the tip of the western breakwater, then proceed to the entrance. Fog and haze may reduce visibility especially during summer months. Natural oil seepage results in gas bubbles, blobs of oil, or a thin film of oil on the water in an area 1 1/2 to 4 miles offshore.

Though no transient slips are available from the harbormaster, a large area inside the south end of the breakwater affords good anchorage. To anchor, one must obtain the harbormaster's permission; bow and stern anchors are required and there is a 72-hour limit. When available, transient berths can be obtained from the private marinas, and two yacht clubs are based in the harbor. Fuel, marine supplies, hoists and most cruising needs can be met in the vicinity.

REDONDO BEACH, CA

0   ½   1
Approx. Scale n.m.

Not to be used for navigation

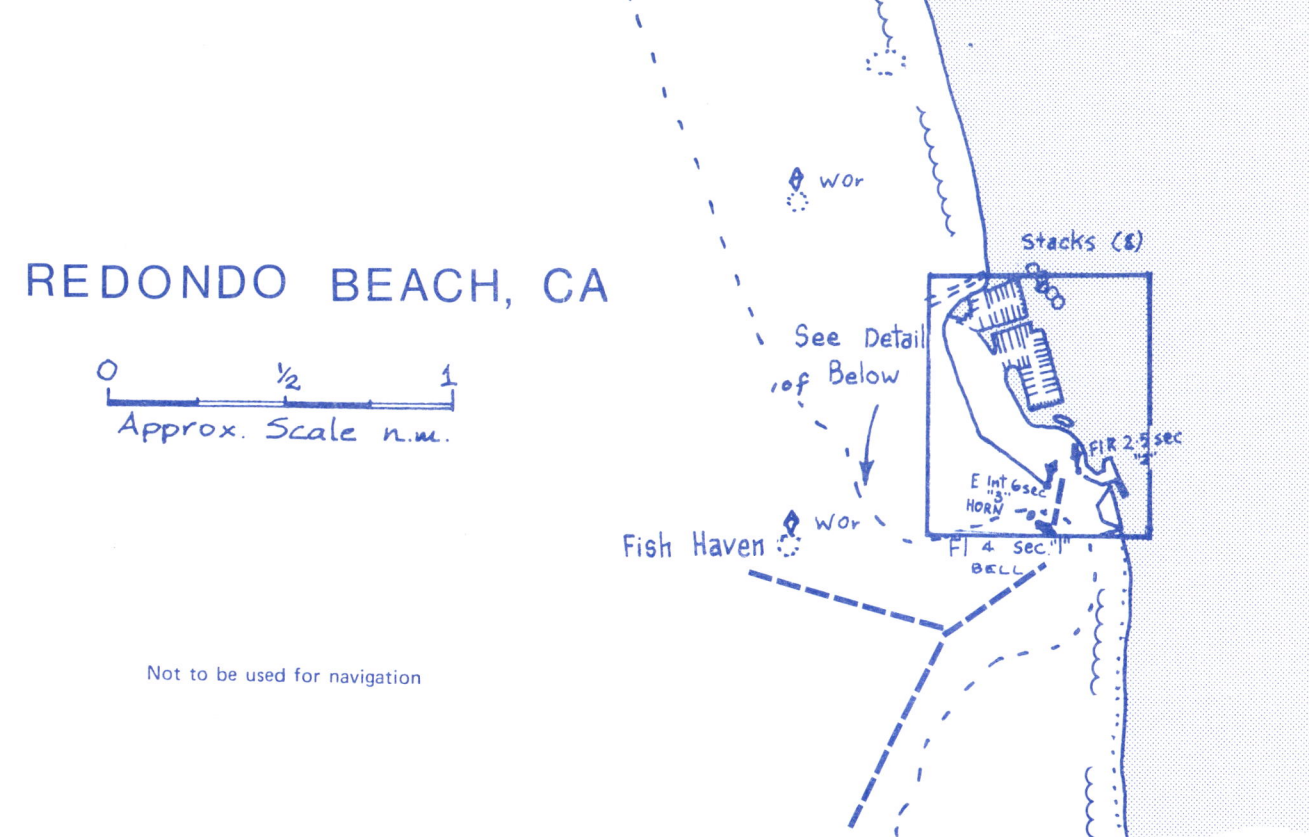

Stacks (8)

See Detail of Below

Wor

Fl R 2.5 sec "4"

E Int 6sec "3" HORN

Fish Haven   Wor

Fl 4 sec "1" BELL

King Harbor Y.C. Fl G "7"

Redondo Beach

5

Fl R "2"

Harbormaster
Pump-out
FG "1"

Mooring buoys

Fuel

Fl R "3"

Breakwater

7

Fl R

7

Fl R 2.5 sec "2"

Fuel

7

E Int 6 sec "3"
HORN

KING HARBOR

0   1000'   ¼m
Approx. Scale n.m.
Not to be used for navigation

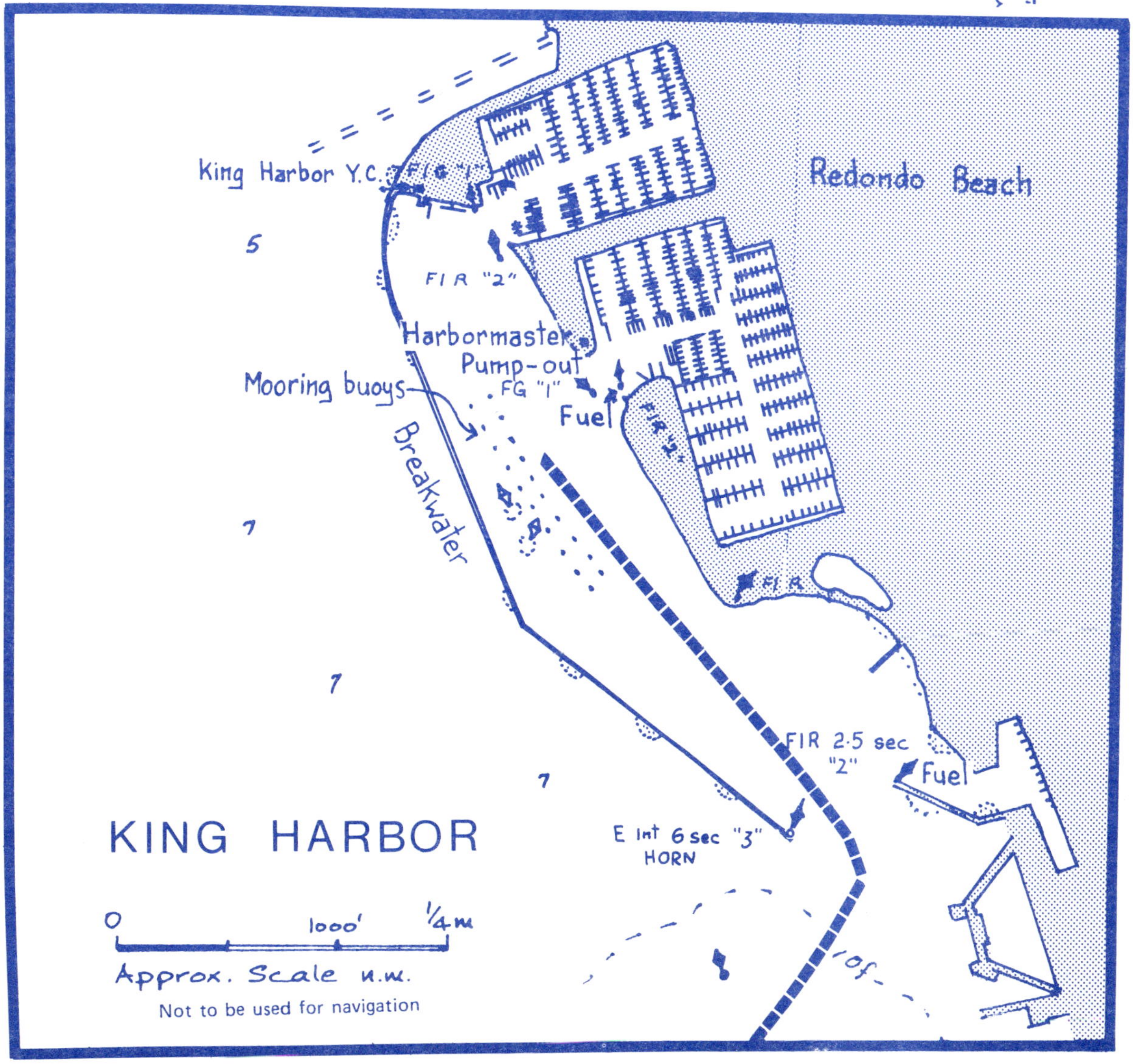

LOS ANGELES HARBOR

Los Angeles Harbor has extensive port facilities developed for commercial purposes. Yacht slips, now numbering over 4,000, have had to compete for space in a long-established port. Transient cruising vessels are not a high priority to this busy harbor and as a result there is a grand total of 1 public slip allocated for visiting yachts. Many private marinas have waiting lists for as much as 3 years for permanent moorage. As berths become temporarily available transients may obtain moorage at these marinas on an overnight basis. Unless a cruising vessel has made prior arrangements this is not a harbor to visit expecting to find moorage without a search.

Located just to the east of Point Fermin, Los Angeles Harbor is adjacent to Long Beach Harbor. When fog or haze are not present San Pedro Hill, about 3 1/2 miles northwest of Point Fermin, is the most noticeable feature in the San Pedro Bay area. Atop the hill are two white radar domes. Point Fermin, the southern end of San Pedro Hill, has a light, and the eye-catching pavilion housing the Korean Bell of Friendship is just to the north of the light. Other prominent landmarks are shown on the sketch.

The harbor area is protected by two large breakwaters: San Pedro Breakwater curves out from Point Fermin for almost 2 miles and has a radiobeacon, fog signal and Los Angeles Light at its tip. Middle Breakwater (detached) protects the outer Los Angeles and Long Beach Harbors for about 3 miles: it has a light at each end. Another short breakwater gives protection to the moorage area at the western end of Cabrillo Marina, while a launching ramp and short fishing pier are built out from Cabrillo Beach.

Great care must be taken not to impede the flow of traffic when transiting the harbor entrance. Facilities in San Pedro are under the jurisdiction of the Los Angeles Harbor Commission and Cabrillo Marina is the newly constructed public marina, having one slip available for transients. The rate charged is 30 cents per foot for a maximum of 3 days. Temporary emergency anchorage is available off Cabrillo Beach but one must apply for a permit at the Port of Los Angeles Administrative Office, 425 South Palos Verdes (or phone 519-3566). The buoys in the outer basin are for use with permission of the harbormaster who may be contacted on Ch. 16.

Of the numerous interesting and varied attractions in Los Angeles a few are listed here: the Los Angeles Museum of Natural History, Los Angeles A Museum of Art, George C. Page Museum of La Brea Discoveries, Los Angeles State Arboretum, Virginia Robinson Gardens, South Coast Botanic Garden, and the Descanso Gardens. Attractions of an entertainment nature include: Magic Mountain, tours of Universal Studios or NBC Studio, Marineland, Knott's Berry Farm, Disneyland, as well as countless nightclubs, bars, and other attractions.

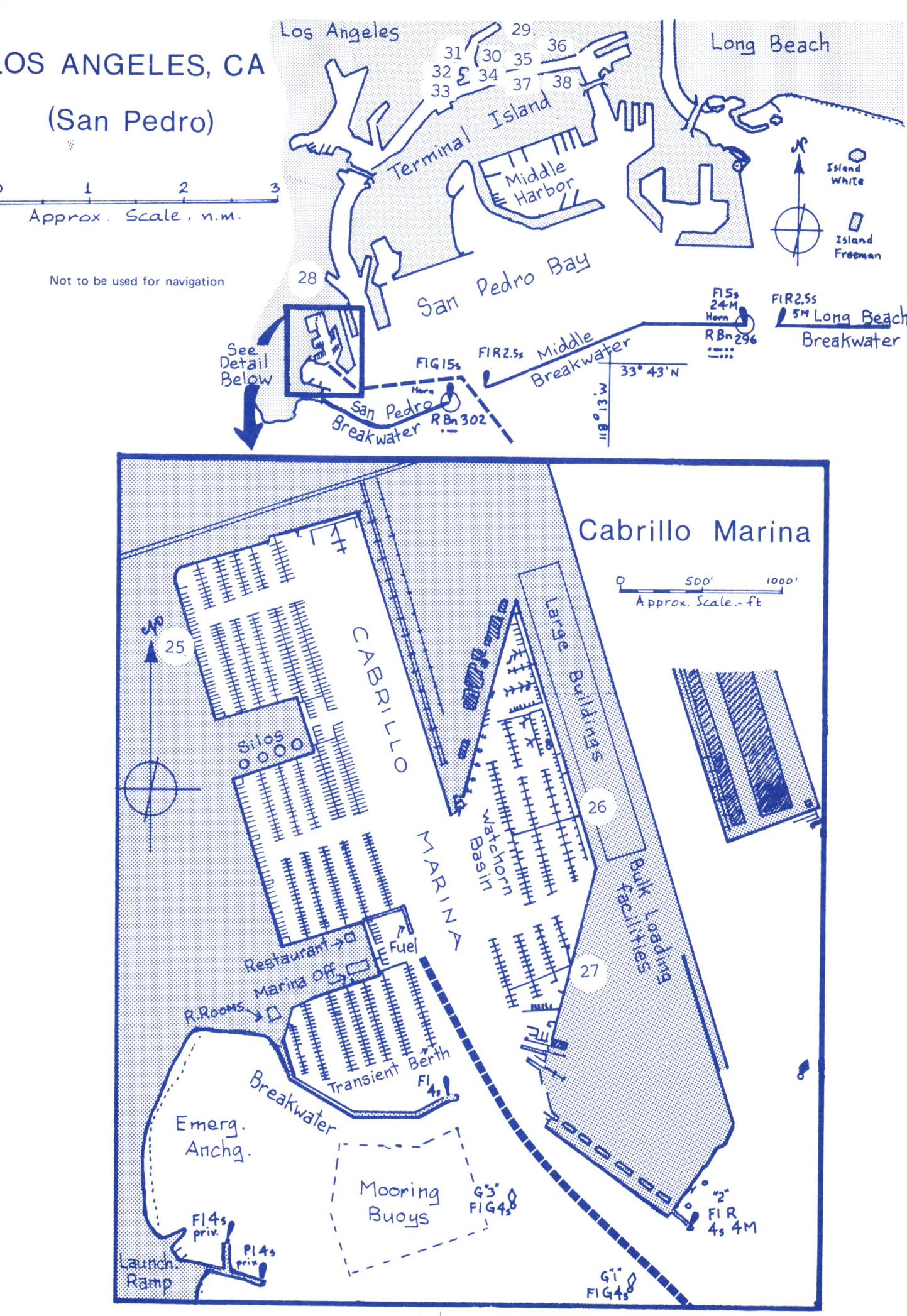

LOS ANGELES, CA

(San Pedro)

Approx. Scale, n.m.

Not to be used for navigation

Los Angeles

Long Beach

Terminal Island

Middle Harbor

San Pedro Bay

Island White

Island Freeman

Fl 5s 24M Horn
R Bn 296

Fl R 2.5s
5M Long Beach Breakwater

Fl G 15s
Fl R 2.5s Middle Breakwater

33° 43'N

118° 13' W

See Detail Below

San Pedro Breakwater
Horn
R Bn 302

Cabrillo Marina

Approx. Scale - ft

CABRILLO

MARINA

Large Buildings

Silos

Watchorn Basin

Bulk Loading Facilities

Restaurant
Fuel
Marina Off.

R.Rooms

Breakwater

Transient Berth

Fl 4s

Emerg. Anchg.

Mooring Buoys

G"3"
Fl G 4s

"2"
Fl R 4s 4M

Fl 4s priv.

Fl 4s priv.

Launch Ramp

G"1"
Fl G 4s

LONG BEACH

The Long Beach Harbor entrance is just 4 miles east of the Los Angeles Harbor entrance. Protecting the harbor is the Long Beach Breakwater which is about 2 miles long and is lit at both ends. The 4-mile long Middle Breakwater gives protection to both Long Beach and Los Angeles Harbors. Terminal Island, a cluster of huge port facilities shared by both harbors is beyond this breakwater. The two most eye-catching landmarks are the white dome of the Spruce Goose and the massive bulk of the Queen Mary.

The entrance to the harbor lies between the eastern end of Middle Breakwater and Long Beach Breakwater. As this is a very busy container cargo port a cruising vessel must take care not to impede the large vessels moving about the harbor. The entrance to small craft facilities is shown on the sketch.

There are two municipal small craft facilities in Long Beach Harbor: the **Downtown Marina** on Queensway Bay and Long Beach Marina in **Alamitos Bay**. In addition there are many private marinas, yacht clubs and small craft facilities scattered around the various channels. Over 6,000 pleasure craft moor in Long Beach waters. Both municipal marinas allow transients to berth at end-ties at 50 cents per foot for a maximum of 15 consecutive days per month. A $15 refundable deposit is required for washroom keys. Reservations two weeks in advance (with the first day prepaid) are allowed for vessels whose home port is 100 or more miles distant. For reservations write to: Downtown Marina, 450 Eaast Shoreline Drive, Long Beach, CA 90802.

The entrance to the Downtown Marina is between Island Grissom and the curved breakwater which forms the southwestern edge of the basin. Do not attempt to enter between the NE side of Island Grissom and the breakwater forming the eastern edge of the basin. A dangerous wreck is 1/2 mile SSW of the entrance and a sunken wreck is reported about 1/5 mile to the west.

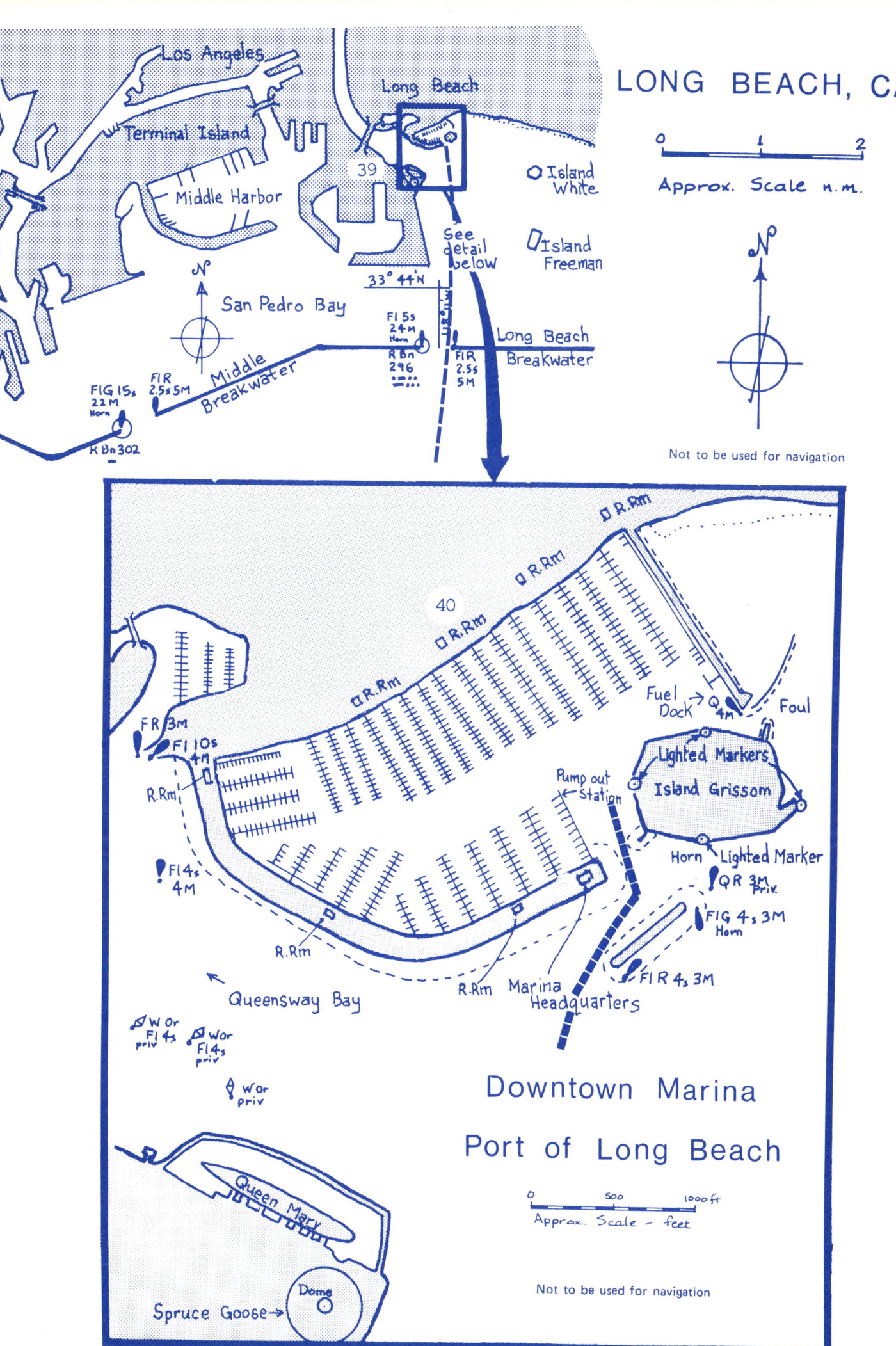

LONG BEACH, CA

Los Angeles
Long Beach
Terminal Island
Middle Harbor
39
See detail below
33° 44'N
San Pedro Bay
N
Middle Breakwater
Fl 5s 24m Horn
R Bn 296
FlR 2.5s 5M
Long Beach Breakwater
FIG 15s 22M Horn
FlR 2.5s 5M
R Bn 302
Island White
Island Freeman

0   1   2
Approx. Scale n.m.

N

Not to be used for navigation

40
R.Rm
R.Rm
R.Rm
R.Rm
R.Rm
R.Rm
R.Rm
Fuel Dock
Q 4m
Foul
FR 3M
Fl 10s 4M
R.Rm
Fl 4s 4M
R.Rm
Lighted Markers
Island Grissom
Pump out station
Horn   Lighted Marker
QR 3M Priv.
FIG 4s 3M Horn
R.Rm   Marina Headquarters
FlR 4s 3M
Queensway Bay
W Or Fl 4s priv
W Or Fl 4s priv
W Or priv

Downtown Marina
Port of Long Beach

0   500   1000 ft
Approx. Scale - feet

Queen Mary
Spruce Goose →
Dome

Not to be used for navigation

The **Long Beach Municipal Marina** in **Alamitos Bay** is 3 1/4 miles to the south of the Downtown Marina and 15 miles northwest of Newport Bay. Three man-made offshore oil drilling islands in the vicinity are named after astronauts who died while on duty, Islands White, Freman, and Chaffee. Entrance to the bay is between two jetties which are about 1/2 mile north of Seal Beach pier. Both jetties are lit at their seaward ends, and the western jetty also has a fog signal. Propane is reported to be available in Alamitos Bay at the fuel dock.

The two attractions unique to Long Beach are the Spruce Goose and the Queen Mary; a visit is very interesting though at $14.50 per person it is expensive for a large crew. Moorages most convenient to the Queen Mary are the 40 buoys in the Queensway Bay Moorage. During weekends and holidays the chances of picking up a mooring are unlikely, but reservations may be made by contacting Queensway Bay Hilton Marina, 700 Queensway Drive, Long Beach, CA 90801 (Ph. 213-436-0411). The charges vary with the length of vessel; 1988 fees are $14 per day for a 34 ft. boat with a 30-day limit.

Other points of interest accessible from Long Beach are listed in Los Angeles at the end of the preceding page. In the immediate area, Shoreline Village (directly across the harbor from the Queen Mary) has many fascinating shops as well as an operating wooden carousel dating from 1906.

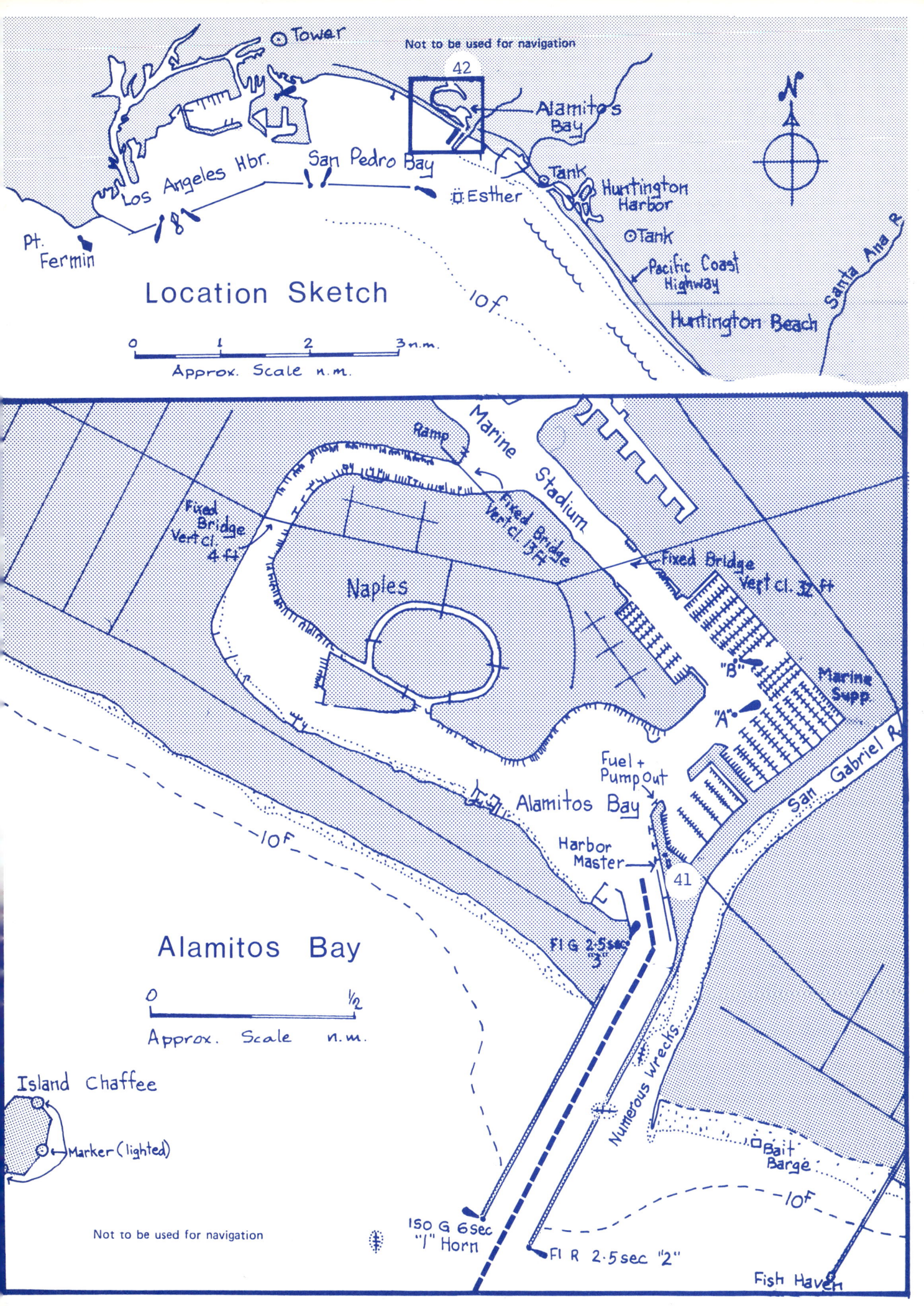

Location Sketch

Tower

Not to be used for navigation

42

Alamitos Bay

Los Angeles Hbr.   San Pedro Bay

Pt. Fermin

☐ Esther

Tank

Huntington Harbor

Tank

Pacific Coast Highway

Santa Ana R.

Huntington Beach

10f

N

0   1   2   3 n.m.

Approx. Scale n.m.

Ramp

Marine Stadium

Fixed Bridge Vert cl. 4 ft

Fixed Bridge Vert cl. 15 ft

Fixed Bridge Vert cl. 32 ft

Naples

"B"

"A"

Marine Supp.

Fuel + Pump out

Alamitos Bay

San Gabriel R.

Harbor Master

41

Fl G 2·5 sec "3"

Alamitos Bay

0   ½

Approx. Scale   n.m.

Island Chaffee

Marker (lighted)

Numerous wrecks

Bait Barge

10f

10f

Not to be used for navigation

Iso G 6 sec "1" Horn

Fl R 2·5 sec "2"

Fish Haven

ANAHEIM BAY (HUNTINGTON HARBOUR)

A coastal cruising vessel may well bypass this harbor since it is the site
of a U.S. Naval Weapons Station and as a result has numerous restrictions.
Another factor limiting use of facilities is the 23 ft. vertical clearance on a
bridge crossing the channel leading to the marinas. Close to the Los Angeles/
Long Beach conglomeration, Anaheim Bay is only 1 1/2 miles south of the
entrance to Alamitos Bay, and 14 miles northwest of Newport Bay. It has
accommodation for about 600 power boats and is the home of two yacht clubs.

In order to pass through the Bay a vessel must have a Certificate of Number
assigned by the California Division of Small Craft Harbors. In addition, the
vessel must be registered in the Security Office and display the required
decal. A specific route must be followed when traversing the danger zone, where
rowboats, kayaks, and smoking are prohibited. Sailboats must use their engines
in the inner harbor.

When approaching the harbor pick up lighted bell buoy "1" and lighted
whistle buoy "2" which are a little less than a mile west of the entrance to
the outer bay. Two additional markers indicate the direct course to follow to
the entrance. Two long jetties protect the outer part of Anaheim Bay; lights
are at the seaward ends and a fog signal is also at the end of the west jetty.
The enclosed waters are within a danger zone, while an explosives anchorage is
east of the channel. The channel is marked by buoys, lights, and a lighted
range. Anchorage is not permitted in Anaheim Bay.

Huntington Harbour is a private development composed of waterfront homes,
each having a private dock. Two private marinas operating in the harbor offer
the usual amenities, while a number of boat supply and repair businesses can
satisfy most boating needs. Recent dredging of the harbor has made a
considerable improvement, particularly at low water.

The Huntington Beach Pier which is less than 1/2 mile north of the entrance
to Anaheim Bay, was a victim of the January, 1988 storm which struck the coast.
The outermost 250 ft. of the pier were destroyed along with the restaurant
perched at the seaward end, appropriately named, "The End Cafe."

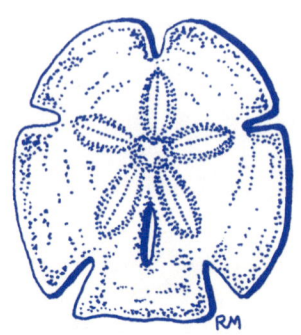

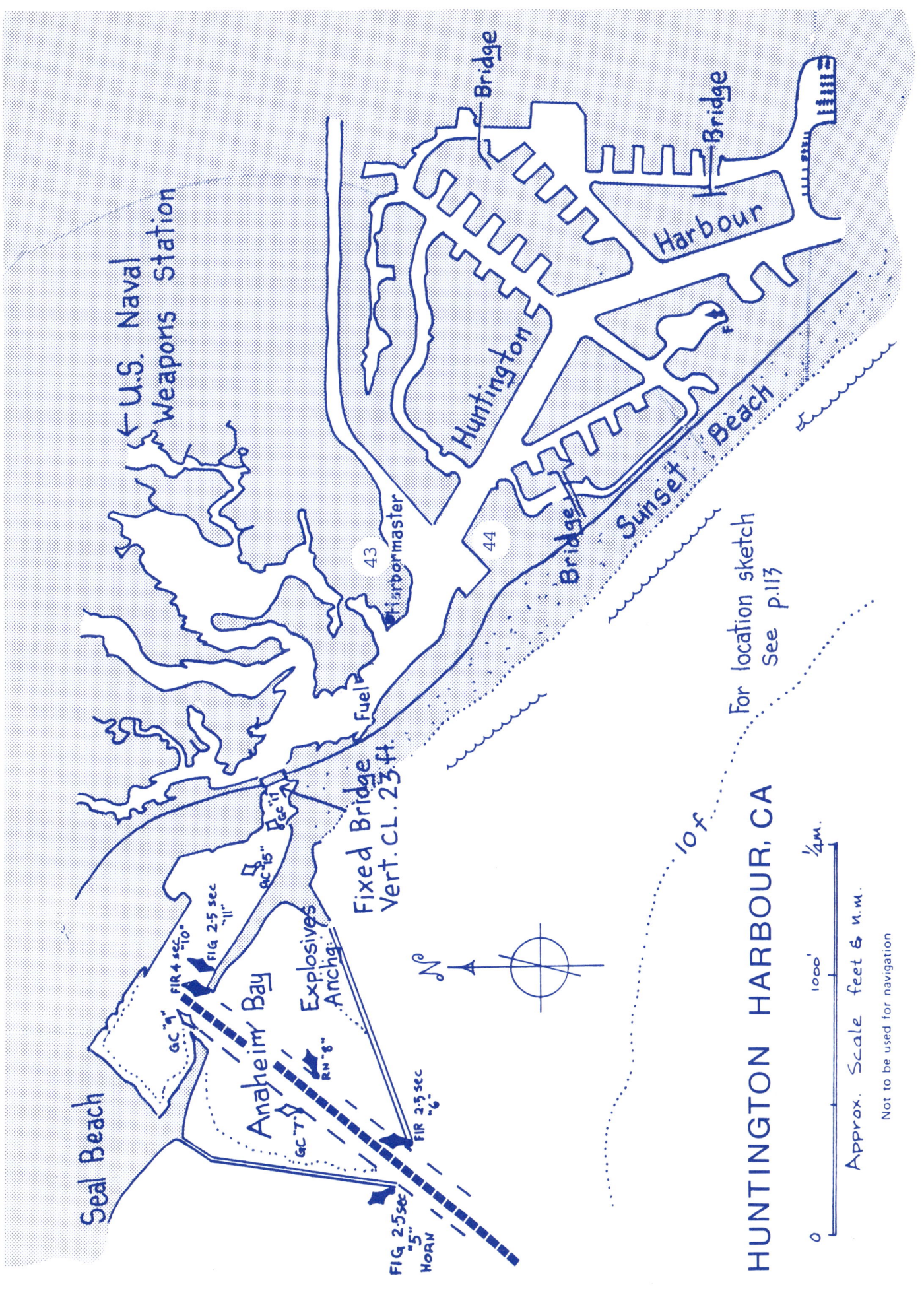

Seal Beach

← U.S. Naval Weapons Station

Harbour

Huntington

Bridge

Bridge

Bridge

Bridge

Sunset Beach

43 Harbormaster

44

Fuel

Fixed Bridge
Vert. CL. 23.4

Gc "17"

Gc "15"

Fl G 2.5 sec "11"

Fl R 4 sec "10"

Gc "9"

Anaheim Bay

Explosives Anch'g.

Rn "8"

Gc "7"

Fl R 2.5 sec "6"

Fl G 2.5 sec "5"
HORN

10 f

For location sketch
See p.117

N

HUNTINGTON HARBOUR, CA

Approx. Scale feet & n.m.

0   1000'   ¼ n.

Not to be used for navigation

NEWPORT BEACH

What appears to be a natural land-locked harbor at Newport Beach was until 1870 a quiet lagoon from which periodic shipments of livestock and grain were made. The first dredging of the entrance was done in 1876, but it wasn't until 1936 that the jetties were built and the present channels and turning basins were dredged. Opulent waterfront homes, manicured gardens and neat, clean, organized spaces are now the norm.

Next door to the Los Angeles/Long Beach area, the prosperous city of Newport Beach is only 14 miles southeast of Huntington Beach and 12 miles north of Dana Point. It is a very busy yachting center, being home to over 9,000 vessels, seven yacht clubs, and numerous sportfishing and marine oriented businesses. A Coast Guard rescue boat is based in the harbor.

The high-rise office towers in downtown Newport -- about 1 1/2 miles north of the entrance -- make good landmarks. Balboa Pier (800 ft. long) is over a mile northwest of the harbor entrance while Newport Pier (950 ft.) is about 2 miles further up the coast.

The channel leading into the harbor is protected by two jetties, both having lights at their seaward ends. The west jetty also has a fog signal and radiobeacon at the light. Shoal areas are marked by buoys.

Moorage within the harbor is under the jurisdiction of the Orange County Harbor Patrol. In contrast to most marine developments, boats are moored (fore and aft) rather than being tied up to docks. Five berths for transient vessels (maximum length - 40 ft.) are available at the Guest Dock near the Harbor Patrol Office. As available, buoys in other parts of the harbor may be assigned to transients for a flat rate of $5 per night, 20-day maximum stay. Restrooms and showers are available, but the nearest laundromat is located on Balboa Island on Agate Street.

Anchorage may be taken in the area east of Lido Island for a maximum of 5 days. To use this free anchorage one must obtain the permission of the Harbor Patrol. However, someone must be left on board at all times; the Harbor Patrol may board the vessel to check that this rule is being followed. Take care that the vessel does not swing out of the specified area -- if it does, the Orange County Police may issue a ticket. When anchoring here, it is a 1 1/2 mile trip by dinghy to the showers (or 3 miles overland). Since the shoreline is privately owned, landing by dinghy is difficult though one may get permission to land at the Sea Scouts base or at the Orange County Rowing Club.

All boating needs can be met by the many marine oriented shops in the bay except for replenishing the vessel's propane -- the closest outlet for it is at Orange Coast Trailer Supply on 16th Street in Costa Mesa.

A shore trip to the "fun zone" near Hills Fuel Dock will take one to a collection of eateries and many tourist oriented shops and entertainment outlets. Dinghy dockage is provided for clients at the many first-class harborside restaurants. Attractions in Los Angeles are easily accessible by bus.

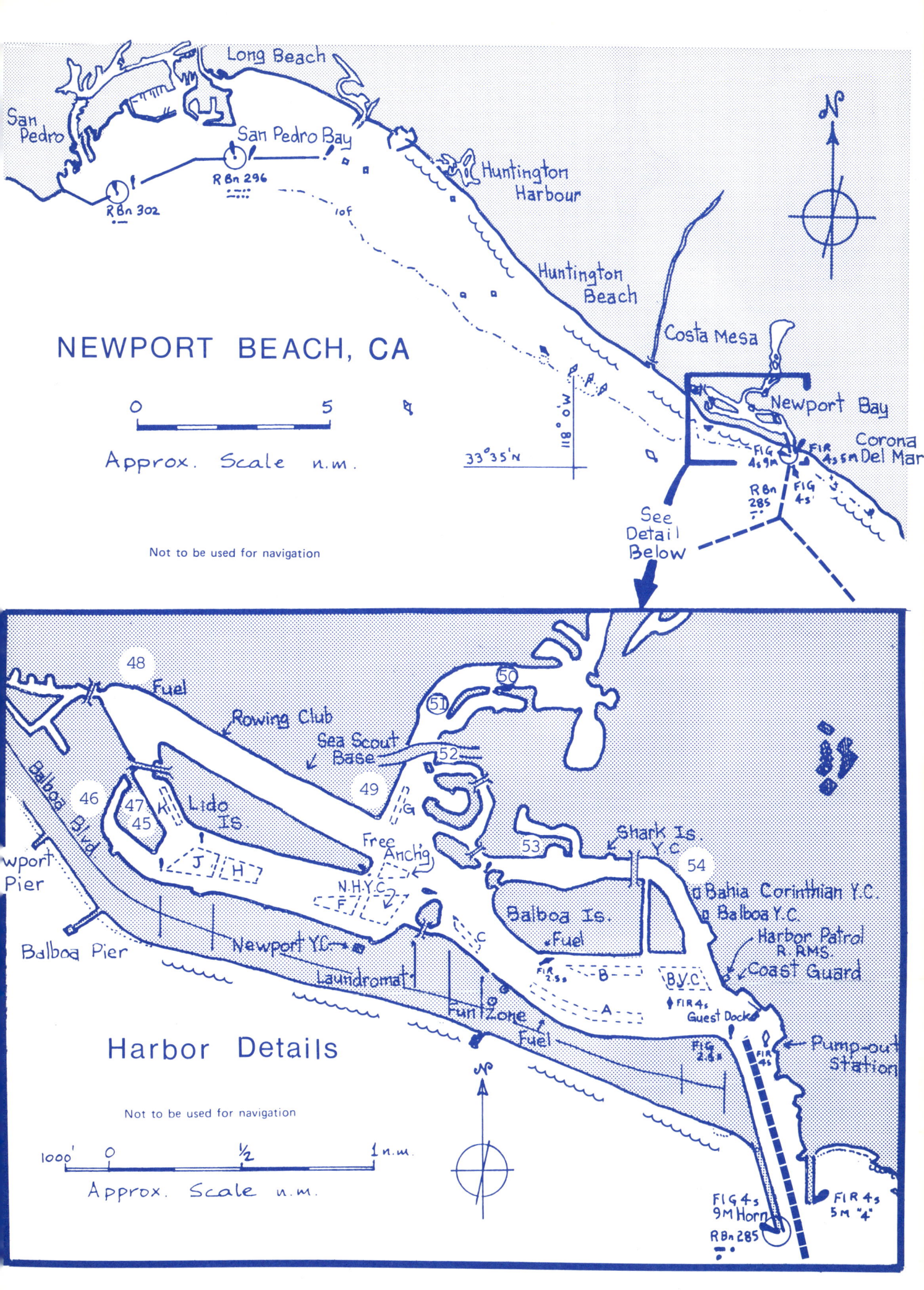

NEWPORT BEACH, CA

0 ——————— 5

Approx. Scale n.m.

Not to be used for navigation

San Pedro

San Pedro Bay

R Bn 302

R Bn 296

Long Beach

Huntington Harbour

Huntington Beach

Costa Mesa

Newport Bay

Corona Del Mar

33°35'N

118° 0'W

10f

FIG 4s 9M

FIR 4s 5M

FIG 4s

R Bn 285

FIG 4s

N

See Detail Below

---

48 Fuel

Rowing Club

Sea Scout Base

50

51

52

49

Balboa Blvd

46

47 45

K

Lido Is.

J H

F

N.H.Y.C.

Free Anch'g

n G

53

Shark Is Y.C.

54

Bahia Corinthian Y.C.

Balboa Y.C.

Harbor Patrol R.RMS. Coast Guard

Newport Pier

Balboa Pier

Newport YC

Laundromat

Fun Zone

Fuel

C

Balboa Is.

Fuel

FIR 2.5s

B

A

B.Y.C.

FIR 4s Guest Dock

FIG 2.5s

FIR 4s

Pump-out Station

Harbor Details

Not to be used for navigation

1000' 0 ——————— ½ ——————— 1 n.m.

Approx. Scale n.m.

N

FIG 4s 9M Horn

R Bn 285

FIR 4s 5M "4"

DANA POINT

The harbor at Dana Point is a well protected, easy to enter, scientifically designed facility which was constructed in the 1970's. It is the first man-made harbor on the coast to be tested and redesigned while in scale model form. With almost 2,500 slips it has helped to satisfy the ever-growing demand for pleasure craft accommodation.

In the lee of Dana Point, the harbor is 12 miles southeast of Newport Beach and about 24 miles northwest of Oceanside. Two breakwaters (having lights at their seaward ends) protect the entrance to the harbor; a fog signal and radio beacon are also located at the south light.

When approaching, pick up Dana Point lighted whistle buoy "2" which is about 1/2 mile southwest of Dana Point. Avoid the buoyed rock which is about 300 yards northeast of the south breakwater light. About 300 yards east of this light is a submerged sewer outfall pipe extending about 1/2 mile from the shore; it too, should be given clearance when approaching from the south. The entrance to the harbor is between two breakwaters. A bridge with a clearance of 20 ft. separates the East and West Basins. Private buoys mark the shoaling which occurs near the entrance to the West Basin.

Since all transient moorage is under the control of the harbormaster one must report to him for permission to use the guest slips or to anchor. He may be contacted on Ch. 12 and 16, by phone (714-496-2242) or by reporting to the office in person. Guest slips are available at $5 per day or one may drop a hook in one of the two anchorage areas after having obtained permission from the harbormaster. When anchoring in the East Basin Anchorage keep to the breakwater side of the yellow cans. There is a 5-day limit for use of the anchorages and someone must be aboard at all times. Vessels under 65 ft. are not required to show an anchor light. Rafting of vessels must have the harbormaster's permission.

Two marinas operate in the basin, **Dana Point Marina** (in the east basin) and **Dana West Marina.** Dana Point Marina has transient slips available for vessels under 28 ft. When berths are available, Dana West offers "hot-berthing" privileges to boaters from the two "sister" marinas at Ventura West and Harbor Island West in San Diego.

Mariners Village and Dana Wharf feature a variety of interesting shops and restaurants and a $1 shuttle service makes it easy to reach the commercial establishments in the city or at the top of the hill on Pacific Coast Highway. If time permits, a beautiful side trip can be taken to the Mission at San Juan Capistrano which is only 4 miles distant. Famous for the return of the swallows on March 19, it was established in 1776 by Father Junipero Serra. The Orange County Marine Institute, an education facility, is located at the west end of the harbor. Anchored nearby is a full-sized replica of Richard Henry Dana's square-rigger which is used as a stage for concerts and various other functions.

DANA POINT, CA

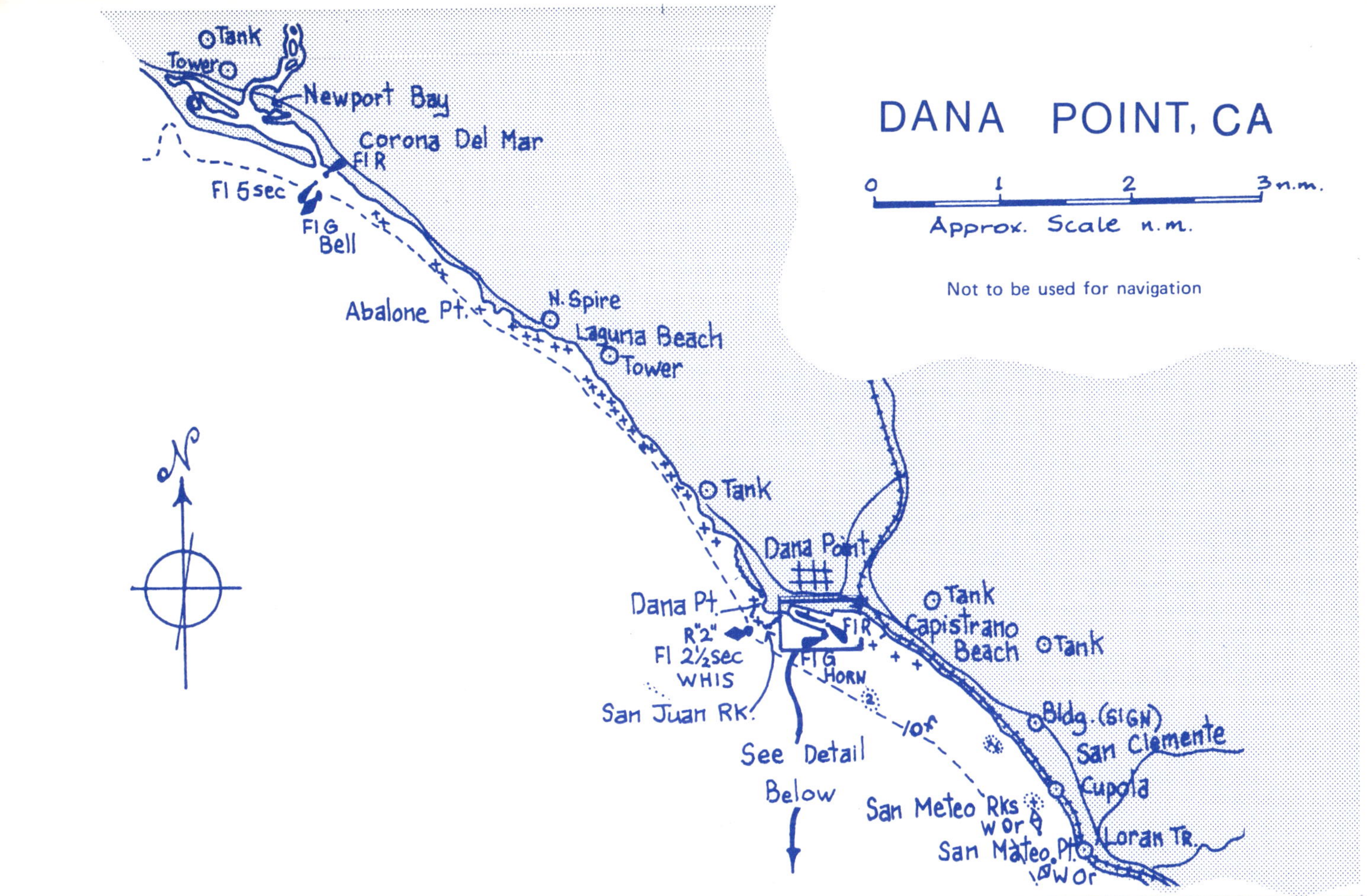

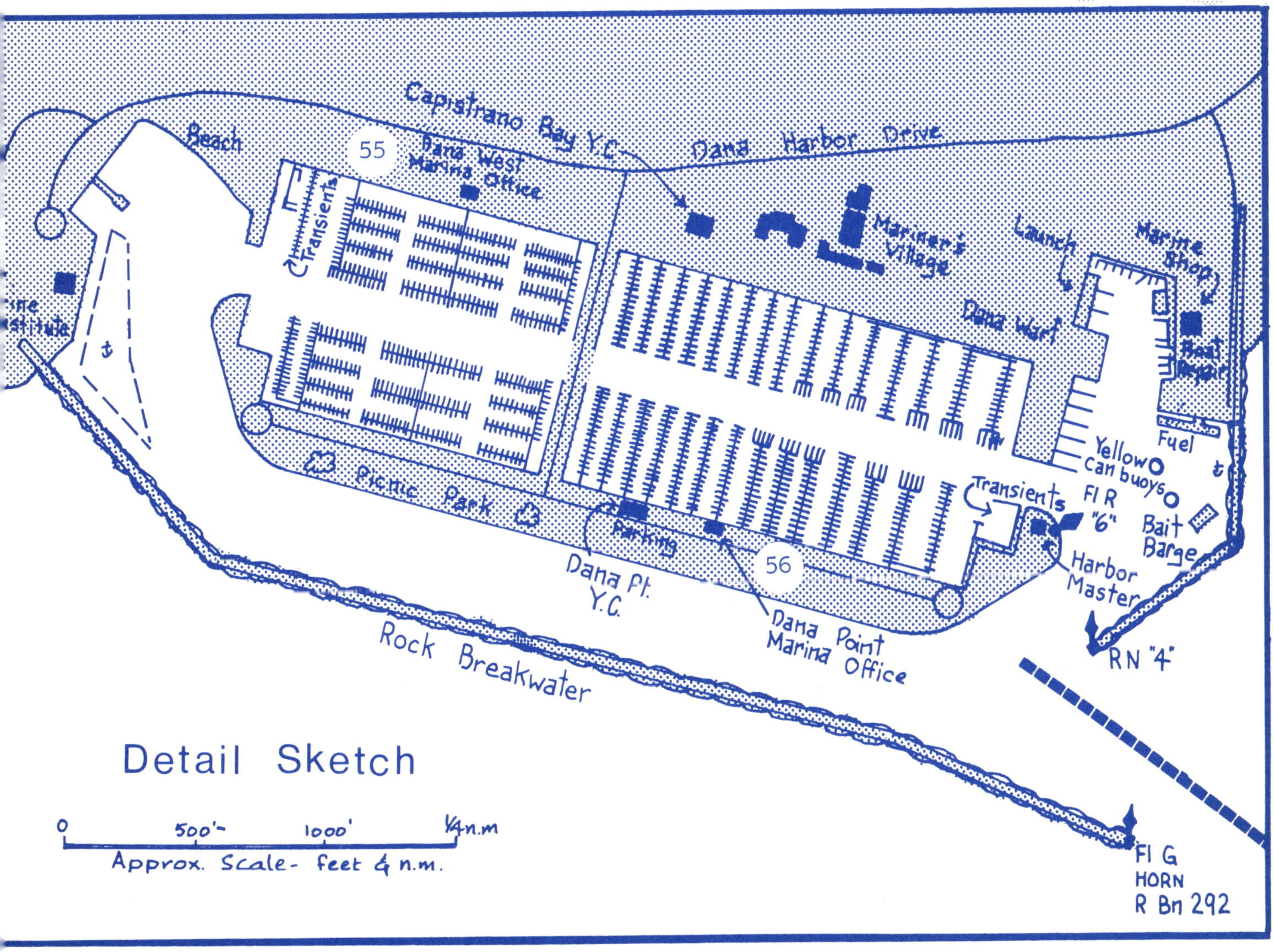

0   1   2   3 n.m.

Approx. Scale n.m.

Not to be used for navigation

Upper map labels:

- Tank
- Tower
- Newport Bay
- Corona Del Mar
- Fl R
- Fl 5 sec
- Fl G Bell
- Abalone Pt.
- N. Spire
- Laguna Beach Tower
- N
- Tank
- Dana Point
- Dana Pt. R"2" Fl 2½ sec WHIS
- San Juan Rk.
- Fl R
- Fl G Horn
- See Detail Below
- Tank
- Capistrano Beach
- Tank
- Bldg. (SIGN)
- San Clemente
- Cupola
- Loran Tr.
- San Meteo Rks W or R
- San Mateo Pt. W or R
- 10 f

Detail Sketch

- Capistrano Bay Y.C.
- Dana Harbor Drive
- Beach
- 55
- Dana West Marina Office
- Transients
- Mariner's Village
- Launch
- Marine Shop
- Dana Wharf
- Boat
- ne Institute
- Picnic Park
- Parking
- Dana Pt. Y.C.
- 56
- Dana Point Marina Office
- Transients
- Yellow can buoys
- Fl R "6"
- Bait Barge
- Fuel
- Harbor Master
- RN "4"
- Rock Breakwater
- Fl G HORN R Bn 292

0   500'   1000'   ¼ n.m.

Approx. Scale- feet & n.m.

OCEANSIDE

There are three bays in the coast on the north side of the city of Oceanside. The northernmost bay is the Del Mar Boat Basin which is restricted to use by the Camp Pendleton Marine Corps, while the two to the south provide space for over 900 slips in the Oceanside Small Craft Harbor. Located 22 miles south of Dana Point, Oceanside is 30 miles north of Mission Bay. Various landmarks are shown on the sketch but the most obvious is the large lighted sign, "OCEANSIDE," on a hill overlooking the harbor.

When approaching the entrance, pick up lighted bell buoy "2" which is about 1,000 yards southwest of the end of the east jetty. The entrance to all three basins is protected by two jetties -- the longer western jetty which is almost parallel to the beach also protects the channel to the Del Mar Basin, and the shorter, eastern jetty which angles out from the beach. Both have a light at their seaward ends. The east jetty has a fog signal at its tip and another light and a radiobeacon are about 200 ft. further along where the jetty bends in a more easterly direction. Buoys, lights, and a daybeacon mark the entrance to the harbor. Give good clearance to the submerged jetty marked by a buoy labelled as such.

Caution is advised as this can be a treacherous entrance when a heavy southerly swell is running and the tide is ebbing. Breaking waves across the entrance may cause a vessel to broach and be carried on to the breakwater. Though dredging of the channel is done regularly, shoaling is constantly occurring. Contact the Harbor Patrol (Ch 16) for advice on channel conditions. A Coast Guard cutter is stationed at the dock on the south side of the entrance.

Berths for 48 transient vessels are available at the Harbor Headquarters Dock. It operates on a first-come, first-serve basis and the rates are 45 cents per foot during summer months. The usual amenities are available.

A short walk around the harbor takes one to a collection of shorefront shops, fast food outlets and restaurants clustered around the southern basin.

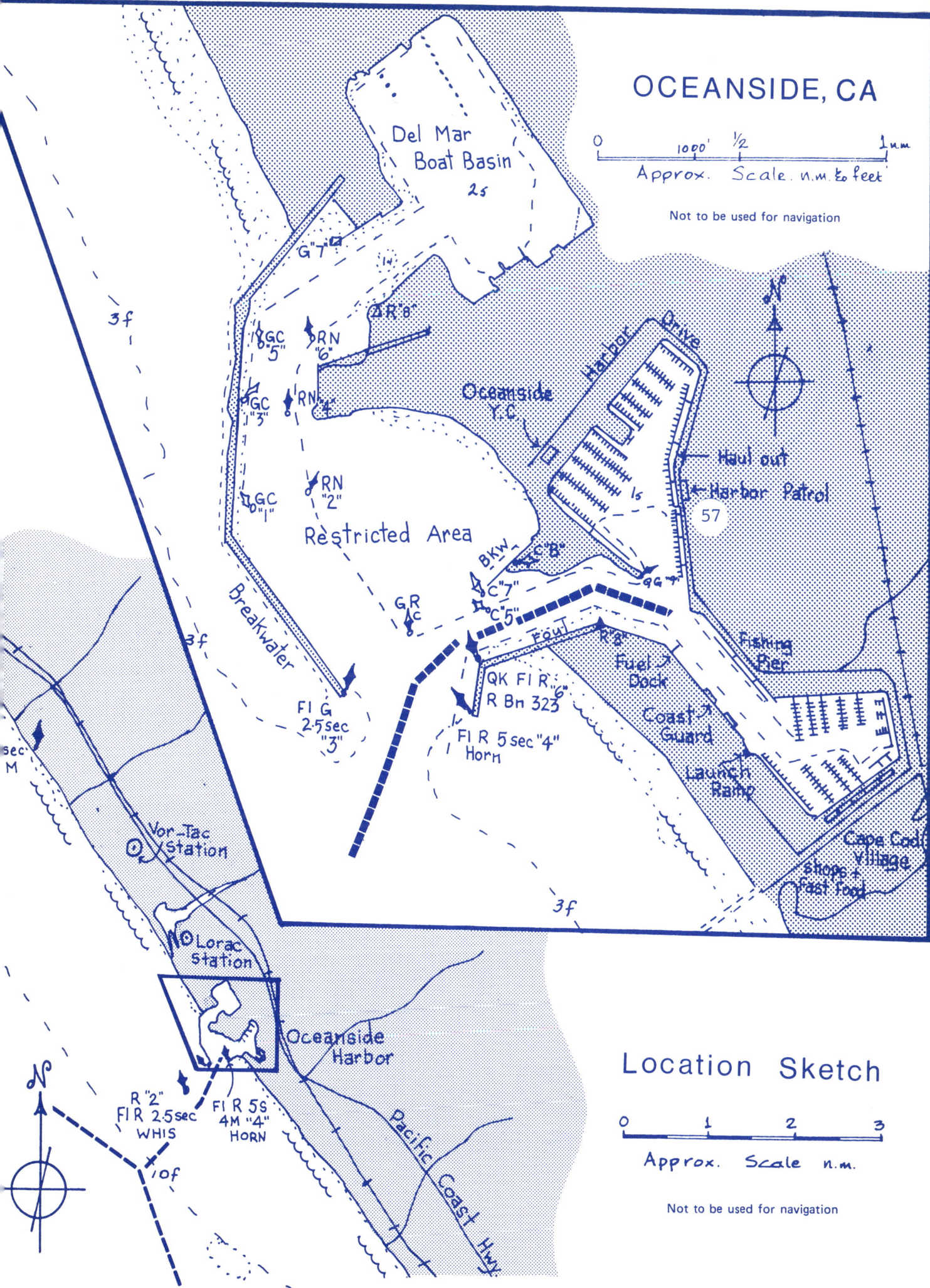

OCEANSIDE, CA

Approx. Scale n.m. to feet

Not to be used for navigation

Del Mar Boat Basin
2s

3f

G"7"

ΔR"8"

GC "5"
RN "6"

GC "3"
RN "4"

Oceanside Y.C.

Haul out

Harbor Patrol

57

GC "1"
RN "2"

Restricted Area

BKW

C"B"

C"7"

QG"9"

Harbor Drive

ls

Breakwater

G R C

C"5"

Fout

R"8"

Fuel Dock

Fishing Pier

3f

Fl G 2.5 sec "3"

QK Fl R "6"
R Bn 323

Fl R 5 sec "4"
Horn

Coast Guard

Launch Ramp

Cape Cod Village

Shops + fast food

3f

3f

sec M

Vor-Tac Station

Lorac Station

Oceanside Harbor

R "2"
Fl R 2.5 sec
WHIS

Fl R 5s 4M "4"
HORN

Pacific Coast Hwy

10f

Location Sketch

Approx. Scale n.m.

Not to be used for navigation

N

N

MISSION BAY

Most of the waterfront and all of the waters and islands within Mission Bay are a 4,600-acre park administered by the city of San Diego. It is surrounded on all sides by the residential areas of Pacific Beach, Morena, Loma Portal and Ocean Beach which are all within San Diego city limits. Though it covers a large area, most of its inner waters are shallow (6 ft.) and much of it is blocked off by the Mission Bay Bridge (Cl. 38 ft.) which joins two lobes of land in the southwest corner of the park. Two other bridges having clearances of 29 ft. and 24 ft. further restrict traffic in the bay.

Located 30 miles south of Oceanside, Mission Bay is most easily identified by the high Sea World Tower and the Hyatt Islandia Hotel. A U.S. Navy Ocean-ographic Platform is 1 mile north of the entrance while a fishing pier at Ocean Beach is about 1/4 mile south of it.

Two jetties protect the entrance channel leading to the small craft facilities in Quivera Basin, Mariners Basin, and beyond. Both jetties have lights at their seaward ends and fog signals are at the north jetty light, the fishing pier, and the U.S. Navy Platform.

There is no problem in entering the bay under normal conditions, but this can be a dangerous entrance which must be avoided if a moderate to heavy swell is running. At such times breakers occur at the entrance and roll in along the south jetty. Favoring the northern side of the channel is advisable when seas are choppy.

On entering the bay report to the Harbormaster (Ch. 16), or briefly tie up at the dock while reporting in person. No transient slips are available at his dock but one may obtain permission to anchor in the special anchorage in Mariners Bay where good anchorage may be taken, sand and mud. There is no charge, but a maximum of 72 hours per week are allowed; the dinghy may be beached anywhere to go ashore. Public restrooms are on the beach.

Three large private marinas line the waterfront in Quivera Basin. **Islandia Marina** is adjacent to and is operated by the large luxury hotel, Hyatt Islandia. Transient berths are available at $15 per day. Use of all hotel facilities including swimming pools, jacuzzi, etc. is included. Next door is **Seaforth Marina** which may have transient slips (max. 35 ft.) at a flat rate of $10 per night. Showers and restrooms are available but there are no laundry facilities. **Knight and Carver Mission Bay Yacht Center** and **Marina** (formerly Mission Bay Marina) is a combination of a large marina, shipyard, and ship chandlery. Transient berths are usually available at $15 flat rate for up to 30 days; all amenities are conveniently located close to the docks.

Beyond Mission Bay Bridge (Cl. 38 ft.) are two small boat marinas in Dana Cove (**Dana Landing** and **Dana Inn Marina**), and around the corner in Perez Cove is **Sea World Marina.** All slips are booked by permanent tenants and no transient berths are available at these marinas.

The exhibits and shows at Sea World are worth seeing once. Other attractions in the area that may be of interest are listed on the page which describes San Diego, and because of a good bus system they are accessible from Mission Bay.

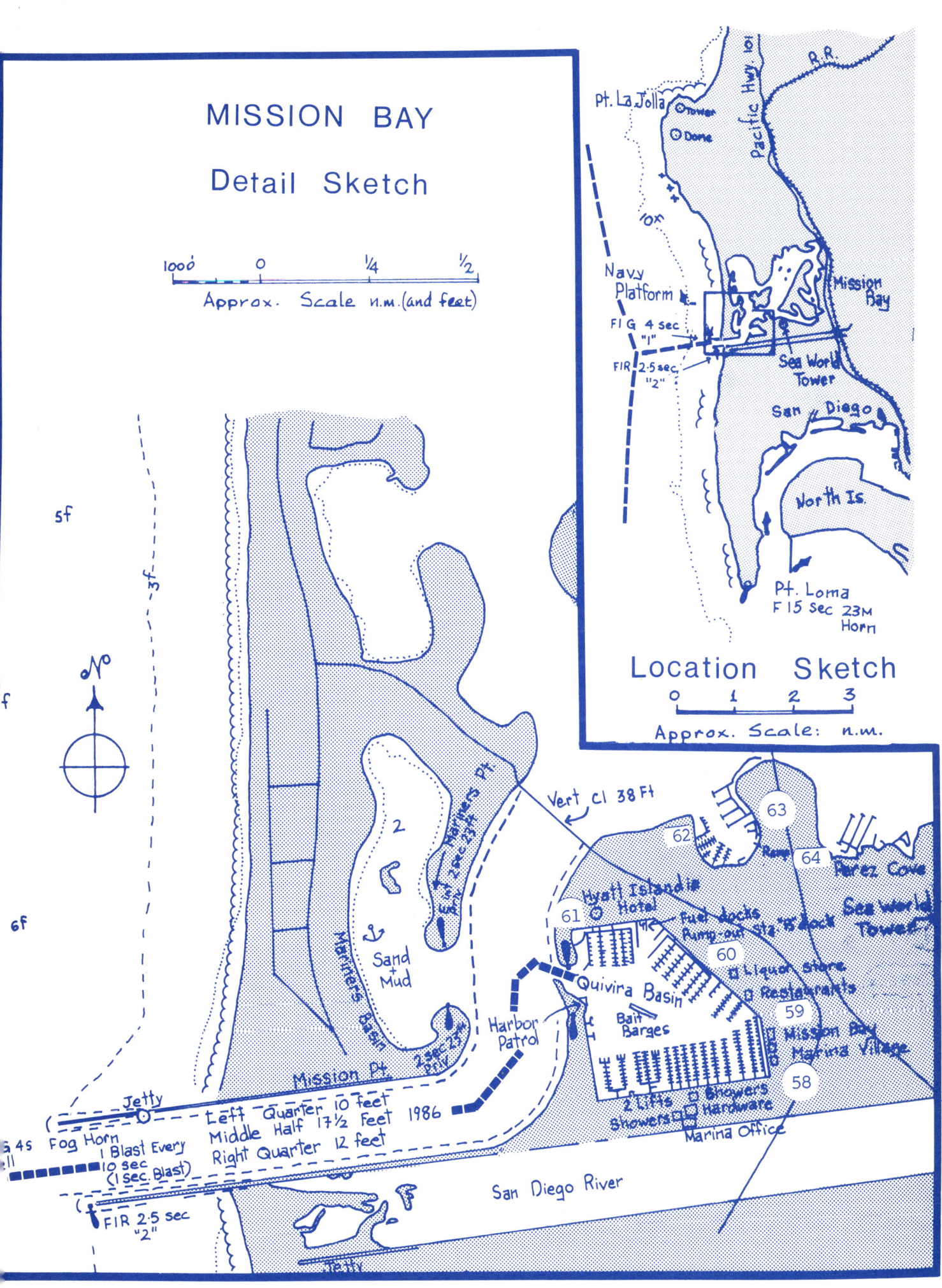

MISSION BAY

Detail Sketch

1000   0   ¼   ½

Approx. Scale n.m. (and feet)

Location Sketch

0   1   2   3

Approx. Scale: n.m.

Pt. La Jolla
Tower
Dome
Pacific Hwy 101
R.R.
"O"
Navy Platform
Fl G 4 sec "1"
Fl R 2·5 sec "2"
Mission Bay
Sea World Tower
San Diego
North Is.
Pt. Loma
F 15 Sec 23M
Horn

5f
3f
f
6f

N°

2
Sand + Mud
Mariners Pt.
Mariners Basin
Fl R 2 sec 23 Ft
Fl R 2·5 sec 23 Ft
Mission Pt.

Vert Cl 38 Ft

Hyatt Island Hotel
61
62
63
64
Perez Cove
Sea World Tower
Fuel docks
Pump-out sta "B"dock
60
Liquor store
Restaurants
59
Mission Bay Marina Village
58
Quivira Basin
Bait Barges
Harbor Patrol
2 Lifts Showers
Showers Hardware
Marina Office

Jetty
Fl 4s Fog Horn
1 Blast Every 10 sec
(1 sec. Blast)
Left Quarter 10 feet
Middle Half 17½ Feet 1986
Right Quarter 12 feet

San Diego River

Fl R 2·5 sec "2"

SAN DIEGO BAY

Less than 10 miles north of the Mexican border, this area was first visited in 1542 by Juan Rodriquez Cabrillo. It was the site of the first of the 21 missions built by Father Junipero Sera linking Catholic outposts to present-day San Francisco. Following the defeat of Mexico in the Mexican-American war in 1847, it became part of the United States. Most of the city's development has taken place since 1900 with the fastest growth since World War II.

This large natural harbor has seen much development of pleasure craft facilities in recent years. This is fortunate, for San Diego is not only home to over 4,000 boats and 9 yacht clubs, it is also a destination for vessels from as far away as Alaska. The annual migration to warmer climes sees hundreds of boats of every size and shape stop to take on provisions, top up water tanks, repair gear, and rest up before the next leg of the cruise commences. Consequently, dock accommodation and anchorages are stretched to the limit, especially from September to December when the main stream of transients arrive and await the end of the hurricane season.

The high, steep-sided peninsula ending in Point Loma protects the entrance from northwesterly winds. Point Loma Light, as well as a fog signal and radiobeacon, is located at the south end of the point below the ridge on which is an abandoned lighthouse. If it is too foggy to see either lighthouse, extensive kelp beds offshore are a good sign that Point Loma is close by. Fifteen miles south of Point Loma and 7 miles offshore are the stark and undeveloped Coronado Islands which are Mexican territory. When approaching from the south one sees the long beaches of Silver Strand Park with a backdrop of tall condominiums and crowded city buildings.

A jetty extends for 1 mile south of the southwestern tip of North Island from Zuniga Point. This is a dangerous area since the outer 2/3 is submerged at high water and is marked by only 3 lights along its length and a light and fog signal at its end. Within 3 miles to the south of Point Loma there are 3 buoys, the last of which marks the beginning of the channel leading into the harbor. Another light and fog signal are off Ballast Point which is almost 1/2 mile NE of the east side of Point Loma. The large U.S. Navy submarine base with its many imposing structures and tenders is just beyond.

If a vessel is of foreign registry or is arriving from a foreign port it must go directly to the Harbor Police Dock at the western end of Shelter Island and make a formal entry through Customs for San Diego is a **Port of Entry.** If entry is made from Monday to Friday between 8 a.m. and 5 p.m. there is no charge, but at any other time there is a $25 fee. One may stay at the Municipal Dock (adjacent to the Police Dock) until all formalities -- Customs, Immigration, Public Health, and Agricultural Inspection -- have been completed. A flat rate of $5 per day is charged for the first 5 days, $10 per day for the 6th to 10th day. Restrooms and showers are available, but no laundromats.

If Customs clearance is not required, a first-time visitor is advised to call the Harbor Police (Ch. 16) to verify current anchoring rules and regulations. The stress of finding one's way around a new harbor can be reduced by taking the first convenient anchorage to allow the crew time to tidy up the boat, have a meal, clean up, and get their bearings.

Right: The beauty of the days of sail have been recaptured in this lovely replica based at Ventura.

Below: Any bar can be dangerous as is shown by the entrance to Oceanside.

Even the well protected roadstead anchorage at Shelter Island does not forgive poor anchoring techniques or inadequate ground tackle.

The Coronado Islands in Mexico seen from Point Loma invite one to travel south. (But first, have you got a copy of CHARLIE'S CHARTS of MEXICO?)

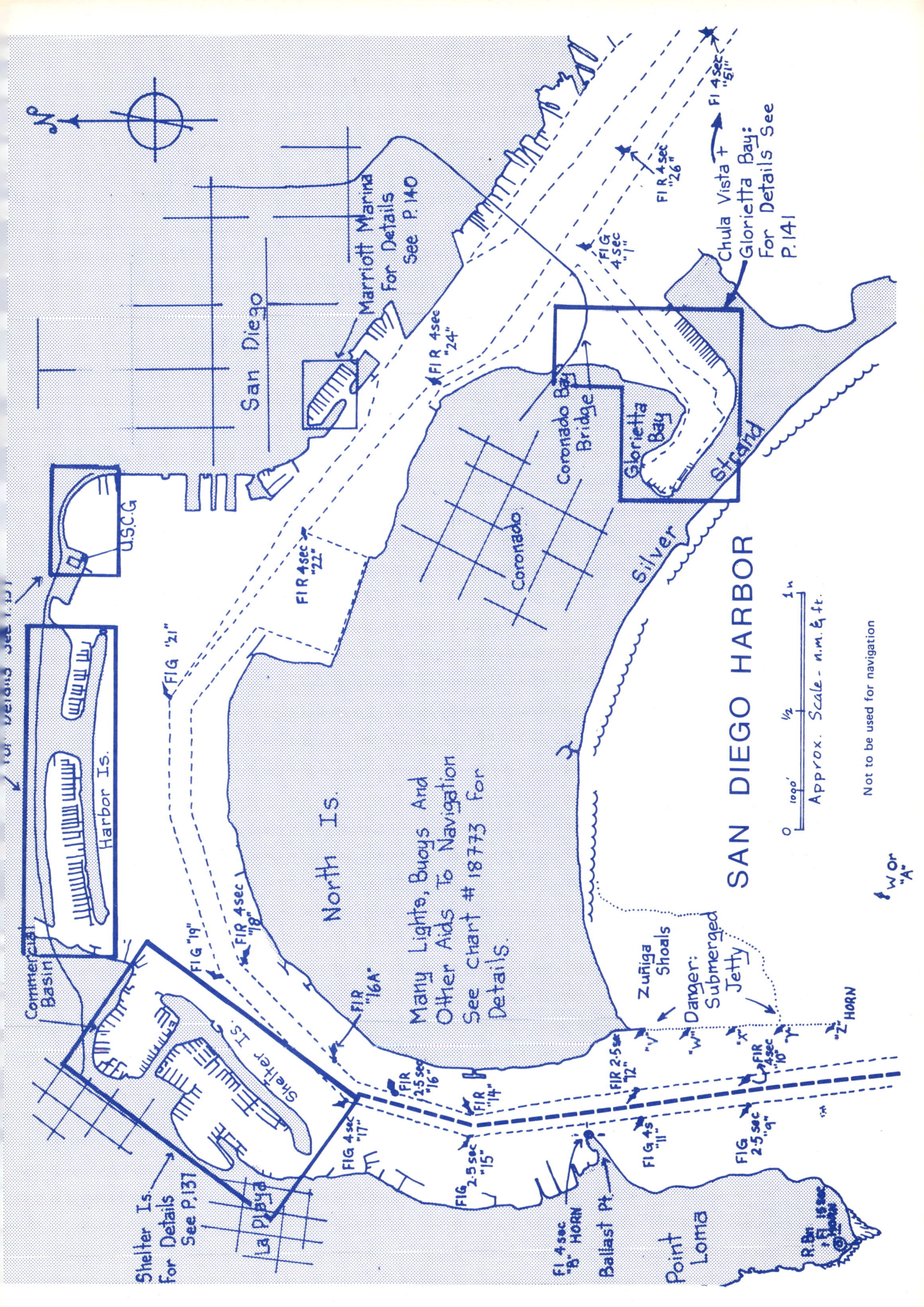

SAN DIEGO HARBOR

Marriott Marina For Details See P.140

San Diego

Fl R 4sec "24"

Fl R 4sec "22"

Fl G "21"

U.S.C.G.

Harbor Is.

Commercial Basin

Fl G "19"

Fl R 4sec "18"

Fl R "16A"

Shelter Is. For Details See P.137

La Playa

Shelter Is.

Fl G 4sec "17"

Fl G 2.5sec "15"

Fl R 2.5sec "16"

Fl R "14"

North Is.

Many Lights, Buoys And Other Aids To Navigation See Chart #18773 For Details.

Coronado

Coronado Bay Bridge

Glorietta Bay

Silver Strand

Fl R 4sec "26"

Fl G 4sec "1"

Chula Vista → Glorietta Bay: For Details See P.141

Fl R 4sec "51"

Zuñiga Shoals

Danger: Submerged Jetty

"V"

"W" HORN

"X"

"Y"

"Z" HORN

Fl R 2.5sec "12"

Fl R 4sec "10"

Fl G 4s "11"

Fl G 2.5sec "9"

Fl 4 sec "B" HORN

Ballast Pt.

Point Loma

R Bn ● Fl.15sec ● HORN

W Or "A"

Approx. Scale - n.m. & ft.

0 — 1000' — ½ — 1n

Not to be used for navigation

SHELTER ISLAND

Three anchorages are in the vicinity of Shelter Island, the easiest to find being off the **roadstead** on the south side of the island. Located about 1 mile east of Point Loma, it is a rather rough anchorage because of the wake of vessels passing up and down the channel. On the plus side, it gives access to Shelter Island facilities and landing is easy on the beach or at the dinghy landing near the launching ramp. The vessel must show a proper anchor light at night and display an anchor ball during the day. The Harbor Police sometimes check at odd hours during the day or night to see that all rules are being followed. At present, there is no time limit on the length of stay at anchor.

The forest of masts seen on the north side of Shelter Island is a dense accumulation of 3 yacht clubs, 3 fuel docks, 5 marinas and 1 anchorage. The **La Playa Cove** anchorage is between the San Diego Yacht Club (a large brown clubhouse) and Southwestern Yacht Club. To anchor here the vessel must have a holding tank and a permit issued by the Harbor Police whose office is at the tip of Shelter Island. Sometimes anchoring is permitted only on week-ends so check current rules regarding length of stay.

A complete range of yacht services is available on Shelter Island: boat-yards (Eichenlaub Marine, Driscoll Custom Boats, Kettenburgs, and Shelter Island Yachtways), numerous chandleries, specialty stores, sailmakers, chart retailers, and yacht brokers. Transient berths are sometimes available at 3 marinas (Bay Club, Half Moon Anchorage, and Kona Marine). Rates depend on the vessel's length -- 1988 charges for a 34 ft. vessel are about $18 per day.

Although the area northeast of Shelter Island is known as the **Commercial Basin,** it is for small craft use. The 2 marinas here do not have transient berths and the anchorage area is filled with houseboats and local vessels (many of which are live-aboards). In any case, the bottom is cluttered with sunken vessels, anchors, lines, and other garbage. Permission to anchor here must be obtained from Marine Operations Dept. (Ph. 291-3900, Ext 212).

Though all of a vessel's needs are within walking distance of yachting facilities, the closest large grocery store (Von's) is several long blocks east of Shelter Island Drive on Rosecrans Street. Convenience stores and restaurants are in the immediate area while a laundromat is close to Baskin-Robbins Ice Cream Parlor. Membership in the Price Club gives one access to a discount food warehouse which is an excellent place to stock up.

There are many pleasurable things to see and do while one is in San Diego and its calm pace and excellent climate make it a city that calls one back. Some attractions are: the world famous San Diego Zoo, the Wild Animal Park, Ruben H. Fleet Space Theatre, Sea World, San Diego Mission, "Star of India" and other vessels at the Maritime Museum, Mission San Diego de Alcala, and Old Town. For shopping, try Seaport Village, Horton Plaza and Fashion Valley.

From Point Loma and Lighthouse Park one has a marvelous view of San Diego Harbor and Coronado Islands. Enroute one passes through Fort Rosecrans National Cemetery where acres of white tombstones mark the graves of military personnel killed during wartime. One can't help but feel a tremendous sadness, and appreciation for the sacrifices made by so many which have made it possible for us to enjoy the way of life we take so much for granted.

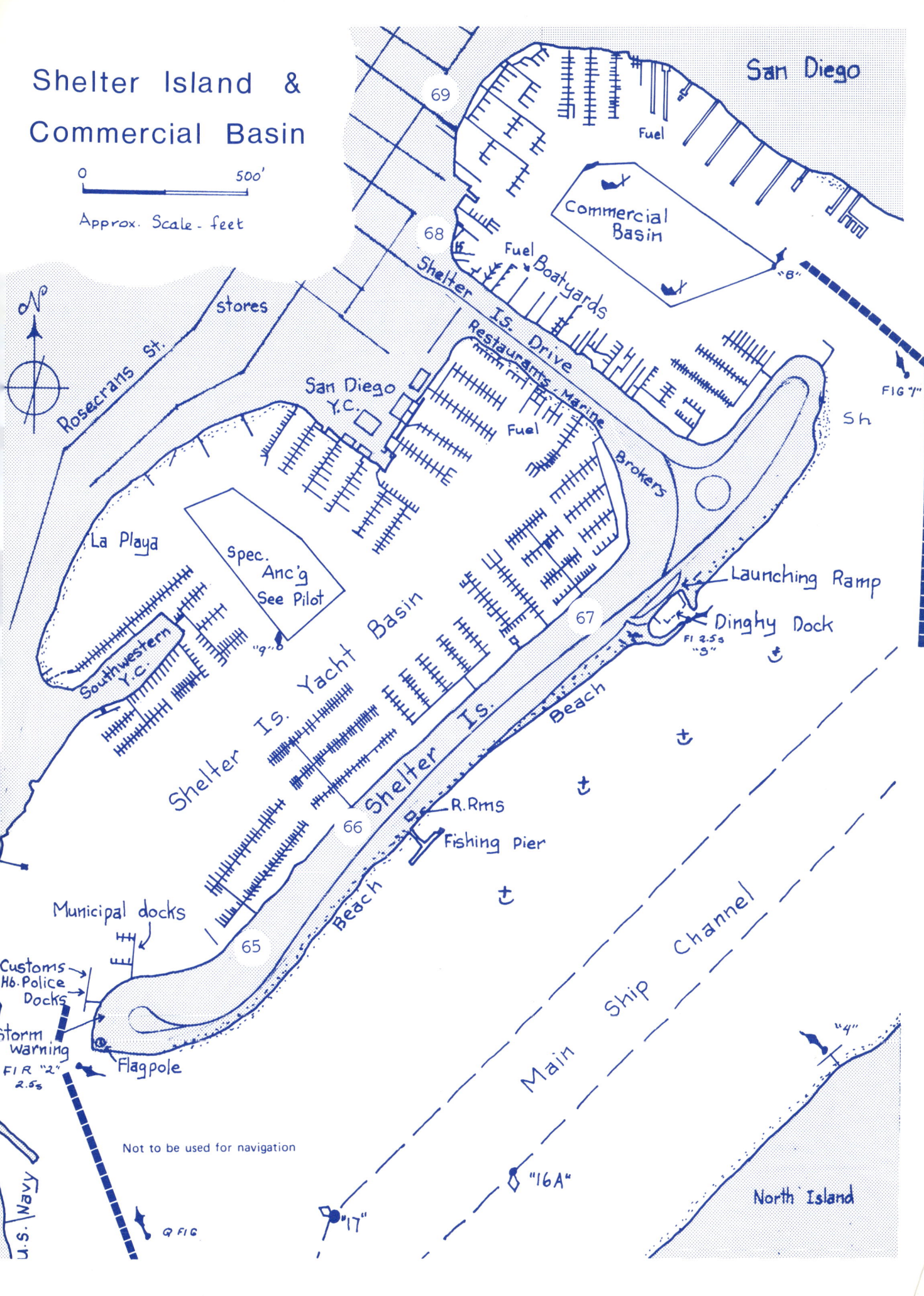

Shelter Island & Commercial Basin

0   500'

Approx. Scale - feet

N

San Diego

69

Fuel

Commercial Basin

"8"

68

Fuel Boatyards

Shelter Is. Drive

Restaurants Marine

stores

Rosecrans St.

San Diego Y.C.

Fuel

Brokers

FIG "7"

Sh

67

La Playa

Spec. Anc'g See Pilot

"9"

Launching Ramp

Dinghy Dock

Fl 2.5s "9"

Southwestern Y.C.

Shelter Is. Yacht Basin

Shelter Is. Beach

Municipal docks

66

R. Rms

Fishing Pier

65

Beach

Customs Hb. Police Docks

Storm warning

Flagpole

F I R "2" 2.5s

Main Ship Channel

"4"

Not to be used for navigation

U.S. Navy

Q FIG

"17"

"16A"

North Island

HARBOR ISLAND

As one travels further into San Diego Bay, the next pleasure boat
facilities are at the massive man-made development of Harbor Island. In the
west basin are 3 marinas (**Harbor Island West, Marina Cortez,** and **Cabrillo Isle
Marina)** having over 1,600 slips, while the east basin has the newest facility
(**Sunroad Marina)** with 540 slips. Transient berths are usually available at all
of the marinas; rates vary with the length of vessel. (In 1988 the charges for
a 34 ft. vessel were from $17 to $23 per day, depending on the marina used.)
There is considerable variation in what one gets for the rental so it is wise
to enquire about such things as charges for electricity, use of the pool,
whether or not the deposit on the key to showers is 100% refundable, or if
there is a liveaboard charge. See Appendix 2 for telephone numbers.

Two fuel docks are located in the west basin and there are several small
marine shops on the Island. The nearest repair facilities are on Shelter
Island. Though there are several restaurants ashore there are no grocery
stores, so one must go downtown. Guest docks are provided for patrons of
several Harbor Island restaurants. It is well to call ahead for reservations:
Boathouse Restaurant (291-80810), Tom Hams Lighthouse Restaurant (291-9110),
and Sheraton Harbor Island Hotel (291-1900).

Just a short distance away is a large Coast Guard Airstation and to the
south of it is the **Embarcadero.** There are 24 mooring buoys where one may tie
up Mediterranean style for a maximum of 30 days. Fees are payable in advance;
rates are $5 per day for the first 15 days, $10 per day for the 16th to 30th
day. To determine if any buoys are available call the Wharfinger's Office at
291-3900, Ext. 340, 8 a.m. to 5 p.m. on weekdays or after hours call 291-1799.
Dinghy docks along the Embarcadero provide access to restroom facilities
ashore. Noise and air turbulence from the Coast Guard Station can be a
nuisance,while jet traffic at the International Airport on Harbor Island add to
the sound effects.

Southeast of the Coast Guard Station is the **Laurel Street Anchorage** area.
There is seldom space for transients here as it is normally filled with local
tenants.

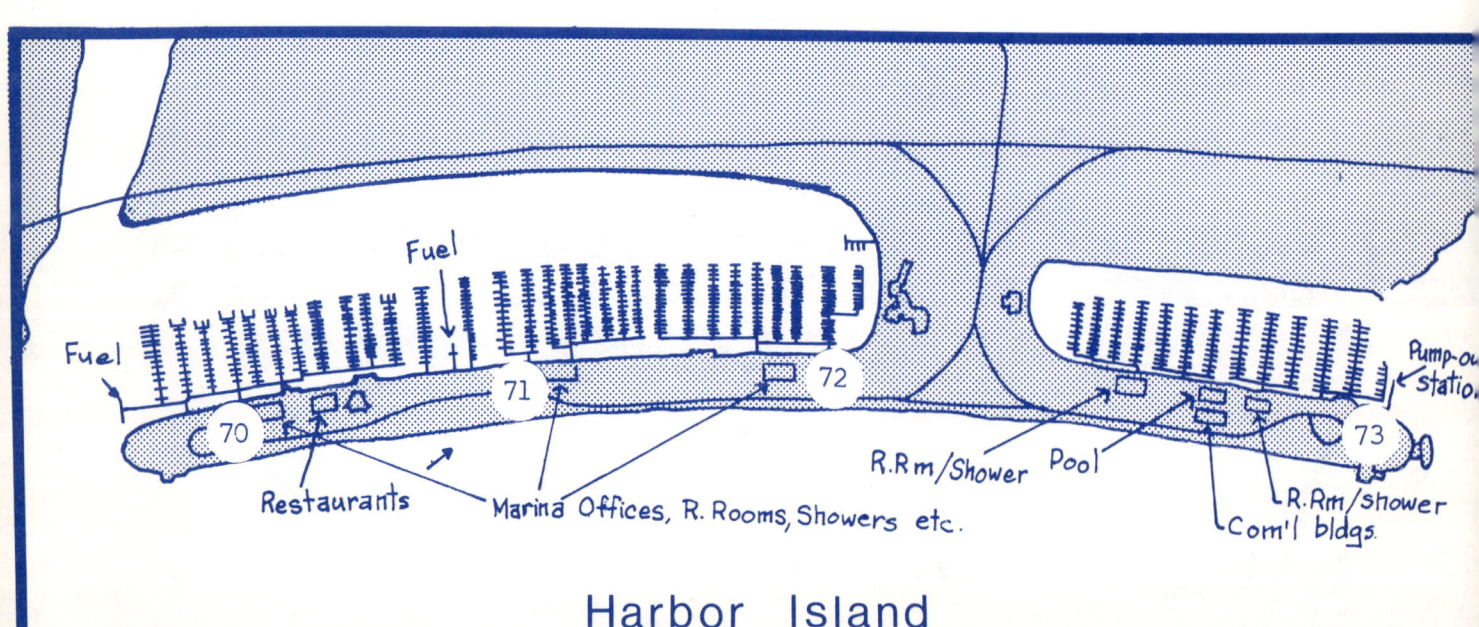

Harbor Island

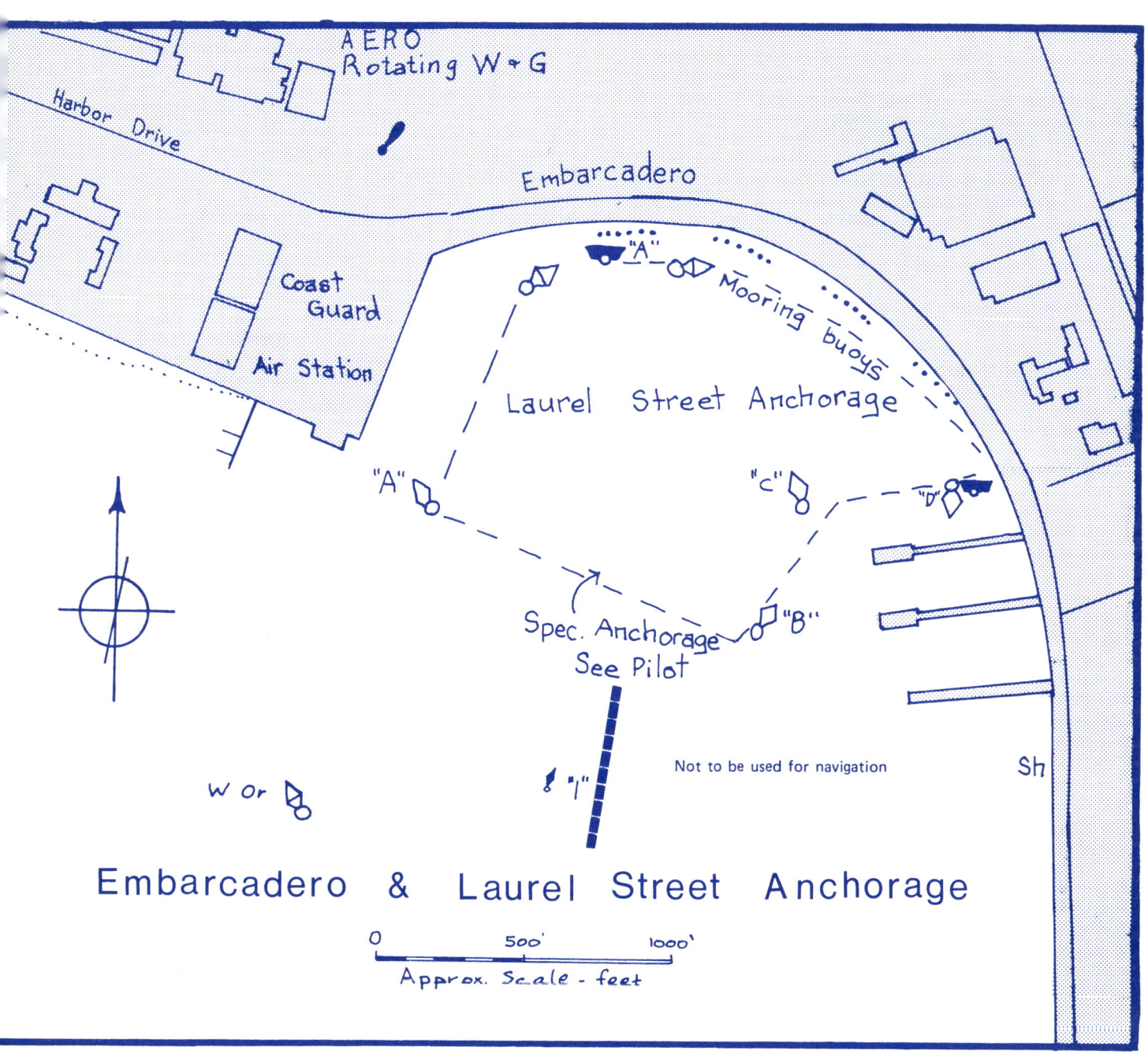

AERO
Rotating W & G

Harbor Drive

Embarcadero

"A"

Mooring buoys

Coast
Guard

Air Station

Laurel Street Anchorage

"A"

"c"

"D"

"B"

Spec. Anchorage
See Pilot

Not to be used for navigation

Sh

W or

"I"

Embarcadero & Laurel Street Anchorage

0   500'   1000'

Approx. Scale - feet

Marriott Marina is the new name for the 445-slip facility formerly known as the Intercontinental Marina. When space is available transients are welcomed at $1 per foot per day with a $100 refundable deposit on each key. One has the use of the luxurious swimming pools, jacuzzi, and a first-class restaurant is close by. To make berthing arrangements, phone ahead, or tie up at the pump-out station and contact the dockmaster. Next door is a very interesting collection of shops and restaurants in the rambling bayside development of Seaport Village.

As one proceeds south in the bay, two anchorage areas are available: the **Bay Bridge roadstead** has two areas on either side of the Coronado Bay Bridge near its Coronado End, and a very pleasant one at **Glorietta Bay,** across from the boat launching ramp. Officially, there is a 72-hour limit for anchoring here. The Glorietta Bay Marina has transient berths, though no fuel. Rates depend on the vessel's length -- a 34 ft. vessel costs $29 per day. Another anchorage further south in the bay is at Crown Cove; since regulations change it is advisable to check on the current rules. The anchorage and dock area adjacent to Silver Strand Park is for military personnel only.

Transient slips are often available at the two marinas in the southern bay area: **Coronado Cays Marina** and **Chula Vista Marina.** One should call ahead (Ch.16) to verify availability as it's a fair distance from other moorage areas. Coronado Cays Marina has a fuel dock though no laundry facilities. Rates vary with boat length -- 34 ft. charges are $25 per day (1988).

When approaching Chula Vista, use a current H.O. chart and stay well within the buoyed channel. Lights mark the entrance to the marina. Constructed in 1987, Chula Vista Marina has over 500 slips. Rates are $14 per day for vessels under 40 ft., $18 for those over 40 ft. At present the closest fuel dock is at Coronado Cays Marina.

Chula Vista Marina is one of three homeports for the state tallship, "Californian" which is a spectacular replica of the mid-19th century revenue cutter, "Lawrence." Sponsored by the Nautical Heritage Society, it is a cadet training ship for young people between the ages of 16 and 21 who have the opportunity to experience 11-day training cruises at a cost of $700.

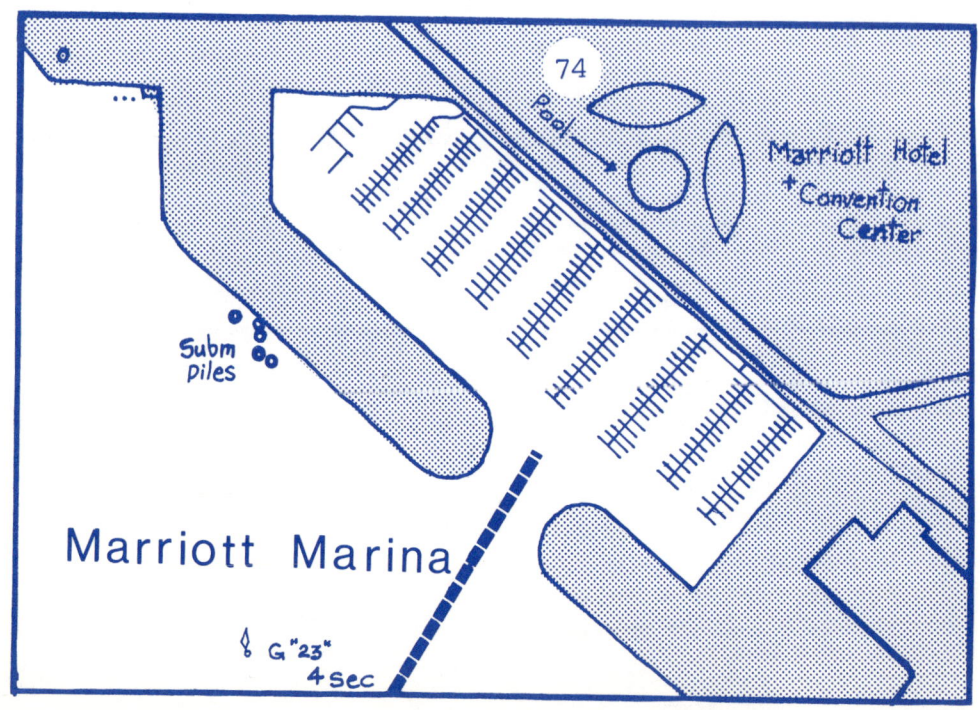

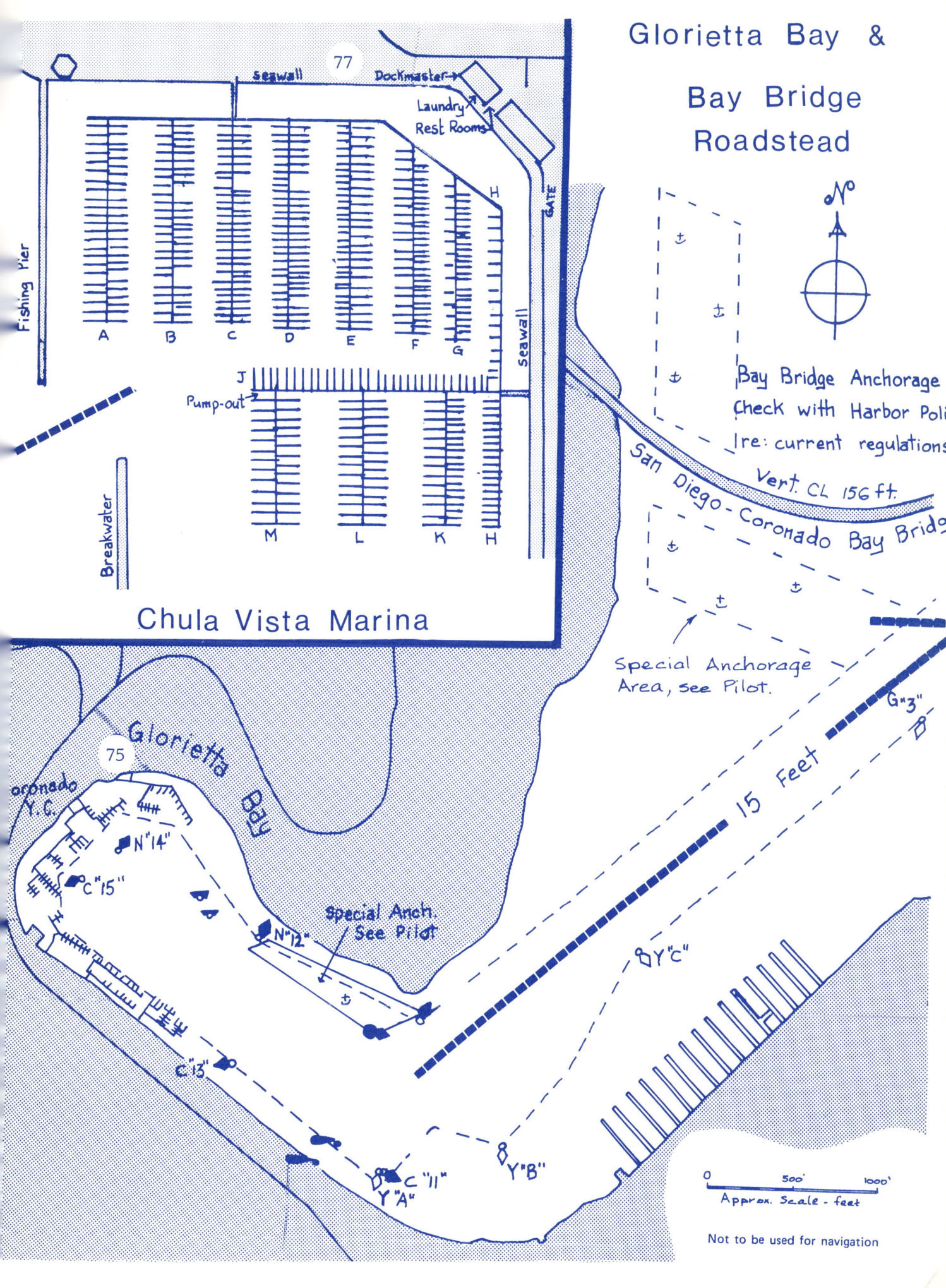

Glorietta Bay &
Bay Bridge
Roadstead

Fishing Pier

seawall

77

Dockmaster→

Laundry
Rest Rooms

GATE

H

seawall

A   B   C   D   E   F   G

J

Pump-out

seawall

M   L   K   H

Breakwater

Chula Vista Marina

N

Bay Bridge Anchorage
Check with Harbor Poli
re: current regulations

Vert. CL 156 ft.

San Diego–Coronado Bay Brid

Special Anchorage
Area, see Pilot.

75

Glorietta Bay

oronado
Y.C.

N "14"

C "15"

Special Anch.
See Pilot

N "12"

15 Feet

G "3"

BY "c"

C "13"

Y "B"

C "11"

Y "A"

0	500'	1000'

Approx. Scale - feet

Not to be used for navigation

APPENDIX I: CHARTS AND PUBLICATIONS

Coastal Charts

18473	Oak Bay to Shilshole Bay
18471	Approaches to Admiralty Inlet
18427	Anacortes to Skagit Bay
18465	Strait of Juan de Fuca - Eastern Part
18480	Approaches to Strait of Juan de Fuca (includes Destruction Island)
18500	Columbia River to Destruction Island
18520	Yaquina Head to Columbia River
18580	Cape Blanco to Yaquina Head
18600	Trinidad Head to Cape Blanco
18620	Point Arena to Trinidad Head
18640	San Francisco to Point Arena
18680	Point Sur to San Francisco
18700	Point Conception to Point Sur
18721	Santa Cruz Island to Purisima Point
18725	Port Hueneme to Santa Barbara
18740	San Diego to Santa Rosa Island

Detail Charts

18450	Seattle Harbor, Elliott Bay, Duwamish Waterway
18443	Approaches to Everett
18468	Port Angeles
18484	Neah Bay
18502	Grays Harbor
18521	Columbia River
18558	Tillamook Bay
18561	Approaches to Yaquina Bay
18581	Yaquina Bay and River
18583	Siuslau River
18584	Umpqua River
18587	Coos Bay
18588	Coquille River Entrance
18589	Port Orford to Cape Blanco
18601	Cape Sebastian to Humbug Mountain
18602	Pyramid Point to Cape Sebastian
18603	St. George Reef and Crescent City Harbor
18605	Trinidad Harbor
18622	Humboldt Bay
18626	Elk to Fort Bragg
18643	Bodega and Tomales Bays
18645	Gulf of the Farallones
18647	Drakes Bay
18649	San Francisco Entrance
18682	Half Moon Bay
18685	Monterey Bay
18703	Estero Bay
18704	San Luis Obispo Bay
18744	Santa Monica Bay
18749	San Pedro Bay
18754	Newport Bay
18765	Approaches to San Diego (includes detail of Mission Bay)
18774	Gulf of Santa Catalina (includes detail of Oceanside)
18773	San Diego Bay

NOTE: This list is presented to assist boaters in choosing charts which cover the areas of their interest. Since NOAA charts and chart numbers are constantly being revised, some data will be outdated soon after publication of this guide.

U.S. Coast Pilot 7: Pacific Coast (California, Oregon, Washington, and Hawaii)
Tide Tables, WEst Coast, North and South America
Tidal Current Tables, PacificCoast of North America and Asia
Light List, Vol. III - Pacific Coast and Pacific Islands

APPENDIX II: MARINAS IN SOUTHERN CALIFORNIA

Ventura   Area Code: 805

1 Ventura Isle Marina   644-5858
2 Ventura West Marina   644-8266

Channel Islands Harbor   Area Code: 805

3 Bahia Cabrillo Marina   985-0113
4 Channel Islands Marina   985-7558
5 Vintage Marina   984-3366
6 Anacapa Isle Marina   985-6035
7 Peninsula Yacht Anchorage   985-6400
8 Channel Islands Landing   985-6059

Marina del Rey   Area Code: 213

9 Marina Harbor 1 & 2   822-1659
10 Tahiti Marina   301-6535
11 Islander Marina   823-4593
12 Neptune Marina   823-4555
13 Deauville Marina   823-4655
14 Villa del Mar Marina   823-4644
15 Bar Harbor Marina   823-4689
16 Dolphin Marina   578-6666
17 Tradewinds Marina   823-2026
18 Holiday Harbor Marina   821-4582
19 Mariner's Bay   822-2001
20 Marina City Club (ext. 313)   822-0611
21 Catalina Yacht Anchorage   822-0669
22 Marina del Rey Hotel   823-4593
23 Pier 44   823-4593
24 Aggie Cal   823-8964

Los Angeles (San Pedro)   Area Code: 213

25 Cabrillo Marina   519-3166
26 Fleitz Bros. Watchorn Harbor   832-0334
27 Holiday Harbor Marina   833-4468
28 San Pedro Marina   519-8177

Los Angeles Harbor   Area Code: 213

29 Leeward Bay Marina   830-5621
30 Holiday Harbor Marina   835-3952
31 Yacht Haven   834-6892
32 Pacific Yacht Landing   830-0260
33 Al Larson Marina   832-0526
34 Colonial Yacht Anchorage   830-1161
35 Lighthouse Yacht Landing   834-9595
36 Cerritos Yacht Anchorage   834-4737
37 Island Yacht Anchorage   830-1111
38 Terminal Island Marina   432 3387

Long Beach Harbor   Area Code: 213

39 Queensway Bay Moorings   436-0411
40 Downtown Marina   437-0375

Long Beach Harbor Con't. Area Code (213)

41 Long Beach Marina (Alamitos) 594-0951
42 Cerritos Bahia Marina   431-6575

Huntington Harbour   Area Code: (714)

43 Sunset Aquatic Marina   846-0179
44 Peter's Landing   840-1387

Newport Harbor   Area Code: (714)

45 Lido Yacht Anchorage   673-9330
46 Twenty-eighth Street Marina   673-6606
47 Little Inn on The Bay   673-8800
48 Newport Arches Marina   642-4644
49 Bay Shores Marina   644-9730
50 Marina Dunes   644-0126
51 De Anza Bayside Marina   673-1331
52 Balboa Marina   644-9730
53 Balboa Yacht Basin   673-1761
54 Bayside Marina   644-9730

Dana Point Harbor   Area Code: (714)

55 Dana West Marina   493-6222
56 Dana Point Marina   496-6137

Oceanside   Area Code: (619)

57 Oceanside Small Craft Harbor 722-1418

Mission Bay   Area Code: (619)

58 Marina Village   224-3124
59 Knight & Carver Mis. Bay Mar. 222-6488
60 Seaforth Marina   224-6807
61 Islandia Hotel Marina   224-1234
62 Dana Inn Marina   222-6440
63 Dana Landing   224-3221
64 Sea World Marina   226-3915

San Diego   Area Code: (619)

65 Kona Marina   224-2489
66 Shelter Island Inn Marina   222-0561
67 Half Moon Anchorage   224-3401
68 Shelter Cove Marina   224-2471
69 Sun Harbor Marina   222-1167
70 Harbor Island West Marina   291-6440
71 Marina Cortez   291-5985
72 Cabrillo Isle Marina   297-6222
73 Sunroad Marina   622-SLIP
74 Marriott Marina   230-8955
75 Glorietta Bay Marina   435-5203
76 Coronado Cays Marina   423-4982
77 Chula Vista Marina   691-1860

APPENDIX III: TABLE OF MILEAGES – COASTWISE DISTANCES

Entrance buoy to San Diego . . . . . . 8.3 miles
Entrance buoy to Long Beach . . . . . 4.3 miles
Entrance buoy to Los Angeles . . . . . 3.8 miles
Entrance buoy to San Francisco . . . . 15.0 miles
Humboldt Bay entrance buoy to Eureka . 5.5 miles
Entrance buoy to Coos Bay City . . . . 13.3 miles
Yaquina Bay entrance buoy to Newport . 3.3 miles
Columbia River Large Navigation Buoy
  to Astoria . . . . 17.8 miles

From \ To	San Diego, CA	Newport Beach, CA	Long Beach, CA	Los Angeles, CA	Santa Barbara, CA	Port San Luis, CA	Monterey, CA	San Francisco, CA	Eureka, CA	Crescent City, CA	Coos Bay, OR	Florence, OR	Newport, OR	Depoe Bay, OR	Astoria, OR	Cape Flattery, WA	Seattle, WA
San Diego, CA	—	78	94	95	174	259	370	455	653	704	817	848	881	891	989	1104	1228
Newport Beach, CA		—	25	27	108	193	304	389	587	638	751	782	815	825	922	1038	1162
Long Beach, CA			—	3	94	179	290	374	572	624	736	768	800	810	908	1024	1148
Los Angeles, CA				—	90	175	286	371	569	620	733	764	797	807	904	1020	1144
Santa Barbara, CA					—	91	203	287	485	537	649	681	713	723	821	937	1061
Port San Luis, CA						—	121	205	403	455	567	599	631	641	739	854	978
Monterey, CA							—	96	294	346	459	490	522	532	630	746	870
San Francisco, CA								—	232	283	396	427	459	469	567	683	807
Eureka, CA									—	64	180	212	244	254	352	468	592
Crescent City, CA										—	125	156	188	199	296	411	535
Coos Bay, OR											—	59	92	101	201	321	445
Florence, OR												—	43	54	153	273	397
Newport, OR													—	16	115	235	359
Depoe Bay, OR														—	101	222	346
Astoria, OR															—	153	277
Cape Flattery, WA																—	124
Seattle, WA																	—

The intersection of columns between two places is the approximate distance in nautical miles. For example: Santa Barbara is 713 nautical miles from Newport, Oregon.

INDEX

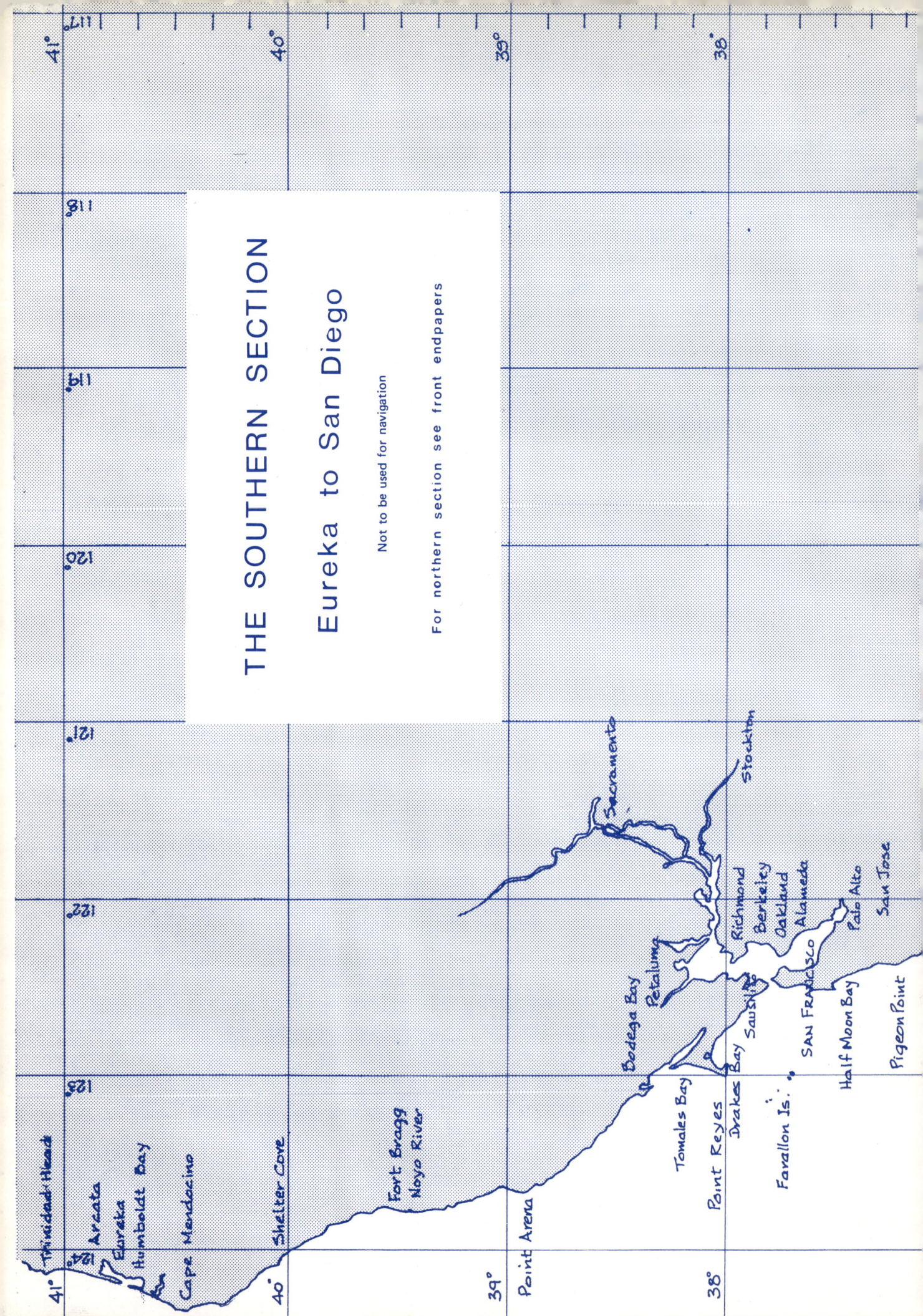

THE SOUTHERN SECTION

Eureka to San Diego

Not to be used for navigation

For northern section see front endpapers

41° 117

40° 117

118

119

120

121

122

123

39° Point Arena

38°

Trinidad Head
Arcata
Eureka
Humboldt Bay
Cape Mendocino
Shelter Cove
Fort Bragg
Noyo River

Sacramento
Stockton

Richmond
Berkeley
Oakland
Alameda
Palo Alto
San Jose

Bodega Bay
Petaluma
SAN FRANCISCO
Sausalito
Half Moon Bay
Pigeon Point

Tomales Bay
Point Reyes
Drakes Bay
Farallon Is.

41°
40°
39°
38°